BOTTOMS UP!

I began to look at the assembled girls. They were all remarkably attractive. And they were all young. I don't suppose there was one there over the age of about twenty-five. Most were in some form of lingerie. One or two were completely naked. None was fully dressed. As I looked around the room, my eye was caught by a tall, lithe, long-legged redhead. She was at least five ten, five eleven, with legs all the way up to her shapely bottom, which itself was lusciously full and firm. She had what I'd call a spanker's arse. It just cried out to be chastised. Her strikingly auburn hair was long, almost down to her waist, and she was wearing white, semi-transparent panties of some kind.

'That's the one,' I said, pointing. 'That one over there . . .'

Also in New English Library paperback

In the Pink 1: Stripped for Action
In the Pink 2: Sin City
In the Pink 3: Getting It

Vampire Desire
The Ruby: volume 1
The Ruby: volume 2
The Ruby: volume 3

The World's Best Sexual Fantasy Letters: Volume 1

Edited and compiled by David Jones

NEW ENGLISH LIBRARY
Hodder and Stoughton

Introduction and compilation copyright © 1997 by David Jones

First published in 1997
by Hodder and Stoughton
A division of Hodder Headline PLC

A New English Library paperback

The right of David Jones to be identified as the Compiler of
the Work has been asserted by him in accordance with the
Copyright, Designs and Patents Act 1988.

10 9 8 7 6 5 4 3 2

All rights reserved. No part of this publication may be reproduced,
stored in a retrieval system, or transmitted, in any form or by any
means without the prior written permission of the publisher, nor be
otherwise circulated in any form of binding or cover other than that
in which it is published and without a similar condition being
imposed on the subsequent purchaser.

All characters in this publication are fictitious and any resemblance
to real persons, living or dead, is purely coincidental.

British Library Cataloguing in Publication Data
A CIP catalogue record for this title is available from the British
Library.

ISBN 0 340 67227 7

Typeset by Avon Dataset Ltd, Bidford-on-Avon, Warks

Printed and bound in Great Britain by
Mackays of Chatham PLC, Chatham, Kent

Hodder and Stoughton
A division of Hodder Headline PLC
338 Euston Road
London NW1 3BH

INTRODUCTION

Fantasies are what inject the life into most of our sex lives. At dinner parties, when the food is cleared away and the coffee, port and brandy are served, the subject, sooner or later, turns to sex. And one of the most frequent, and most popular, of sexual topics is, inevitably, where does real sex stop, and where do fantasies begin? There have always been two distinctly opposing views about fantasies. There is the one that says the best advice is to keep your fantasies as exactly that, for once you have turned them into experiences, they will lose their magic. And then there is the opposing view that says that the only worthwhile reason for having a fantasy is to be able to look forward to turning it into reality. And enjoy doing just that.

The trouble is, of course, that one man's sexual fantasy can be another man's complete sexual turn-off. But herein, perhaps, lies the magic. Many young men and women, at the outset of their sexual experience, find the thought of performing either cunnilingus or fellatio distasteful. Literally. Whereas most sexually mature men will leap at the opportunity. Many older men actually complain of the lack of opportunity to indulge in oral sex. My own view has always been that taught to me, years ago now, by a delightful young woman called Ann Summers. Which is that, whatever two people do together in their sexual relationships is perfectly acceptable, *provided* that both of them want to do it, and that no physical or mental harm results to either. I accept that there are people who consider that sex in anything other than the missionary position is abnormal, and that to them those of us who like to experiment with our sexual partners are the worst kind of deviants.

Be that as it may, in a career in men's magazine publishing as a journalist, editor, and publisher, spanning over thirty years, my experience was that the readers' letters columns were always a mainstay, a linchpin, of the textual content of all the magazines upon which I ever worked.

These included Paul Raymond's *Men Only* and *Club International*, back in the days when they quite properly assumed that their male readers had partners of the opposite sex, at least for some of the time, rather than the – to me – seemingly single-minded preoccupation with single-handed sex that appears to obsess whoever edits their columns these days.

We also, back then, published the finest writers and artists that money could buy, to produce and illustrate the features, fiction, reviews and interviews that were as essential a part of the magazines as were the girl sets. Strangely, it is a fact that in the 1970s and 1980s, we paid more for the words and pictures than those magazines do today. And I think it shows.

Frank Norman, Wolf Mankowitz, Irma Kurtz, Jeffrey Bernard, Daniel Farson, Molly Parkin, George Melly, Sandy Fawkes, the late Kingsley Amis and his son Martin Amis, all wrote for me in the United Kingdom. Ralph Steadman, James Marsh and George Underwood used to illustrate fiction for the magazines, as did Brian Froud and Brian Grimwood. Fluck & Law, the originators of *Spitting Image*, built models that we photographed for humorous features, long before they'd even thought of *Spitting Image*. Tom Hustler and Patrick Litchfield photographed for us. So did David Parkinson and Geoff Howes. In the United States, William Burroughs, Clifford Irving, Andrew Sarris and F. Lee Bailey were regular contributors, amongst many others. Perhaps the audience today is different. But I don't believe so. Today, magazines like *GHQ*, *Esquire*, and *FHM* still perpetuate that old, up-market, quality approach to men's magazines, showing respect for the intelligence of their readers. Thank God someone does.

In the United States I eventually ran Paul Raymond's flagship American magazine *Club*, whose circulation went from four hundred thousand copies a month when I took it over from my old friend Tony Power to one million, two hundred thousand copies a month under my editorship. I also ran another magazine from the same stable, one that attempted to be all things sexual to all people sexual, and that was entitled *Club Quest*. It almost succeeded. I treasure the copies that I still have.

Back here in Britain, I subsequently took over the European editions of *Penthouse*, of *Forum* and of *Variations*. Not forgetting, of course, *Omni*, then the world's best science magazine for laymen, edited in those days by Professor Bernard Dixon, the ex-editor of *New Scientist*.

Forum, of course, started its life in England, as did *Penthouse*. It was originally the brainchild, back in the late 1960s, of Professor Albert Z. Freedman, who still works with Bob Guccione in the United States (where *Forum*'s current associated publisher and editorial director is a protégé of mine, V. K. McCarty). Al had the intelligence to see that the correspondence columns of *Penthouse* could spawn a magazine offshoot of their own, and thus was *Forum* born. In the past, the UK version has had many distinguished names upon its editorial staff, including – after Al Freedman – Philip Hodson, Anna Raeburn, and the late Roger Baker, the respected author of what is still the definitive book on drag. Sadly, he died recently.

Over the years, the main difficulty with publishing readers' letters – and, most particularly, readers' fantasy letters – has always been the question of space. Almost every reader's letter published in men's magazines, anywhere in the world, upon whatever topic, is edited down from its original length. With fantasy letters, this is often to the detriment of the letter. And to the disappointment of the reader. It is simply a sad fact of magazine editorial life. Now, New English Library is publishing two volumes of the world's best fantasy letters – of which this is the first – collected from over the years, and which permit – for the first time ever – the best of these letters to be published in their original, unedited, full-length state. An historic event! Enjoy.

David Jones. Hampstead, London. 1996.

ALICE IN KNICKERLAND

I love to look at young girls walking in the street, sitting on buses, or travelling on the Underground, and wonder to myself what kind of underwear they are wearing. I fantasize about their knickers, and try to decide, by looking at their faces, what they might be wearing. Are they wearing tiny little silky G-string-style knickers? Perhaps in black, with little red lace bows? Or have they got on bikini-style knickers, with high-cut sides and low-cut fronts? Maybe in pink? Or maybe they are wearing totally transparent white nylon lace knickers that show their pubic hair and their little pink cunt lips through the front?

In my daydreams, I order the girls into my bedroom, one at a time, and they lift up their short skirts and show me their knickers. Of course I reach out and stroke and feel their pussies through their knicker crotches, and I remark on it when the knickers are wet from the girls' pussy juices. If they're really wet, I make the girls take them off, and I make them hold their damp knicker gussets up to my nostrils, so that I can breathe in the delightful smell of cunt. And while I'm sniffing their knickers, I'm fingering their wet cunts.

It's a sort of competition, really, and in my fantasy, depending upon the style of knickers worn and the amount of dampness between their legs, and the specific aroma of their pussy, they will either be rejected, in which case they simply leave, or they are selected, in which case they are short-listed for fucking – and other sexual acts – later on. Sometimes I fantasize that a girl might be wearing a pair of old-fashioned knickers. You know, the kind that schoolgirls wear. Navy-blue, heavily textured, woolly ones. And I put my fingers underneath the leg elastic, and slip them into their pussy, which is always wet and warm, and very accommodating, and then I masturbate them. Do you think this is a peculiar fetish?

A. J. Stroud, Glos.

Absolutely not. Whatever turns you on.

KNICKER KICKER

My husband has always been a dyed-in-the-wool knicker fetishist, from long before we ever got married. The vulgarly sexy tart's knickers that he buys me on every possible occasion – birthdays, Christmas, St Valentine's Day, and so on – mean far more to him than they do to me, and for that reason I'm beginning to wonder if it's me he wants to fuck, or the knickers. Black is obligatory. Black satin, black nylon, black lace. Camiknickers, French knickers, teddies. You name it. Rather like Henry Ford's cars, I can have any colour I like, provided that it's black. In one way I don't mind. I'd much rather that he bought the knickers for me than for some other woman. But on the rare occasions when I've either chosen to wear a different colour, or have refused to wear black, or suggested that I take my knickers off before we get into bed, he doesn't seem to be able to get it up. I simply can't win. No black knickers, no sex. It seems vital to him that our fucking has to begin with him sucking my pussy through my knicker crotch. If he isn't allowed to do this, he doesn't get an erection. Or he doesn't even attempt to make love. What shall I do?

P.A. J. Lincoln, Lincs.

Make love, not war. It may be irritating, but I think you're stuck with it. At least he's not into rubber *knickers. His preoccupation with black underwear is what fetishism is all about. My dictionary defines fetishism as '. . . the irrational worship, or reverencing, of an inanimate object, for its magical powers . . .' If it magics up his hard-on, it can't be all bad, can it?*

NIX TO KNICKS

I very recently began my first live-in love affair. I'm twenty-three and have just come down from university, where I read psychology. I'm not a virgin, but nor am I very sexually experienced. I appreciate that I have a lot to learn about life, but at least I thought that my theory, with regard to sex, was fairly well grounded. My boyfriend is five years older than I am and has lived with a number of girls before me. I do love him, but I find some of his habits strange, to say the least.

He's very up-front, and tells me all about his fantasies. He says that the idea of prostitutes excites him, but he also says that he's never had one. The main problem is that he wants me to dress up as one and perform certain sexual acts that I basically find distasteful. He wants me to wear crotchless knickers and peep-hole bras – two items of underwear of which I was ignorant until he recently brought them home. I'm not totally against wearing them. If it gives him pleasure, then why not? They seem, in themselves, harmless. But then he wants me to take these knickers off and masturbate him with them while I talk dirty to him. This seems to me to smack of his having a knicker fetish. Is there anyone else out there who has been through this experience? Is he simply going through a phase, or is this something that could stay with him throughout his life? I'm disturbed that he's basically sexually immature.

L. C. Ipswich, Suffolk.

The World's Best Sexual Fantasy Letters: Volume 1

You're right, he is sexually immature. And, yes, he is a knicker fetishist. And, yes, the chances are that he will retain these preferences throughout his sexual life. Please see my comments in answer to the letter above.

PANTIE FREAK

I just adore women's intimate lingerie. In my home town, I can't keep out of the lingerie departments of places like Marks and Spencer's, for example. When I go down to London, my friends want to go to the Tate, or to the National Gallery, or to see some show or other. All I want to do is to go to stores like Dickens and Jones, or Ann Summers, and look at sexy knickers.

And whenever I fuck my girlfriend, the most exciting part of all, for me, is pulling her knickers down. I just love it. I love the feel of the soft, silky material under my fingers, and I love the scent that lingers around the gusset of her knickers. If I ever become rich, I shall pay young girls to let me pull their knickers down. I'd love to actually tear them off. Rip them off. I sometimes dream of sniffing girls' knickers without their owners knowing what I am doing, and then I wake up with a huge boner. I read the advertisements in girlie magazines offering women's worn knickers for sale, and I'm tempted to send off for them. But I strongly suspect that they would simply keep my money, and I wouldn't get any knickers. Do other male readers have this penchant for ladies underwear?

S. E. Carshalton, Surrey.

In a word, yes.

LADIES' CHOICE

I'm a girl who's happily into sex (with the opposite sex) but it never ceases to surprise me that my girlfriends don't seem to fantasize about men as much as I do. Your columns are always full of male erotic fantasies. May a mere female be allowed to voice her favourite fantasy? Thank you.

I love to imagine that I'm a royal princess and that I'm at some well-attended charity dinner. I spend the earlier part of the event, before the actual meal, selecting the male whom I'm going to take back home with me afterwards. I do this by reaching out and feeling the men's cocks in a perfectly straightforward manner whilst I'm talking to them. When I find one that feels as if it will stiffen nicely, given a little TLC later on, I tell the guy that he is to accompany me back to my luxury home at the end of the evening, and that this is a royal command. There is no question of his saying no, or pleading a headache!

In my fantasy, I start to feel the man up in my limousine on the way home. I quickly undo his fly and pull his gorgeous cock out into the open, where I begin to masturbate it up to a full erection. When it is fully erect, I lean down and begin to give him head. Not to the point of ejaculation, but simply as an exercise in controlled oral sex. If you think about it, it wouldn't *do* to come in a royal mouth, would it? I mean, not on our first date. I use my lips and my tongue, as well as my fingers. Sooner or later the man always says something like 'I simply don't believe that this is happening to me,' or (my favourite one, this) 'I never imagined that one of the highest in the land would give the best blow job in Christendom.'

When we get back to my place, I take him straight into my royal bedroom, where I have thoughtfully arranged for a bottle of vintage champagne to be left on ice. I get him to open the bottle and pour two glasses and, after a sip, I command him to take the royal knickers down. This involves him kneeling in front of me. I then hoist the royal skirt, and he slowly pulls down my naughty black bikini knickers, revealing my curly royal blonde – and highlighted – pubic hair, in the midst of which pinkly nestles the royal slit. It is, of course, by now oozing royal pre-come juices, and I sit down on the edge of the bed, spread the royal legs, and command him to suck the royal pussy. I always make certain that I've taken my knicks away from him, and put them away somewhere safe. Well, just imagine what a tabloid would pay for an opportunity to photograph the royal knicks! David Mellors's Chelsea strip wouldn't be in it. They'd probably run them as a special royal scratch-and-sniff centre spread.

Speaking of which, the royal legs are still spread, and our manly volunteer is by now sucking and licking the royal clit. After I've come a few times, I command him next to lie on the bed, where I wank him a little just to make certain that he's good and stiff before I lower myself slowly down onto his pole – and fuck him senseless. I'm never sure, in my fantasy, how to thank the object of my desire that particular evening. Offering him my knickers as a souvenir is obviously out, for the reasons stated.

Eventually, I get out my Polaroid camera. First, I toss him off until he's good and stiff again, and then I take a photograph of his erect cock to add to my rapidly growing collection. Queen Victoria's gamekeeper would have loved it. Then I spread my legs wide again, hold my cunt lips open with my fingers, and tell him to take a picture of the royal gynaecological apparatus. When it has developed, I check it out, to make certain that there is nothing in the photograph to identify my apparatus as actually being mine, and then I give the picture to the man as a souvenir. 'Remember,' I tell him, 'that a lot of the crowned heads of Europe have been down there between my legs. And now so has yours. To say nothing of your cock.' And off he goes, as chuffed as anything. When he's gone, I often ring my philandering husband. Just to ask him if he's actually getting any. Usually, he just puts the 'phone down. Fuck him.'

S. F. Pewsey, Wilts.

You forgot to say that you always give your guests a knighthood, in the interests of safer sex.

GIVING A TOSS

I'm using your columns to ask, if I may, whether there are any other young girls like me (I'm eighteen and a half) who have an obsession about masturbating. Themselves, that is. I like to fuck, and I think I probably get more than my fair share, but I'm still as horny as hell almost all of the time.

In the office, I'm constantly slipping into the loo and slipping my fingers into myself to bring myself off. If there's no one in my office, I'm regularly to be found with my fingers up my knickers, wanking myself slowly to orgasm. My boss opened his connecting door unexpectedly the other day, and found me playing with myself. *Ooops*, I thought. 'Excuse me,' I said to him. 'I had an uncomfortable itch.' Well, it was true, really, wasn't it? On buses, I always go upstairs and take a back seat so that I can attend to my aching pussy without anyone noticing. Failing that, I always carry a largish shopping bag which I can put on my knee and use to cover up my manipulative sex.

When I'm in the bath, I simply lie there wanking away, having orgasm after orgasm, to my heart's content. The moment I've finished, I want to start again. Am I ill? Do I need to see a doctor? Or a psychiatrist? I was lucky enough, last St Valentine's Day, to get quite a selection of Valentine cards from admirers. It occurred to me then that perhaps my fingers should have sent one to my pussy. What's your advice?

(Name and address supplied.)

Let your fingers do the wanking. We all do it. It's not a problem.

ANAL RETENTION

My fantasies are all about fucking girls in the arse. It's something I've never done, but in my fantasies beautiful girls come up to me in the street, at parties, on public transport, and say things like, 'Hi. My name's Andrea. Are you doing anything right now?' And I say, 'Why do you ask?' And then they say, 'Well, you'll probably find this fairly disgusting, but I love anal sex, and my current boyfriend won't fuck my arsehole. He thinks it's dirty. I wondered maybe if I could come home with you, and if you'd bugger me silly when we get there?'

Of course I agree. I call a cab, we get to my place, I offer them a drink, and then we go into the bedroom. They say, 'Don't bother to undress me. I'll just bend over this chair and pull my skirt up, and you can pull my knickers down. Then we'll get at it.' And then I say, 'Have you got any lubricant? You know, K-Y jelly. Something like that.' And they say, 'No. But anything will do. Vaseline. Butter. Olive oil. Lard. Anything greasy.' And then they pull their knickers down, take their arse cheeks in their hands, and pull them apart, showing me the shiny, pink inside of that beautiful little brown arsehole. I dash off into the bathroom, grab a tin of Vaseline, go back into the bedroom, and carefully and lovingly anoint that puckered little centre of anticipated pleasure with the care of someone repairing a delicate antique.

Then the girl says, 'That feels good. I'm well greased, and I'm ready for you. Bugger me now. Please.' And she stands up, turns around, undoes my flies and takes out my

John Thomas, which she squeezes and pulls until it's fully erect and throbbing in her hand. Then she'll kneel down, take it in her mouth, and just simply suck it, very, very gently, for a few moments. And next she takes it out of her mouth, stands up and bends over the chair again, pulls her arse cheeks apart again and says, 'Let me feel it up my arse, baby. But slowly at first. I haven't had my arsehole stretched for a very long time. Too long. So take it carefully. If I say "Stop," then stop. Immediately. OK?' 'Don't worry about a thing, my darling,' I say. 'Just leave everything to me.'

I take my swollen prick in my hand and I guide it carefully to the dead centre of her lovely, forbidden arsehole, pressing my cock up against its soft, puckered skin. Then I slowly begin to ease my cock in, and she says, 'Oh, God. That's good. Oh, darling, that feels so good. That's lovely. You're buggering me. I love it. Bugger me harder.' And I obediently thrust my tool harder up her arsehole, she relaxes her anal sphincter, and I slide deeply into her. She feels warm, and soft, and wet, and tight. I begin to fuck her properly. I'm in her up to the hilt, and she's beginning to move against me, thrusting her buttocks backwards against me. I can feel the suction as she begins to work her arse muscles up and down the full length of my cock. My balls are slapping against her cunt. I can't believe that my dick is where I've wanted it to be for so long. Up a girl's anus. And the bum of a really pretty girl, at that. Not that I care. I'd fuck a slag right now, so long as it was up her arse. I wonder, while I fuck her anally with long, strong strokes, if perhaps I should ask her to marry me, while I have the chance.

She is grunting and muttering to herself as I bugger her, wriggling her arse, and then she reaches behind her, takes the base of my cock in her hand, and begins to wank me into her rectum as I thrust in and out of her. I can smell the acrid scent as my tool thrusts deeply up her arse – and at that moment she lets go of my cock. Putting her hand between her own legs, she begins to frig herself, her fingers busy at her clit, bringing herself to orgasm as I begin to feel my own ejaculation gathering deep in my groin.

I look down at what I'm doing. Here's this lovely young woman, her short skirt up around her waist, her white nylon knickers pulled down below her knees. I can see a dark stain at the cotton lining of her knicker gusset as I look down, confirming that she was sexually excited at the thought of what we were going to do when we arrived, as we sat in the taxi on the way here. In my fantasies, the girls are always as randy as I am at the thought of anal sex. They may not think of anal *rape* as excitedly as I sometimes do! But then, if it was going to be rape, they wouldn't be here in my fantasy anyway, would they?

Maybe that's a thought for another fantasy. Right then, I am distracted as I feel my ejaculation rising suddenly, spurting through my cock and into the girl's arse, jetting up inside her. She squeezes me with her rectal muscles as she feels me coming inside her. She shouts out and frigs herself feverishly as I orgasm into her, joining me finally with long, shudderingly enjoyable vaginal convulsions. 'Oh, my God,' she shouts. 'I'm coming. I'm coming as you spunk up my arsehole. I'm coming as you bugger me. Oh God. I love it. Do it again. Fuck my arsehole again. Now, baby. Now. Please.' I stay up her until every last spasm has been extracted from my rapidly shrivelling dick, and I finally pull out of her.

'Thank you, darling,' I say. 'That was wonderful.' She stands up, turns around, and puts her arms around me. 'Wonderful?' she says. 'What do you mean, wonderful? It was fucking marvellous. We'll do it again, just as soon as you're ready. Is there anything you'd like, as a little sexual treat, while we're waiting? Is there anything that your other girls won't do for you? Would you like me to suck your cock? Strap a dildo on, and fuck *you* up the arse? Anything?' She grins at me as she hugs me.

'You've just done the one thing I seriously fantasize about,' I tell her. 'None of the girls I know will let me even put my finger up their arse, never mind allowing me to actually bugger them. But if you're serious . . .' She interrupts me. 'I'm serious, darling,' she tells me. 'Anything you want. Absolutely anything. You can fuck me when I've got my period. I'll wank you with my tits. You can come in my mouth. Anything. You only have to ask.' I feel embarrassed. I've never actually asked any girl what I am about to ask this girl. 'Could you . . . would you . . . give me a wank?' I ask her. 'You know . . . a plain, old-fashioned J. Arthur. One off the wrist. I'd love that.' She laughs. 'Oh, sweetheart,' she says. 'What a lovely request. I thought wanking had gone out of fashion. It'll be my pleasure. I was the champion school wanker when I was in the fifth form. They used to pay me fifty pence, which included showing them my pussy – no touching, mind you – and letting them sniff my dirty knickers whilst I wanked them. They used to queue up around the back of the gym, waiting for me to toss them off. Just come here, my darling. I'll give you the wank of your dreams. With the greatest of pleasure.'

She bends down, pulls her knickers all the way down her legs, and off, and then hands them to me. 'Let's do it in proper fifth-form fashion,' she says. 'You've probably looked up more pussies than I've had hot dinners, but I bet it's a very long time since you sniffed a girl's knickers. Have a sniff of those. From the way I was wetting myself coming here in the taxi, thinking about you buggering me, I wouldn't mind betting you that they smell pretty sexy. The real aroma of sexually aroused cunt. All the fifth-form boys used to get was the scent of over-wanked teenage pussy. And there *is* a difference.' She laughs.

'What else should we do to bring back all those happy

memories? Oh, yes. Of course. I know. You should feel me. Starting with my tits. Shouldn't you?' She takes a deep breath, standing there in front of me. 'They're a lot bigger than they used to be, but they're still not exactly blockbusters,' she says. 'But have a good feel. I used to wear a bra in those days. We all did. It made us feel grown up, even if we didn't really have any tits. These days I don't. Wear a bra, that is. Which perhaps ought to make it a little bit more interesting for you. What do you think?' She comes and stands up against me, taking my flaccid cock in her hand. I reach up, and take her right breast in my own grasp. Her breast is warm, and soft, and firm, and I can feel her nipple hardening beneath the thin material of her blouse.

'You had a far more sophisticated education than did I,' I tell her. 'I never touched a breast whilst I was at school. Nor looked at a pussy. Nor sniffed a pair of knickers. I did all those things at college. I fucked girls too. But I was in my twenties. All I did before that was think about it. And wank, of course. But for myself. By myself. I used to buy *Men Only*, and jack off looking at the pictures. So what you're going to do for me is something of a first. Quite an historic first, in fact.' 'How lovely,' she says. 'I'll do my best to make it memorable for you. I promise. But you were a bit backward, you know. When I was growing up, I gave many a wank to men who wanted to fuck me, simply because it was an easy way out.

'They didn't actually care, as long as they got their rocks off. And then it was a sort of tradition that I grew up with. If I had my period, I'd give a man a wank. Or if I simply didn't feel like a fuck, I'd do it. I know it seems lazy, and I know it would drive any feminist potty. But it simply was the accepted thing in the world that I lived in, in those days. I mean, if a man's got a hard-on, and he wants to fuck, it's only going to take a few seconds to wank him off. It's no big deal. But if you just flatly refuse him, you're probably going to lose a friend. You've heard of date rape?' I nod. 'There wouldn't be such a thing as date rape, if only more girls had the sense to give a man a quick one off the wrist at the end of the evening. It takes all the stress and passion out of the event. No one is offended. Nobody's hurt. What's the worst that can happen? You get sticky fingers.' She laughs again. 'No big deal, eh? Now come here, my darling, and I'll show you what a serious wank is about.' She starts to move my foreskin slowly up and down, and as she does, I go on feeling her breasts through her blouse. They are small, but nicely full and well-shaped, and both her nipples become rock-hard with my manipulation of them. I know before she starts that I shall come very quickly once she begins seriously to masturbate me. And I do.

'There you go, baby,' she says, as I spurt my semen all over her hand. And that is where my fantasy usually ends. When I open my eyes, the girl of the day (or night) has disappeared, of course. Along with her receptive arse and her masturbatory expertise. But it is always fun while it lasts. One day, perhaps, it will come true. I sincerely hope so.

L. P. W. Dublin, Republic of Ireland.

That's one fantasy that is probably better kept as *a fantasy. It's still illegal in the UK for a man to have anal sex with a woman. But between consenting males of legal age, it's OK. Strange, isn't it?*

LESBIAN LOVE

I've always wanted to experience the classic male fantasy – that of watching two girls making love together – and I recently began talking to my new girlfriend Sarah about this dream. To my surprise, she told me that there had been a period in her adult life when she had been into other women, sexually, and that she still found some women sexually attractive. If I was serious, she said, it wouldn't be too difficult to contact one of the lesbian women she knew from that time and arrange a demonstration for my benefit. But she warned me to think about it carefully and seriously before agreeing to it.

There was the obvious danger, she said, of my being jealous of her having sex with another woman. That was something that I must admit hadn't occurred to me. And the second thing she wanted me to consider was, she said, the fact that not all lesbian women are, as she was – and still is – bisexual. If I felt like joining in at any stage (usually part of the classic male fantasy in this situation) I would need to know beforehand that the other woman in the threesome was agreeable to that kind of relationship. If she wasn't into it, it was positively *verboten*.

I took her advice to heart and gave due consideration to her warnings. After deliberation, I felt that I could cope with all the points that she had raised, and my overwhelming wish was still to be able to be a voyeur at a lesbian love-nest. Some weeks later, Sarah came home one Friday evening and told me that she had contacted one of her friends, and that the friend had agreed to allow me, as Sarah's husband, to be present while the two girls made love. Any participation by me was to be by general agreement at the time. There was no automatic agreement, but neither was a sexual threesome forbidden in advance. Sarah had agreed that the session would take place at the woman's home, since various items of equipment that might be used were difficult to transport. I felt my prick stiffening at the thought. A week later (a week of intense sexual excitement and anticipation for me, and one during which my sexual activity with my girlfriend reached a new peak), at six on the Saturday evening, we arrived at Sarah's girlfriend's place. She had a flat in a large, converted house in a residential suburb of North London. The house had walls thick enough to ensure total privacy.

Sarah's friend answered the door and welcomed us both in. She was an attractive woman of about twenty-three or twenty-four, with short dark brown hair, long legs, and a good figure. Sarah introduced her as Margie. She led us down a short hallway and into her living room. There was plenty of light, but it was of low intensity. There was music playing softly – gentle, romantic music. Margie had opened a bottle of red wine, and she poured glasses for Sarah and for me. She raised hers to both of us. 'Lovely to see you again, Sarah darling,' she said. 'And good to meet you, Charles,' she said to me. We all drank. 'Shall we get on with it before any of us loses our nerve?' Margie asked Sarah. Sarah agreed. 'Why don't you sit over there, Charles?' Margie suggested, indicating a sofa that was placed diagonally across from the fireplace, with its matching twin opposite.

I settled down quietly on the sofa, my glass of wine on a small table beside me. 'Shall we have a drink the way we used to, darling?' said Margie to Sarah. 'Oh, yes. That would be nice,' Sarah said. They were both standing together in the middle of the space between the two sofas. Margie took a mouthful of wine from her glass, but I noticed that she didn't swallow it. She put her mouth to Sarah's, and they kissed. As they kissed, Margie passed the wine from her mouth to Sarah's, and Sarah swallowed it as they continued to kiss. It was intensely erotic. And it was certainly something that Sarah and I had never done. I got an immediate erection.

Sarah then did the same thing in reverse: she passed a mouthful of wine from her mouth into Margie's. Margie drank it, thirstily. They then put their glasses down on a side table, and began to undress each other. They were kissing and hugging, in between starting to take off each other's clothes, which extended the time that it took for them to get down to their undies. Margie was wearing a short black leather skirt, which only just covered her bum, and a tight black T-shirt. This basic outfit was finished off by black nylon stockings or tights (I couldn't see which, at this stage) and black high-heeled patent leather court shoes. Sarah had on a navy blue wool suit, with a shortish skirt (but not as short as Margie's!) and underneath her jacket she was wearing a white blouse. She had on (I knew, because I'd seen her put them on) black silk stockings, held up by a suspender belt, and she was wearing highly polished navy blue leather court shoes.

Sarah undid the zip at the side of Margie's skirt, and she then knelt down on the floor and pulled the skirt down around Margie's ankles. Margie stepped out of it. She next took off her own T-shirt, pulling it up over her head and throwing it onto the floor. She wasn't wearing a bra of any kind. Her naked tits were fantastic. I noticed that her nipples looked fully erect. Patently she had the hots for Sarah. She was wearing thin, pure white cotton bikini panties, with lace inserts at the sides, and more lace all around the waist. (I believe that 'broderie anglaise' is the proper name for this kind of decoration.) The cotton was so thin that I could see her dark brown pubic hair through it. Her black nylon stockings, I could now see, were of the hold-up kind. Self-supporting, in fact. Sarah took off her own suit jacket, and Margie quickly relieved her of her skirt, showing that Sarah, too, was braless, and revealing to my gaze her pretty black lace suspender belt, with its long, thin, black suspenders holding up her silken stockings, and her matching sexy black silk French knickers. Her stocking tops were heavily patterned, as is the fashion of today, according to her. Sarah is a natural blonde. She shaves her pubic hair, which I find a tremendously erotic pleasure. I could suck her shaven pussy all night.

So there they were, two pretty girls, naked from the waist up, and wearing only panties, stockings, and shoes, with one of them – Sarah – also wearing a tiny suspender belt. As I watched, Margie put her hand between Sarah's legs and began to rub her fingers up and down Sarah's crotch. Sarah responded immediately by doing the same with her long, slim fingers, excitedly rubbing the translucent material between Margie's legs. Her white cotton knickers soon became stained with whatever liquid was now flowing generously from her aroused cunt.

They continued to kiss as they rubbed each other's pussies through the crotches of their knickers. After a while, Margie pulled her face back from kissing Sarah and looked into her eyes. 'Oh, darling,' she said. 'I have to kiss your lovely cunt now. I can't remember when I last sucked your lovely bald little cunt, but I must do it again. Now. Please. Don't keep me waiting.' I knew exactly how she felt. Sarah didn't say anything right then, but she smiled at Margie and, standing back for a moment, she pulled her black lacy French knickers down her thighs, down her long, slim legs, and took them off. She left her suspender belt and her stockings on, went over to the sofa opposite the one that I was sitting on, and lay down upon it. She didn't even glance at me, but she lay back, spread her legs, began to finger her hairless pussy lips, and said to Margie, 'Come on then, Margie darling. I'm ready for you. Wet and willing. Come and suck me.' She was frigging herself quite hard as Margie came and knelt down on the carpet in front of Sarah's spread legs.

Margie pulled down her white cotton knickers, and, looking at me for the first time since the two girls had started touching each other, she grinned at me, threw me her knickers, and said 'There you are, Charles darling. Toss yourself off into those.' I caught them and held them up to my nose, inhaling deeply. They smelt divine. Of unadulterated, beautiful clean cunt. I was tempted to do as Margie suggested, but I was fascinated by the sight of Sarah's fingers busy at her shaven pussy. Her cunt lips were full and fleshy, and palely pink. They obtruded far more out from her plump pudenda, in its complete hairlessness, than they would have been seen to do had she had a strong pubic growth. Her outer lips were pulled back, showing her full inner lips at their most succulent. I wasn't exactly jealous of Margie, as she knelt down, and took Sarah's pussy lips into her mouth, but I would have been happy to do exactly that which she was doing at that particular moment. Instead, I put Margie's knickers up to my nostrils again and breathed in her lovely cunt smell. At least I could enjoy the scent of cunt, if not the taste. It was fascinating for me to watch Margie's pink little tongue lapping my Sarah's bald, pink cunt. She was doing a terrific job with it. As a bit of a specialist cunt-lapper myself, I could tell that she was thoroughly enjoying what she was doing. And certainly Sarah was having a grand time.

She was lying right back, her legs spread wide, her eyes shut, moving her hips to the rhythm of Margie's tongue while she used both hands to play with her nipples. From where I was sitting, I had a tremendous view of Margie's lovely little bum. I could see her hairy cunt. Inside her dark brown hairy little pubic nest, her lips were much smaller than Sarah's. Sort of neater. Tidier. Know what I mean? But still extremely kissable. And fuckable, of course. Given the opportunity. I wondered for a moment what the chances were, and then I thought, the hell with it. Enjoy this while you can. Whatever happens, happens.

Looking once more at Margie's bum, I could see her tiny, pinky-brown arsehole, tucked in between her arse cheeks, about an inch above her pussy. It was tightly clenched (as most arseholes are) and classically puckered. I itched to ease my middle finger deeply into it. That's something that girls' arseholes do to me. Do they have that effect on you? Her lovely bum was framed by her shiny black hold-up stockings, with her sexy, lacy patterned tops. I love that part of girls' stocking tops where there is a plain band of heavier weight nylon between the patterned top and the basic leg part of the stocking. It's the bit you always want to slip your hand up and stroke and feel when you see a girl in black stockings and a really short skirt. She's probably bending over something, and you can see this lovely, darker stocking band, and – if you're lucky – a bit of tightly-stretched knicker crotch. That aside, Margie's buttocks were moving lecherously as she moved her head up and down Sarah's slit, and she was simply asking to be raped. In both entrances. At that point I was distracted by the fact that Sarah started to orgasm, which she did with the maximum amount of thrashing about on the sofa upon which she was lying, and also with the maximum amount of noise. It occurred to me for a second or two that she never came as loudly as that when *I* was fucking her, but then I realized that I had never been an audience on those occasions but had always been very much part of the act. So it wasn't a fair judgement. That's my story, and I'm sticking to it.

Margie leaned back and stretched as Sarah's multiple orgasms died slowly away. Then she stood up – not glancing in my direction, or saying anything to Sarah – and went to a cupboard at the far end of the room. She opened the door, reached inside, took something out, shut the door again, and came back to our end of the room. This time she did look at me. 'Have you ever seen one of these, Charles?' she asked me, holding the object out to me. 'It's one of the reasons why I prefer girls to boys.' She laughed. 'You meet a better class of prick, if you see what I mean.' I took hold of it, to discover that it was a large pink rubber dildo. A lifelike, knurled, extremely phallic, double-ended dildo, with a leather harness at one end. Its dimensions were indeed impressive. It was certainly larger than any live male penis, erect or otherwise.

'Mmmmm,' I said, slightly self-consciously. 'I do see what you mean.' It was at that moment that I realized that Sarah had just seen what Margie and I were talking about. She sat up. 'Oh, Margie, darling,' she said. 'You're going to fuck me. And with that dildo that we bought together in Soho. Oh, darling. How lovely.' 'I wondered if you'd remember it, darling,' Margie said, grinning at me. 'Especially since you've been getting the real thing recently.' Sarah *almost* blushed. But not quite.

Whilst we all laughed, Margie was greasing the dildo with some kind of emollient out of a tube that she had taken out of a near-by drawer. She then inserted one end of it slowly and carefully into herself, holding her labia apart with the fingers of one hand, while she fed the rubber prick up her love-hole with the other. I could see how it stretched her: she grimaced slightly as she worked it up and down a few times, after which she relaxed, smiled, and began to do up the leather harness around her thighs and waist.

Sarah at this stage was lying back on the sofa, her legs splayed, playing idly with herself as she watched Margie intently. When Margie had satisfied herself that she had adjusted the dildo straps to her complete satisfaction, she walked over to Sarah, the dildo standing up rampant in front of her, and handed Sarah the tube of lubricant. 'You grease your end, darling,' she said. 'And then you'll know for certain that it isn't going to hurt you.' Sarah took the tube, and squeezed some of the jelly-like substance out onto her fingers. She then carefully anointed the rubber prick, stroking and rubbing it as if masturbating it. I found the sight of her doing that strangely erotic. Almost as if she were masturbating the rubber tool. The low lights in the living room reflected off the knobs and whorls of the now well-greased weapon, and Margie gave Sarah a small towel on which to wipe her hands. Neither of the girls said anything at this stage, but Sarah lay back, her legs apart, her knees drawn up. Margie knelt between them and fed the other end of her dildo up Sarah's pussy. Sarah groaned, holding her pussy lips apart as the tool entered her. Whether with pain or pleasure, I wasn't too sure. Perhaps both.

My immediate reaction was the thought that if this was what Sarah was accustomed to being fucked with when she first met me, then it was something of a surprise that she managed to get off at all when I fucked her. I've never felt under-endowed in that department, and I've not had too many complaints. But the dildo that was now enthusiastically fucking Sarah, its rhythm building rapidly as Margie moved her hips faster and faster, was something that I could never, physically at least, compete with. But – unless Sarah was a past-mistress at faking orgasms – we enjoyed a happy and fulfilled sex life. We fucked long and hard, and frequently. Sarah was now groaning almost continually, and as I watched, Margie leaned down and began to kiss her passionately.

The sight of the two naked girls on the sofa, bucking and writhing in their lesbian ecstasy, their tongues thrust down each other's throats, Margie's fingers tweaking and pulling at Sarah's engorged nipples, and Sarah now inserting a finger up Margie's arsehole as they both began to orgasm, was terrific.

I wanted to leap on the two of them, sucking and fucking at every available orifice. But there was no indication from either of them that they even knew that I was there, so, with considerable effort, I simply sat there watching, storing up mental images for the next time that I was fucking Sarah. And then, suddenly, it was all over. The girls lay side by side for a while, not speaking, but holding each other, and then, eventually, Margie suggested that they go and shower, which they did. When they came back, they were fully dressed, made-up, and chattering away about supermarket prices. That was the sum of their lesbian sex for the evening and, after another glass or two of wine, we all took off for a meal at a local restaurant. On reflection, I did enjoy the experience. Very much. Whether or not I shall ask if it can be repeated, I don't yet know. Certainly my sex with Sarah has been even better since that evening.

C. D. Earls Court, London.

Sounds like the best of both worlds to me.

KNOTTY PROBLEM

My boyfriend and I have known each other for almost a year now, and over that period of time, it has become evident – quite slowly – that he is seriously into bondage, and also, to a degree, into sadomasochism. My problem is that I don't know to what specific extent he is into S&M. Up until recently, I didn't mind him tying me up. In fact, I quite enjoy it. I love the feeling of submitting to him, sexually. But I'm not at all into pain, or real S&M of any kind, and I'm worried now that if I continue to let him tie me up, the time will come – even if it isn't intentional – when he'll be overcome by his sadistic tendencies, and hurt me. I've tried discussing it with him, but he clams up the moment I get onto the subject. It's not any great love affair, but we like each other's company, and the sex is good, apart from this particular worry. What is your advice?

K. A. L. Croydon, Surrey.

If he won't discuss it with you, find yourself a new boyfriend. Better to be safe than sorry.

SPANKS FOR THE MEMORY

At the age of thirty-seven, I've discovered an avenue of sexual activity that is entirely new to me, and which I never thought I would ever even experience, never mind enjoy. I've become addicted to being spanked. It started off, strangely enough, in Kingston, Jamaica. I recently divorced my husband of twelve years. Whilst our sex life was perhaps, at best, acceptable, it was finally destroyed – as far as I was concerned – by the fact that he was consistently unfaithful to me. Mostly with prostitutes. But actually with anything to hand. Or perhaps that should be with anything to cock. There's a lot of it about, as he always told me. However, be that as it may, I was always faithful to him. Looking back, I realize that I was probably very stupid.

Either stupid to be faithful to him, in the face of the continuing evidence of his unfaithfulness, or stupid to remain married to him for so long, in such unhappy circumstances. Happily, that is now all in the past. I am currently living with a man whom I met whilst staying in Kingston, where I went to spend the last Christmas holiday with friends who live there. John is divorced, three years older than me and, like me, he lives in London. He is a successful solicitor, with a great sense of humour. We like each other a lot, and have fantastic sex. But not long after our first night sharing a bed together, he grabbed me as I took off my dress, which left me wearing just knickers and my hold-up stockings. I don't need to wear a brassiere. He then put me – quite forcefully – across his knee, and started to spank me. 'You've been a very naughty girl, Diana,' he said. 'I'm going to have to punish you.' And he began to spank me on my knicker-covered bottom, with just the flat of his hand. I have to be honest and say that it was more of a statement than a serious spanking. Hurt it didn't. But what it did for his cock made the next part of the evening particularly enjoyable. However, my initial reaction was one of extreme indignation. Who the fuck did this creep think he was? And naughty? What sort of naughty?

I was trying to do a number of things at once. I was trying to wriggle off his lap, but I was firmly held in position there by his left hand. I was trying to look up at him as I shouted at him, telling him exactly what I thought of him and his 'punishment'. 'You're being even naughtier now, Diana,' he said. 'I'm going to have to pull your panties down, and spank your bare bottom.' And so saying, he did exactly that.

He pulled my knickers down to just below my knees, and then he spanked my naked buttocks. His hand stung my naked bottom just a tiny bit, and I wriggled and screamed, with real tears running down my cheeks. More from anger, I realize, looking back, than from actual pain. But slowly, as he spanked away – quite gently, really – I began to realize that my pussy was getting wetter and wetter, and that actually I was beginning to feel seriously horny. 'Oh, John darling,' I said to him. 'That's very exciting. You're making me feel very sexy. You're going to have to fuck me very soon. And fuck me properly. With your great big stiff prick, all the way up my tight, wet little cunt. Oh, I love it. Please don't stop. Please go on spanking me. Please.' I could feel that my pussy was getting wetter and wetter as he spanked me, and I was worried that I was going to make a sticky mess on his trousers, but he didn't seem bothered. 'Your bottom's getting all red as I spank you,' he said to me. 'I'm going to have to stop spanking you, and start *massaging* your naughty bottom. We don't want to cause permanent damage, do we?'

'Sod massaging my bottom,' I told him. 'Get out your great stiff prick and fuck me. Fuck my tight little cunt. Or fuck my tight little arse. Or would you rather that I sucked your swollen cock in my mouth, until you shoot your spunk down my throat? Or would you like me to toss you off as you spank me? I'll do anything for you. Anything. Just don't stop spanking me. Spank me, wank me. Anything you want to do to me. I love you spanking me. I love you wanking me. I love you fucking me. I love it when you fuck my mouth, and come down my throat. I just love it. All of it.' 'That's very generous, Diana my darling,' he said. 'I think I will go on spanking you for a little while, then, if that's all right with you.' He hadn't stopped stroking my buttocks ever since he'd actually stopped spanking me. I loved the feel of his firm, hard palm on my bottom. He stroked and rubbed and felt my posterior for what seemed like fifteen minutes, but it was probably a lot less.

'Do you like anal sex?' he asked me. 'It very much depends upon who's asking me,' I told him. Quite honestly. 'If they've got a huge prick, like yours, the thought of it tends to make me a bit nervous. But if it's someone I can trust, with a rather smaller cock than yours, they can fuck me anywhere they like. At least, they certainly can if they've wound me up first, as you have, by spanking my naked bottom.' And so he fucked me. Deliriously. But not up my arse. That'll come later. I hope. Now he's talking about buying a cane. I love it. Whatever next, I wonder? Yours,

D. P. Henley-on-Thames, Oxfordshire.

You've obviously got to the bottom of your sexual pleasures. Enjoy.

CANE AND ABLE

I'm just an ordinary reader of your excellent magazine, and I enjoy reading the letters in your correspondence columns about your readers' fantasies, their sexual problems, and their sexual successes. I'd love to tell you about my biggest sexual fantasy, in the hope that one of your male readers might get in touch with me, and join in with me in acting it out. Will you indulge me? Please? Then here goes.

I've always had strongly sexual dreams about being used. In every possible way. What I think I mean is that I want to be someone's sexual slave. I want a man to say to me, do this. Now. And I will want to do it. And I will want to please him. Shall I give you some examples? OK. I'd love a man to say to me, 'Sit down in that chair, pull your knickers down, and masturbate yourself until you come. When you've excited me by doing that, then you can masturbate me until I come.' Or, even more deviously, I'd love a man to say to me, 'Bend over, pull your skirt up, pull your panties down, and then reach behind you and stretch your arse cheeks apart. I'm going to bugger you. When I've spurted my load up your bottom, then I'll sit down and you can suck my cock clean.' I want to be sexually humiliated, you see. Is there anyone out there who understands that? Another part of the same fantasy is that I would like a man to see how many ways he could use me, sexually, to continually bring himself to orgasm. It is something to which I would love to give my enthusiastic attention. In no particular order of priority, he could, one, fuck me. Two, I'd toss him off. Three, he could have anal sex with me. Four, he could fuck my breasts. Five, I'd suck him off. Six, we'd start again at the beginning.

There are a number of other things that I've only either read or been told about that I would love to try, even though I know I wouldn't enjoy some of them. But if they turned my man on, I wouldn't object. These include, one, giving, or being given (I don't feel strongly about either option) an enema. Two, pissing on, or being pissed on by, my partner. As with enemas, the idea doesn't appeal very much, but from the Scandinavian magazine pictures that I've seen of both these options, some people seem to enjoy it. Sadomasochism doesn't appeal. At all. But if some guy wants to get his rocks off by putting clamps on my nipples, I'll try anything once. (Provided that he fucks me afterwards of course). I'm not into being caned or whipped or spanked, either. But you can do it to me, or I'll do it to you, if you really want that. And if you promise to love me forever, afterwards. OK?

K. W. Bromley, Kent.

Hey, slow down, baby. You don't have to go to those lengths. Really you don't. Just take it easy. OK?

NO BOUNCE

I've got this rubber fetish. At least, I think I have, in that I'm turned on by the very idea of my girlfriend wearing latex garments. Skirts. Bras. Knickers. Stockings. Arm-length gloves. Dresses even. But I can't persuade her to actually wear anything made of latex. I've bought quite a selection of this type of thing, but she simply refuses to wear any of it. I'm reduced to masturbating over them – or with them – when she's not around. She says that what I want her to do is perverted. What do you think?

A. O. Cardiff, Glamorgan.

I think you should respect your girlfriend's wishes.

QUICK CHANGE

I love to see women undressing. Preferably without them knowing that they are being watched. I discovered this when I happened to be on the woman's fashion floor of one of London's bigger department stores with a girlfriend, and she went into the changing rooms to try something on. I waited just outside, like a number of other husbands and boyfriends, and quickly discovered (we all did!) that, because the curtains weren't properly closed, we had an excellent view into the changing room itself. It was one of those stores that had one large communal room, rather than a number of separate closets, offering an excellent if slightly restricted view of a number of women in various stages of undress. Including, of course, my girlfriend. I found it extraordinarily erotic to see a pretty young woman walk past me, fully clothed, into the changing room, and then watch as she first took off her suit jacket, then her skirt, revealing herself in only tights, knickers and a bra, while she then tried on the dress she had been carrying. This activity was repeated continually as I stood there and watched. A number of the girls were bare-breasted. There were even a couple of girls wearing stockings with suspender belts. There was an interesting variety of underwear, from the strictly functional – plain white cotton – variety, to the truly exotic. There were kangas, French knickers, tiny bikinis, frilly, lacy, sexy panties. The prettier the girl, generally speaking, the plainer her underwear. Whilst we men outside the entrance were all watching for all we were worth, none of us spoke to the others about what was happening.

I didn't tell my girlfriend about this delightful interlude when she finally emerged, for fear that the revelation might prevent her from providing me with another opportunity in the future. But the episode has, in fact, changed my life. Whereas before this happened I was like any other bloke in that, yes, of course I have always enjoyed watching my girlfriends undress, I have now become a real voyeur. I seek out opportunities to see strange women undressing. Often, these days, I go into London's West End and hang about outside women's changing rooms in stores, as though waiting for someone. It's surprising how often I succeed in obtaining glimpses of undressed women. And my fantasies all revolve around secretly watching women undressing. I am a nightwatchman at a girls' boarding school. Or the caretaker at a women's rowing club. Or a teacher at a girls' physical training college. Or I'm a voyeur, a Peeping Tom, spying on ballet dancers as they change into or out of their tutus. Or I'm at a swimming bath, peeping into the women's changing rooms, spying into individual cubicles. If I'm lucky, I sometimes catch a woman playing with herself, her fingers busy up her knickers, tossing herself off. I particularly enjoy it if she sucks her fingers when she's finished. I'd like to suck them for her.

A favourite fantasy is that I get to spy, quite by chance, on a pair of lesbian lovers, who slowly undress each other as they kiss, and who feel up each other's sexes through their knickers, wanking each other off while they are still kissing. Eventually, of course, they peel each other's knickers off (and in my most favourite fantasy, the gusset of their knickers is always so wet that it sticks in the girls' pussies, and is slowly and carefully pulled out of there by each partner). Then they feel each other up with their fingers, exploring, stroking, frigging, until one will pull the other down onto the floor, or onto a sofa, or a bed – depending upon where they are –

and then they start to suck each other off.

I often vary the ending of this particular fantasy. Sometimes the girls just fuck each other with their fingers and their tongues. Sometimes I have them frigging each other with one or other of all those penis-substitute variations that one reads about girls using. Milk bottles. Candles. Cucumbers. Carrots. Occasionally they use vibrators on each other. And, naturally, some of them use dildoes. Sometimes strap-on single ones. Sometimes double-ended ones (so that they can fuck each other at the same time). Naturally enough, I'm beating my meat all the time that I'm watching these delightfully dirty young ladies at their private sex games, but in the very best of these fantasies, where there are two girls, (i) I happily actually let the girls know that I have been watching them, and (ii) they turn out to be bisexual – yes, both of them – and they are always delighted to let me join in with them. Ain't life wonderful?

Sometimes I fuck one of them whilst the second one helps me. She might, for example, hold her friend's labia apart for me as I thrust my swollen cock up her friend's cunt. Or if I'm into anal sex on this occasion, she'll pull her friend's buttocks apart for me as I thrust into the offered, opened anus. Or she might simply French-kiss me, using her agile tongue to excite me, whilst I fuck the other girl doggy fashion. Another favourite is when one of the girls wanks me off into her friend's mouth. These variations, with a couple of really co-operative bisexual lesbian girls, are endless. Think about it.

W. P. S. Hull, Humberside.

I will. I hope your night-watchmen are getting good overtime rates.

DYKE'S DELIGHT

I love to read your letters columns, but I strongly suspect that the vast majority of them represent reader's fantasies. And there's nothing wrong with that. But I thought that it might make a pleasant change for at least some of your readers if, as a young, pretty (I'm told) practising lesbian, I told you what it *really* feels like to make love to girls. So here goes. But first of all, may I please get one thing straight? I don't pretend to speak for all lesbians. Only for myself. I'm the so-called butch half of my relationship. To me, that simply means that I'm the instigator. The male, if you like. And the point that I want to make is that I have never used a dildo, or a vibrator, or a penis-substitute of any kind, in my entire life. Sex for me and my partners is entirely oral, or manual.

I've actually never even seen a dildo. Nor have any of my girlfriends. I think girls fucking each other with penis-substitutes is a mostly male fantasy. Strange, isn't it? I mean, women don't fantasize about men fucking false vaginas. I know they exist, but did you ever know anyone who used one? Like men, I find that pretty lingerie turns me on, and it's always fun for me to buy sexy underwear for my girlfriends. And like men, it's fun, occasionally, to buy really vulgar undies. Tarts' knickers. You know the sort of thing. Red satin, crotchless knickers, with lots of black lace. And then you bury your face in the exposed pussy and suck and lick your way to heaven!

As a lesbian, I've always loved sucking pussy. But it has to be clean. So a bath or a shower together is often the starting place for sex, *chez moi*. I love to soap my girlfriend's pussy and slide the soap right inside her, rapidly followed by my agile, clit-finding finger. I don't seriously suffer from penis envy, but the one thing that I *do* envy men is the ability to have an erection. It's such a magnificent statement of sheer, unadulterated lust. Of desire. It says I WANT TO FUCK YOU in a way that a woman can't. Yes, of course, I know that we show similar feelings by getting our pussies all wet. And I get wetter than anyone I know. But it's not in the same league as walking around with a rampant cock. So we've been through the pretty knickers bit, and I've told you that I like to suck pussy. Freshly washed pussy. What comes next. Oh, yes. Actually doing it. Some men are very expert at cunnilingus. I've been sucked off by a few expert gentlemen in my time, I have to admit.

And when a girl is fortunate enough to meet a guy who likes sucking pussy, she's on to a good thing. No doubt about it. I speak from experience. I haven't always been gay. Nor am I, necessarily, always gay now. But – in my admittedly limited experience – a lot of men won't suck cunt. They love girls to take their dirty, unwashed cocks in their mouths and suck them off. But they won't suck cunt. The thought horrifies them. It's dirty. Disgusting. If girls are made of sugar and spice, and all things nice, they quote, why do they taste of kippers? Har har. Clean cunt doesn't taste of kippers. Take it from me. It tastes of elixir. Sexual elixir. Come and taste mine. Any time.

So, as the evening wears on, when I'm with a new girlfriend, I get more and more excited. We have dinner. Somewhere romantic. I keep trying to touch her. No. Not touch her up. Not yet. Just touch her. You know. A hand on her elbow. An elbow brushing against her breast, as I take my coat off. A hand on her knee, to make a conversational point. And then, after dinner, I love to dance. Yes, of course we go to gay places to dance. I want to be able to relax, just the same as you do. I want to be able to put my arms around her, in the semi-darkness, and stick my tongue down her throat, and dance with my thigh between her legs, grinding it against her sex, and feel and squeeze her buttocks while we dance, just the same as you do. There's not *that* much difference between what you and I like to do, you know. I want to wind her up. Get her feeling sexy. Wanting me. I want her pussy to be wet, just the same as you do. And then I want to take her home in a cab, with my arm around her waist. I probably won't kiss her in the cab, as you would, because London cab drivers are notoriously chauvinist. But I might stick my hand up her skirt, and gave her a quick feel, if the cabbie's not looking in his rear-view mirror.

And then it's pay off the cab, in through the front door, up into the bedroom, and knickers round your ankles, just like Adam Faith used to demand in *Budgie*, all those years ago. And then it's down onto the bed, onto her back, spread her pretty legs, press my lips against her wetness, and lick the divinely tasting fluid that is emanating from her pretty little cunt. And she'll raise her hips up right off the bed as I suck her. She'll writhe, and moan, and say, 'Oh God. I like it. Oh, yes. Oh, Jesus. Oh, darling. Oh, I'm coming. Oh fuck. I'm coming now. Oh yes. Oh, please. Oh, God.' And she'll grind her cunt against my lips as I suck and tongue and lick.

And I'll keep on sucking her, but at the same time I'll slide my forefinger down inside her wet little pussy, and I'll find her clitoris, and I'll masturbate it until she's practically screaming for mercy. But I won't stop, even when she asks me to. I'll keep on, and on, and on. Until, eventually, she'll have a giant orgasm. Which she'll love. And after she's recovered from that, she'll suck my pussy until I'm ready to faint. And she'll be feeling so randy, by this time, that she'll keep going all night. Because, like I said earlier, while I'd love to have a rampant penis, wouldn't *you* like to be able to go on fucking for ever? Without ever needing to stop? Because that's what me and my girlfriends do. We go on sucking all night. And playing with each other's pussies. Who needs cock? Yours very respectfully.

W. T. Bolton, Lancs.

It sounds like a lot of fun. Or should I say a slot *of fun? Good luck.*

RELUCTANT HEROES

Can anyone out there tell me why so many men don't like oral sex? I love to suck pussy, and my girl, Mandy, loves me doing it to her. I can happily suck her off for hours at a time. But she tells me that I am very much in the minority. She says that most men aren't into cunt-lapping. Apparently there are many men who think that the idea of kissing and licking a girl's sexual organ is a disgustingly dirty thing to do. She said one man even said to her, 'How can you possibly expect me to do that? You might just as well ask me to lick your arsehole.' I'm certainly not averse to *that*, but pussies are my favourite.

Let's examine, for a moment, some of the alleged reasons why men don't like to suck pussy. One: some men say that women's vaginas smell nasty. Not if they're clean, they don't. So if in doubt, wash it out. That can be good fun in itself. In my experience, I have never actually gone down on a girl who smelt unpleasant 'down there'. I always wash my cock before a heavy date. I'm sure girls act similarly. But what could be the worst that could happen? If you went down on a girl in the evening who simply hadn't had an opportunity to freshen up since leaving home that morning, well, I guess that you might get just a tiny whiff of urine. I actually find that aroma sexually exciting. I guess it's a matter of association. I know where it comes from, and where it comes from is one of my most favourite female places. I believe that all men love having their cock sucked. It's the same thing, isn't it? I'll bet there's many a man who has had his cock sucked at the end of a hard day at the office without being able to wash it first. So what?

Two: the kind of man who will complain of the smell of the cunt he's sucking will probably also complain about the taste. Me? I love it. It's my favourite flavour. Sexually aroused cunt. Fantastic. I wish they made cunt-flavoured mints. I'd suck them all day long, to remind me what I was going to suck all *night* long. And of course my fantasies are all about sucking pussy. I can't look at a woman in the street, or in a pub, or a restaurant, or anywhere, come to that, without wondering if she likes her pussy sucked. And whether she realizes that she is close to/opposite/standing beside one of the world's great pussy eaters. And I always wonder if her pussy is wet or not.

In my fantasies, I lean across and whisper in her ear that I'd like to suck her pussy, and she gets very excited and makes an excuse to get away from whoever she's with. She meets me outside, and we go off together – usually back to her place – and I watch her undress, which these lovely girls always do very slowly. When they're down to their knicks, I take over, and I kneel down in front of them, and pull their knickers down, very, very slowly, revealing first their pubic hair (or, oh Jesus, sometimes the complete lack of it). And below their plump little pudendas, of course, come their outer labia. You will know as well as I do that no two women have identical pussies. They're all different. And I love the excitement of slowly revealing a new one, in all its erotic glory. I just kneel there, and take in its beauty. The colour of the pubic hair. Thick, blonde, curly pubic hair. Long, strong, straight black pubic hair. Curly black pubic hair like steel wool. Soft auburn pubic hair. Wispy, young, sparse pubic hair. Sometimes, as I said, the beauty of a shaven pudenda, the flesh creamy and soft in its immaculate nakedness. I have to reach out and touch it, feel its smooth baldness. And then, down below, the outer lips, guarding the inner labia. A million different patterns. Almost non-existent lips. Swollen, fleshy lips. Long droopy lips. Little short, tight, thin lips. It is, of course, another mouth, and the varieties of lip are as extensive as they are with the facial kind. I trace their outline with my finger.

As I'm kneeling, my face will be only some six inches or so away from the object of my desire. I look for the tell-tale dribble of colourless, sticky mucus that will tell me that its owner is anticipating the entry of my tongue between her cunt lips. I always have to reach out and part the outer labia with my finger tips. Gently. Lovingly. Revealing her inner secrets. That close, I can also inhale the strong scent of her. Aroused pussy. Pussy aching to be sucked. And – eventually – fucked. For, with me, the one leads, as inevitably as night follows day, to the other.

By now I will be highly sexually excited myself, and my erection will be strong and firm. I will probably have undone my flies, allowing my cock to thrust out and up, freeing it from its restraining clothing. I will almost certainly interrupt the proceedings here and stand up to quickly disrobe, throwing my clothes into a corner so that I may, as quickly as possible, return to kneel before the altar of my sexual desire. I will now thrust a finger carefully into the shining pink centre of my mistress's vagina, parting her lips like the petals of some rare, highly scented, satiny-smooth orchid.

She'll be warm, and wet, and tight. She'll gasp at the unexpected intrusion of my finger, which I'll thrust into her as deeply as I can, burying it into her up to the knuckle. Sometimes I'll be able to feel the entrance to her womb with the tip of my finger. At other times I won't come anywhere near it, for the depth, or length, of a woman's cunt is as varied as is the size and length of a man's cock. I love some of the variations that my examination will by now have revealed. What am I saying? I love *all* the variations that will by now have been revealed. But some particularly. Naturally black pubic hair dyed blonde always excites me. Whilst I love a shaved pudenda, I also love hirsute pudendas, covered thickly by a long-haired, springy pubic bush. I find that very sexually exciting. And I just adore hairy female arseholes. But that's another story. I understand the need, but I am not overly fond, of the fashion model's tendency to cut her pubic hair back, leaving a symbolic tuft of hair immediately above the entrance to her vagina.

I worship big cunt lips. The kind that look like miniature spaniel's ears. Or pink butterflies, perhaps. And I never fail to be surprised at the amazing range of colours in which pretty pussies come. From the palest pink to the darkest blue-black. And every variation of shade in between. And all with matching nipples! At this stage in my fantasies, I usually use both hands and put them between the girl's legs, pressing her thighs apart slightly, indicating that I wish her to spread them for me which she then always does. I next reach behind her and clasp her generous buttocks, squeezing them. I pull her towards me, lean forward, and kiss her directly on her vaginal lips. Softly at first. Lovingly. Gently. Then I lick her copiously oozing slit, starting at the bottom, and I lick it upwards, slowly and delicately, revelling in the taste and flavour of her effluent. It tastes good. Delectable. Nice.

Then I stand up, my erection proudly rampant before me, take her by the hand and lead her over to the bed. She lies down and spreads her legs wide, pulling her knees up to allow me free access to her sex, and I lie beside her, my head down between her legs. And I begin. I make her come. Over and over again. Until she is sobbing with sexual pleasure. I kiss her, suck her. Manipulate her clitoris with my fingers. Masturbate her. Wank her. She orgasms. Again and again. Her orgasms build and merge. Build and merge. Until her womb is erupting in one all-consuming, all-embracing, continual orgasm that has her whole body shaking, and now she is pleading to be fucked. 'I want you inside me,' she says. 'In my cunt. I need your cock. Inside me. Now. Fuck me, darling. Please. Now. Fuck me. Fuck me. Fuck me.'

And I get myself up from my prone position, turn myself around and thrust my prick up her tight, wet, welcoming hole. And I fuck her. Seriously fuck her. Fuck her brains out. And she comes again. Only this time, I come with her. I jet my hot semen up her, and we orgasm together, clutching each other, holding each other, our bodies shuddering as we unite in our mutual climax. I'm in heaven. A heaven that began with oral sex.

P. D. Ipswich, Suffolk.

Helped, obviously, by a flight of angels, who took you for a sucker.

JUST GYMSLIPS

I've always been turned on by the idea of sex with young girls and, whilst I have obviously never indulged in under-age sex, I get a lot of my sexual pleasure by persuading my wife to dress up in a variety of youthful, girlish outfits. First of all is, of course, the ever-fancied, ever-fanciful navy blue gymslip. Ours comes from an Oxfam shop, and is the genuine article. It is very short, and fully pleated. Beneath this she wears a basic, plain white blouse, and a very small pair of navy blue cotton knickers. To these she adds black nylon stockings, sometimes held up by a black satin suspender belt, and on other occasions she will wear self-supporting stockings. She plaits her long blonde hair into two schoolgirl-type plaits, secured with ribbons, and the outfit is complete.

She will be wearing this when I come home from work, and will spend much of the time preparing and serving our evening meal giving me lots of opportunities to see her knickers and that lovely bit of naked thigh between her stocking tops and her knicker edge. She will sometimes come and sit opposite me, her legs wide apart so that I can see her knicker crotch, and pretend that she doesn't know what she is showing. I particularly like this when I can see the moisture darkening the already dark blue material between her legs. When I can't stand it any more, I leap at her, and feel her up, and she pretends to scream, and tries to stop me from feeling her between her legs. She loves to play at being raped, and I enjoy fucking her as she pretends to sob her little heart out.

At other times, she will deliberately be 'naughty'. At first,

I will threaten her with a spanking. She (who loves a little mild 'discipline') will of course go on misbehaving until I take her, put her across my knee, pull down her navy blue knickers, and spank her on her bare bottom. I love to watch it getting redder and redder, and I keep at it until she is pleading with me to stop. Another favourite 'uniform' is that of the Girl Guides. This we got from a theatrical costumier. I expect you can imagine the kind of games we play when my wife is wearing this one. And the final outfit is one she designed herself. It's what she calls her 'Teenage Tart's' outfit.

It comprises a skimpy, extremely tight, very short pair of gold satin hot pants, worn with a white, almost transparent bra top, about two sizes too small. She wears these items with the kind of self-supporting stockings that come just up over the tops of her knees, or else with black nylon stockings with seams. Too much make-up and a wad of gum that she chews enthusiastically complete the picture. I can have any kind of sex I like, but I have to pay for it. I don't often fuck her in this outfit, since she insists that I wear a condom, which I dislike. I usually settle for a blow-job (for five pounds) or a quick one off the wrist (at three pounds). We both enjoy the fun we have with these dressing-up, make-believe games.

D. H. Norwich, Norfolk.

Continue to enjoy.

PROFESSIONAL JEALOUSY!

I am a Professor of English at a women's college at one of the older universities, and I write to tell you of the pleasures offered by a number of my female students. As part of the regular system, I take them in small classes of two or three – tutorials – as well as in larger groups. Sometimes, two of the three girls due to see me together may not turn up, for one reason or another, and I am left with just one student. This happened to me recently. I was having the girl read to me from one of the required texts, and she was doing very well when she put the book down, came over and stood beside me (I was sitting on a chair behind my desk as I usually do). She leaned over the arm of the chair, unzipped my fly, reached inside, and pulled out my flaccid penis. I have to say that I in no way tried to resist her. 'This will be much more fun,' she said, and she began to masturbate me. She was absolutely right, of course.

She is an attractive young woman. About twenty-two or twenty-three, with bold, firm, high-standing breasts, and given to wearing short skirts that show off her lovely long legs to perfection. My cock quickly became fully erect: she then knelt down beside my chair and took my erection into her mouth, where she sucked and wanked it until I came in her mouth. She didn't pull away, but swallowed my juices with seeming enjoyment. When she had finished, I thanked her, and put my cock back inside my trousers, after which we resumed the tutorial. Everything went normally until the end of the session, when she came and stood in front of me and stroked my cock through the front of my trousers. 'If you'd like to fuck me, I'll happily come to your rooms in the evening,' she offered. 'I'm on for every kind of sex. Normal. Oral. Anal. You name it, I like it.' As you can probably imagine, my cock stood immediately to attention again, and I said that yes, I'd like that. How would seven o'clock on the following evening suit? 'I'll be there,' she said. 'I'll look forward to that.' *Not half as much as I will*, I thought. And then she left.

That following evening she arrived, as arranged, at seven o'clock. She smiled as I opened the door. Entering my rooms and shutting the door behind her, she carefully turned the key in the lock. She then came to me, took my head in her hands and pulled my face down to hers, at which point she started to French-kiss me. Her tongue probed mine and we exchanged wet kisses until we both needed to stop for breath. During this exchange, I could feel her full breasts pressing against my chest, and I began to get an erection. 'Shall I do a striptease for you?' she asked, and I said that would be fun.

She was wearing a black skirt, with a white blouse and a black woollen cardigan. She took off the cardigan, then the blouse, exposing her naked breasts. She took hold of her nipples, which were bigger than any I had seen before, and began to pull them, playing with them, and twirling them in her fingers. 'Do you like big breasts, Frank?' she asked, using my Christian name for the first time. 'Have you ever sat astride a girl and let her wank you between her lovely, big, soft breasts?' I admitted that yes, I did like big breasts. They have always excited me. And no, sadly, I have never experienced the joys of what I believe is called a French necklace. 'We'll do that later, if you'd like to,' she said. She then turned around, so that her back was towards me and, unzipping her skirt, she wriggled it slowly down her hips, then down her thighs, and finally down her legs, until it was in a heap on the floor, at which moment she stepped out of it. She stayed bending over for a while longer.

I loved the time that she spent bending over and pulling the skirt down: her black lacy knickers were stretched tightly over her full buttocks which I could clearly see revealed against the translucent material of her knickers. The crotch of this flimsy item was also pulled tightly up into her groin, although I could only imagine what it was so coyly covering, since the cotton lining prevented me from seeing anything more. She was also wearing black silky stockings with lacy bands around the tops, which seemed to keep up of their own volition. I think they probably had some kind of elastic around the tops.

As she stepped away from her skirt, she stood there in front of me, naked from the waist up, with just her knickers and stockings and black, high-heeled shoes on. She said, 'Do you like what you see, Frank?' I said, 'Very much, my dear. Very much.' 'It's all yours, darling,' she said to me. 'It's all yours, to do whatever you like with.' I couldn't believe my ears. I mean, I'm not a young man. I'm fifty-three. And I've not had that many women in my life. Three, to be exact. And here was this beautiful young woman offering her body to me, quite voluntarily, to do with as I pleased. It was a dream come true. She looked at me, and smiled. 'Shall I take my knickers off now, Frank darling?' she said. 'Or would you rather take them off for me?' I felt desperately embarrassed. Of the three women in my life, I had never actually seen any of them totally naked, whether in daylight or electric light. Sex had always been an under-the-covers-with-the-light-out activity, and I had never even seen a bare breast, clearly, for any length of time.

'Er, you take them off, please,' I said, hoping that my embarrassment didn't show. And hoping too – although I knew it was not possible – that she could not see my erection, standing out against my fly. This time she stayed facing me, and she very slowly pulled her knickers down, humming the old classic stripper's song as she did so. You know the one. I think it's actually called 'The Stripper'.

I had to laugh. She was making sex so much fun. As she revealed first her pubic hair (which was thick and black and curly) and then her pubis, and, finally, the lips of her sex, she did the classic American stripper's bump-and-grind routine, shaking her hips and wriggling her bottom, her breasts thrust forward. When she stepped out of her knickers, she was left standing there in just her black, silky stockings. It was, I think, the sexiest thing I had ever seen in my life. She crumpled her knickers up in her hand into a little black silken ball, came over to me, and pressed them against my nose. 'Sniff, Frank,' she said. I drew in a deep breath. They smelt entirely of sex, with overtones of heavy scent. 'What do you smell, Frank?' she asked me, continuing to rub the knickers against my nostrils. 'Er, I'm not sure,' I said, not liking to use the words that came to mind. She laughed again. 'That's cunt, Frank,' she said. 'Unadulterated, nicely wet, sexually stimulated cunt. Feel.' And as she spoke, she took my hand and placed it between her legs. She moved my fingers around amongst the hair that I first felt, until they came to her sex. It felt warm, and very wet. She rubbed my fingers up and down against her wet sex, and then she pulled my fingers up in her hand again, and placed them against my lips.

'Taste that, darling,' she told me. I put my fingers in my mouth. Tentatively at first. Then with enthusiasm. I don't mind saying it now, but right then, I was embarrassed to say that I'd never had oral sex of any kind. I realize now that I'd probably never had what most young people these days would call real sex of any kind. But I'm learning. The wetness on my fingers tasted like elixir to me, and I sucked at my fingers until every last trace had been licked off. 'Would you like some more, darling?' she asked. I nodded. 'Let's go into the bedroom, and make ourselves comfortable,' she said. I led the way through to the bedroom where the girl undressed me in an unfussy, methodical way. When I was naked, she lay back on the bed and opened her legs. She took my hand in hers. 'Let's start gently,' she suggested. 'There's no hurry.'

'First of all, I don't know whether or not you know my Christian name, but it's Pamela. OK?' 'Of course,' I said. I knew she was P. Clarke, but I didn't know – hadn't taken the trouble to find out – that the 'P' stood for Pamela. 'Put these two fingers together,' she commanded, closing together my forefinger and my middle finger. She spread her legs even wider. 'Now, I'll help you to put them up inside my pussy,' she said, and she followed her words with the actions, helping me to slide the two fingers into her. 'Have a little feel around in there, darling,' she suggested. I did as I was bidden. It felt lovely and tight. And warm. And very wet. I could feel sort of ribs in the lining surrounding my fingers, and I could feel a sort of bump at the end. The bottom. I'm not sure of the proper terms.

As I moved my fingers about, she squirmed and wriggled quite a bit, and said things like, 'Ooh. Yes. Mmm. Nice. Lovely.' And so on. After a while, she asked 'Do you know where my clit is?' 'Er, no,' I said. It was true. I knew *what* it was, but I didn't know precisely *where* it was. It is, I'd been told, the hub of all female sexual pleasure. The nub against which a man is supposed to rub his cock, thus stimulating the clitoris, and bringing the woman to orgasm. I'd read all the books, but I'd never had this kind of conversation with a woman.

'Give me your finger again, darling,' she said. 'Just the forefinger this time.' I did as I was told. She took it, and slid it into her waiting pussy. She moved it about for a moment or two, and let it finally come to rest on what felt like a small, raised bump. 'Can you feel that?' she asked me. 'Yes,' I said, moving my finger around. 'If you mean that little bit that I'm touching now.' 'The very place,' she said, laughing. 'Now then, sweetheart,' she said. 'Pay attention. If you stroke and rub that little thing that you can feel there – but gently. Carefully. Then,' she said, 'Then, you'll feel it grow. Become erect. Just like a tiny cock.' I must have looked puzzled. 'No,' she said. 'Don't give up. You haven't tried yet.' I tried to relax, and when she had taken her hand away, I felt for, and found, her clitoris once more. When I got there, I spent all the time in the world stroking it. Very, very gently. Moving my finger around and around in small circles. And, magically, I suddenly felt it growing beneath the pressure of my finger. 'Oh, yes,' said Pamela, breathing heavily. 'Mmmm. Oh, Yes. Good. I like it. That's nice. Oh, God. I'm coming. I'm coming now.' And as I continued to massage her clitoris, she actually came. Noisily. I felt as pleased as a teenager.

'Terrific,' she said, sitting up on the bed. 'I'm the one that's supposed to be teaching you, and you're doing things for me. That was terrific. Thank you. Now then, what would you like me to do to you? Like I said before. Anything, absolutely anything at all. Just tell me.' There were so many things that I would have liked her to do to me – and me to her – that I couldn't prioritize any single one. I stayed silent, not knowing what to choose. 'Shall I run through a few possibilities?' she asked. 'You know... just to warm you up?' 'Please do,' I told her. 'There's so much that I'd like that I can't make a decision.' She grinned at me. Just like the Cheshire Cat. 'Look, Frank,' she said. 'We've got all the time in the world. There's no hurry. We can do absolutely everything that you want to do. And then we can do it all over again. And again. It's not a problem. Just tell me what you want.'

I took her at her word. 'I want to lie on top of you, right now,' I told her, 'and slide my cock right up your lovely wet cunt. And then I want to plain, old-fashioned fuck you. Out of your senses. And out of my mind. That's all I want. But

I've been wanting it all my life. How does that sound to you?' 'If that's what you're after, sweetheart,' she replied, 'then that's what you shall have. Come to Mama.' She beckoned me nearer to her. She lay right back on the bed, and opened her legs wider than I would have thought possible.

I knelt down between her thighs, my rampant cock jutting out at a proud angle. She took hold of it and guided it down, in between her legs. I pressed downwards, to thrust it into her, and she raised her buttocks, seemingly anxious to receive it. Once inside her, she seemed to suck me in, rather like a vacuum cleaner. I could positively feel the suction. She felt tremendous. As I tried to become accustomed to the feelings in my cock, thrust deeply into the pussy of an extremely attractive young lady, I wondered at the circumstances that had brought me here. But my real wonderment came from the sensations that were permeating my entire sexual apparatus. They were the most wonderful that I had ever experienced.

I didn't know what sex was all about, prior to the fucking that I was getting right now. Earlier in my life, it had been like rape legalized by marriage. But Pamela was freely mine, and I could do what I liked with her. Or so her own rule book said. I grabbed her buttocks, squeezing them, and began my long climb up to ejaculation. 'Go for it, baby,' Pamela whispered in my ear. 'Fuck me. Fuck me silly. You've got your huge cock up my cunt, and I'm enjoying it. All I need, soon, is a great wad of your spunk up me. I love spunk. I love to drink it. Suck it out of your cock. Come into me. Now, baby. Now. Fuck me now. Please.' Even as she spoke, I was spurting my ejaculate into her womb. I was so embarrassed at having come so quickly that I apologized to Pamela. 'Don't worry about a thing, Frank,' she said. 'Just leave it in there. We'll have you on the go again in minutes.'

And it was exactly so. That evening and night, I did

everything with Pamela that I had ever fantasized about. I fucked her mouth, her vagina, and her rectal orifice. She, apparently, was enjoying teaching me, and I was more than happy to learn. I finally fell asleep, exhausted, with Pamela by my side. When I awoke the next morning, she was gone, but she had left a note saying, 'See you this evening. Love, P.' The day dragged slowly by, but the evening finally arrived. I had an erection simply thinking about what I was going to do to Pamela when she eventually knocked at my door. Imagine my surprise when, having accepted my offer of a glass of sherry, she told me that she was indeed there for me to do anything sexual to her, or with her, that I wished, but that there was something that she felt she ought to get clear first. 'Of course, my dear,' I said. 'What is it?'

She then spent some time explaining to me that, in return for her sexual favours (which, to be fair to her, she said would be available on a daily – or should that be nightly? – basis, and would, as before, include anything that I wished) she would expect a guaranteed First Class Honours degree at the end of her three years. I was flabbergasted, naturally, and I quickly explained to her that, unfortunately, there was no question of my being able to agree to such a suggestion. My professional ethics simply would not permit an arrangement of that kind. She was sorry to hear that, she said. Because after she had left me in the early hours, she had taken a taxi to a friendly doctor who, by prior arrangement and accompanied by a nurse, had given her a thorough physical examination, including the taking of oral, vaginal and anal swabs. These, through DNA 'finger-printing' techniques, would immediately identify me.

She would, she went on, be perfectly prepared to swear on oath to the college authorities that I had forced her to have sex with me, against her will and under threat of failing her in her examination prospects. She also reminded me that anal sex with a woman was illegal in Britain, and that anal rape was much frowned upon, and heavily punished by, the courts. As she sat there telling me this, she pulled her skirt up and her knickers down. She opened her legs, affording me an attractive view of one of the three parts of her anatomy that had given me so much pleasure the previous evening. 'All you have to do to avoid all that unpleasantness, Frank,' she said, 'is to agree to my suggestion. And then this is yours to play with. Right now. And every day. Whenever you want it.' She looked down, fluttering her eyelids and, I swear, blushing slightly. 'And the other parts, of course,' she said. 'Whenever you want them.' I remembered the joy of buggering her. My rigid cock sunk deep between her bum cheeks. Her anus dilated, its puckered circumference stretched tight by my swollen shaft. And I gave in. I agreed.

She slipped out of her chair, unzipped my fly, took out my cock and, just before she took it in her mouth, she said 'Oh, Frank. I knew you'd see it my way.' And then she sucked me off.

J. L. H. Norwich, Norfolk.

Here endeth the second lesson!

BOTTOMS UP

I love to read the mixture of true stories of sexual exploits and descriptions of individual sexual fantasies printed in your columns as related to you by your readers. I wonder if you would care to read about one of mine? Which of the two types this story is, I shall leave you to judge for yourselves. I recently spent ten days in New York on a business trip, staying at the Plaza Hotel, on the south side of Central Park. You will know that this is one of the city's top hotels. I lunched and dined at some of the better-known New York restaurants, as a guest of my hosts, and I loved all of them. They included Windows on the World, Le Cirque, Palm, P. J. Clarke's, and The Tavern on the Green.

But, much as I enjoyed this hospitality and the chance to see (and eat in) some of the most famous restaurants in the world, what I really wanted to do was to get myself down to Greenwich Village, and suss out one of the New York S&M clubs that I had heard so much about. And then my opportunity finally arrived. I had a free evening, to spend as I wished. So, thinking that the Plaza's concierge probably wasn't the man to ask about S&M clubs, I bought a copy of *Screw* magazine from a bookstall, and ran my eye down the club listings.

I ended up at a basement address on the Lower West Side. It didn't look much from the outside and I almost turned away. But I thought nothing ventured, nothing gained, and rang the bell. It was opened by a very pretty girl wearing classic dominatrice gear: black leather basque, net stockings, black patent leather high-heeled shoes, studded wristlets and anklets. She wore a top hat over her long auburn hair, and she carried a vicious-looking whip. 'Hey, Mac,' she said, opening the door. 'Come in. What can we do for you?' As she shut the door, I heard a terrifying, high-pitched scream echoing hollowly from somewhere out at the back. The girl smiled at me, and held out a hand. 'I'm Victoria,' she said. 'Let me take you through to the bar. Just follow me.' We were standing in what was simply a hallway. It was well decorated, expensively carpeted, and hung with some good contemporary art dealing with sexual subjects. Mostly S&M subjects, reasonably enough.

I followed Victoria through to the bar, which was impressively large, and manned – if that's the word – by two barmaids, dressed like Victoria but without the top hat. There were four other people on my side of the bar. A couple, who seemed to be together, and two men dressed, like me, in business suits. 'What can I get you?' Victoria asked. 'We have most things. Alcohol is on the house. These two girls are Linda' (pointing at the nearest girl, who smiled back) 'and Frances' (pointing at the second girl, who raised a languid hand). 'Either of the girls will pee into a glass for you. Or into your mouth, if you prefer. And in private, of course. That we charge for.'

She looked at me, expectantly. 'Thanks,' I said. 'I'll take a Scotch on the rocks, with branch water.' Victoria passed my request on to Linda, who brought a large Scotch on the rocks, with a small bottle of water, and a Seven-Up for Victoria. I wondered if it had any vodka or gin in it. 'Cheers,' said Victoria. 'Cheers,' I said, opening the water and putting some into my Scotch. 'Now then,' said Victoria, 'shall I run through what's available, or would you prefer to tell me what you're looking for?' I took a long slurp at my Scotch and water. 'I'm looking for a pretty girl to spank,' I told her. 'I'd like to tie her up – or have her tied up – spank her, and then fuck her.' Victoria grinned at me. 'Oh, what a pleasant change for someone to ask me for something normal,' she said – rather ironically, I thought. 'That's no problem. Finish your drink, then we'll go together and you can choose your girl. OK?'

'It surely is,' I told her. I had begun to pick up one or two conversational New Yorkisms. Like 'surely', and 'momentarily'. We both finished our drinks. Victoria stood up and I followed her. We went through the bar, to a door on the far side. As Victoria opened the door, that dreadful scream rang out again. 'That's coming from the torture dungeons, downstairs,' she explained. 'I guess it takes all sorts.' I didn't say anything. I tried not to think about it. She finally led me through a door at the end of a corridor into a tiny room, which had what was obviously a one-way mirror in the centre of the opposite wall. It was a big mirror, and it gave a good view of a large room, furnished with easy chairs, sofas, and tables. There was a small hatchway on the far side of the room, which seemed to be dispensing drinks and snacks.

What was attractive about the room, for me, was the fact that it was occupied by around twenty or so beautiful young girls. Victoria looked at me. 'How serious is your spanking?' she asked me. 'And it's vital, to save a lot of trouble later on, that you answer me truthfully. You can thrash the living daylights out of someone, if that's what you're after. But it's vital that I know beforehand. If you're only going to play at it, then tell me now.' That was easy. 'I'm not seriously into pain at all,' I told her. 'I just love spanking bare bums. Or bums covered with tightly-stretched knickers. Bums in all their taut, globular beauty. I love the feel of firmly fleshed buttocks under my hand. I love to spank, but really only very lightly. But it *does* excite me if the girl cries. Or, at the very least, pretends to cry. And that's it. I'm not into caning, pain, blood, or anything seriously unpleasant.' Victoria smiled at me. 'Well, that's very easily set up,' she said. 'For what you're looking for, any one of those girls you can see through there will be up for it. If you had wanted to use a cane, or a whip, and draw blood, then I would have had to point out to you the girls who will accept that kind of treatment. Of which there are quite a few,' she added. 'But not *all* of them.'

I began to look at the assembled girls. They were all remarkably attractive. And they were all young. I don't suppose there was one there over the age of about twenty-five. Most were in some form of lingerie. One or two were completely naked. None was fully dressed. As I looked around the room, my eye was caught by a tall, lithe, long-legged redhead. She was at least five ten, five eleven, with legs all the way up to her shapely bottom, which itself was lusciously full and firm. She had what I'd call a spanker's arse. It just cried out to be chastised. Her strikingly auburn hair was long, almost down to her waist, and although she was wearing white, semi-transparent panties of some kind, they were of a sufficiently thin material for me to be able to see quite clearly that her pubic hair matched her long tresses.

'That's the one, Victoria,' I said, pointing. 'That one over there. The tall girl, with the long auburn hair.' Victoria smiled. 'Oh, what a terrific choice,' she said. 'You'll enjoy her. That's my younger sister. Her name's Prudence. Pru for short. You'll love her. She gives great head.' Victoria turned and looked at me. 'And she loves to be spanked,' she said. 'I'll go and get her ready. I'll get her to dress in some kind of sexy lingerie. After that, it's up to you. OK?'

'OK,' I said. 'Come with me,' said Victoria. 'I'll show you to a room.' We set off into the softly-lit depths of the building. She handed me a sort of small, menu-like card. 'This is our price list,' she said as we walked along. 'The company prefers me to ask you at this stage how you are going to pay. Travellers' cheques and most credit cards are acceptable. As is cash. We give a small discount for cash. Details are on the bottom of the card.' I looked at the price list. The prices certainly weren't cheap. But then, one didn't expect them to be. Good-quality perverse sexual services with pretty, amenable young girls come highly priced in the world's major cities. 'I'll pay by credit card,' I told her, 'if that's acceptable.' 'Absolutely,' said Victoria, holding out her hand. 'May I take it now? I'll run off a blank form which you can sign as you leave. I'll bring your card back right away.'

I got out my wallet and handed over my platinum card. If she was impressed, she didn't show it. 'Thank you,' she said. She stopped, and opened a door. 'This is your room,' she said. 'Make yourself comfortable. Pru will show you where everything is. Have fun.' And she was gone, shutting the door behind her. I looked around the room. It was large, and well furnished. There was a king-size bed at one end, a bathroom with toilet, bath and shower at the other end of the room, and a small bar with a padded leather top just off to the left. I wandered over to the bar, opened the door of the fridge, and took out a bottle of champagne. It was vintage Veuve Clicquot. Good stuff. I looked around, found a couple of glasses, and opened the bottle. I poured a glass and carried it with me as I continued my trip around the room. There was a small panel with three rows of buttons on one wall, but there was no explanatory text anywhere near them. Looking around, I couldn't see anything which connected to them. Air conditioning, perhaps, I thought.

Just then there was a tap at the door, and it opened without waiting for my answer. It was Pru. 'Hi,' she said. 'I'm Prudence. Call me Pru. And you're Geoffrey. And you're British.' She came over to where I was standing, holding out a hand. You might have thought that we were at a Buckingham Palace garden party, except for the fact that Pru was naked from the waist up and wearing only the briefest, pale-lemon-coloured pair of satin bikini panties, and net stockings with a small, pale-lemon suspender belt. On her feet she was wearing black pumps. We shook hands. 'Champagne?' I asked, indicating the bottle on the top of the bar, next to the empty glass. 'Oh, wow,' she said. 'Champagne. Yes, please.' I poured her a glass, and handed it to her. 'Cheers,' she said. 'I gather I've been a naughty girl.' 'Oh,' I said, not thinking. 'How's that?'

She gave me a slightly old-fashioned look. 'Well,' she said. 'I'm told you're going to spank me. On my bottom. With your hand. So I must have been a *very* naughty girl. To be spanked on my bare bottom. Are you going to take my knickers off?' she asked me. 'Or do you want to spank me with them on? I may wet them, if you do. One way or another.' She laughed, and took another swig of her champagne. 'Keep them on, Pru,' I said. 'At least for the moment.' And then, 'Tell me,' I asked, 'What is that panel for over there, on the wall? The one with the buttons?' Prudence put down her glass and moved over to the panel. 'I understand that you want to tie me up, before you spank me,' she said. I nodded. 'Then you'll want to use one of these,' she said, pressing one of the rows of buttons.

A panel on the wall opposite us slid up, revealing a sort of triangular cell containing a wooden whipping post, complete with leather restraints for wrists and ankles. It was the kind that, when you have strapped your victim to it, they look rather as though they have been crucified, but with their backs to you, leaving back and buttocks available for whatever pleasures you have in mind. She left it in position for a few minutes, whilst I took in its details. I could see that it was well padded, and wasn't, in itself, going to cause its victims any actual pain.

'Or this,' said Pru, pressing another button. The triangular cell swung around, disappearing as another, similar unit came into view. This was a different version of the same kind of thing. A wooden frame, again with restraints, over which your victim would be strapped, but this time very much with her (or his) buttocks presented up in the air, for your delectation and attention. 'And finally,' said Pru, pressing another button, 'here is your choice of implement.' As the last of the three units swung around, I could see that it was equipped with every kind of pain-causing whip, cane, paddle, and riding crop, and even with a couple of cat-o'-nine-tails. There were also nasty things like nipple clamps, electric probes, branding irons, pincers, and the like. It seemed that some of the club's customers took the application of pain seriously. I looked at Pru. 'Actually, Pru,' I said to her, 'I don't really need any of those things. Not the whipping posts, nor any of those nasty weapons. When we're ready, I shall simply put you across my knee and spank you with my bare hand. And then, of course, fuck you. That's all today is about. It's not about causing *real* pain. It's about make-believe. That you've been a naughty girl means that you must be punished. I shall punish you. You will cry. Punishing you, and making you cry, will give me the kind of erection that will then make you very happy. It's the opposite of a vicious circle. It's a happy circle.'

Prudence laughed. 'It sounds like a lot of fun,' she said, draining her glass. 'Shall we start?' She went over to the bed. She was every man's walking sexual fantasy, with her gorgeous body dressed simply in her panties, suspender belt and stockings. I had a serious erection just looking at her and thinking about what was coming next, so that I had difficulty in getting my trousers off. When I was finally naked, I sat on the edge of the bed, took Pru's hand, and pulled her towards me.

'Naughty girls get their bottoms smacked, Prudence,' I told her. 'You've been very naughty, and I'm going to spank yours.' 'Oh, please don't spank me,' she said, beginning to sniffle. 'Please don't spank my bottom. Please don't.' I ignored her, and pulled her down across my knees. I placed my hand on the rounded globe of one buttock, and stroked it through the thin satin of her knickers. It felt warm and smooth beneath my hand. I massaged it, and squeezed it, and then I slid my hand up under the elastic of her knicker-leg and stroked her naked flesh. My fingers ran down into her anal cleft, just touching the puckered flesh of her anus in passing. I could feel her pubic hair, and I allowed my fingers to drop down between her legs, where I felt a wet warmth issuing from her secret place.

'That's very naughty, Prudence,' I said. 'You're practically wetting your knickers.' I pulled my hand out from underneath her knickers, and slowly pulled the flimsy item down her thighs. As I pulled it down, I could see that the white cotton gusset lining the satin crotch of her panties was stained dark with her juices, and as I gazed at it, the delightful aroma arising from it reached my nostrils. I breathed in deeply. She smelt of fresh melons, roses, and just a touch of tropical lime. I left her knickers there where they were, halfway down her thighs, the crotch well positioned to continue allowing its scent to reach me, and stroked her now fully exposed buttocks. I could at last see the soft auburn curls of her pubic hair thickening as they disappeared down towards her sex.

I massaged and rubbed and squeezed, until I felt ready to start spanking her. I raised my hand, and she said softly – almost whispering – 'No. Please. Please don't hurt me. Please don't make me cry.' I brought my hand down, sharply. Her buttocks quivered as my hand made contact, and she burst into tears. They were either real, or she was an impressive actress. I looked down, and I could see the imprint of my hand, fingers spread, rising pinkly on her buttocks. I raised my hand yet again, and slapped her once more, this time on the other buttock. I waited until the imprint started to appear, and then I continued with the punishment. Her buttocks slowly

David Jones

turned from pink to red, and her tears progressed from soft sniffles to what seemed very like the genuine article. She interrupted her crying to speak to me, her voice thick with emotion. 'Oh, please, sir,' she said, 'please don't spank me any more. I'll be a good girl, sir. I'll do all those things you want me to. I'll suck your thing for you. I'll play with it, the way you like me to. But please stop spanking me. I'll do anything you want, sir. Anything.'

I found the thought of what Pru was actually saying to me extremely erotic, and I pulled her off my knee, turned her over onto her back, pulled her knickers all the way down her legs and off, and straddled her, my rigid member standing out before me. She looked up at me with her tear-stained cheeks, grasped my prick in her hand, and guided it between her legs, where I sank it into her. She was wet and slippery, and took me all the way in, up to the hilt. She was hot, tight, and very wet. She was everything any man has ever dreamed of. She was sexually exquisite. Her pussy throbbed, and worked itself around my male muscle as if it were a hand, masturbating me. I felt my ejaculation rising rapidly. I could hear her calling me 'sir' as I spanked her. I remembered the obscene things she had spoken of, and I came, luxuriantly, splendidly, into her receptive, hard-working cunt. 'Oh, yes,' she said, to my surprise, as I pumped my semen into her. 'That's nice. That's really nice. You can come and spank me any time, mister, so long as you promise to fuck me like this afterwards.' What more can I tell you?

P. K. New Cavendish Street, London, W.1.

Not a lot. New York, New York. What a wonderful place. Like the song says.

TONGUE TWISTER

I wonder if I may use the facility of your columns to make a complaint? To make a stand, as it were, for all my sisters out there who may have the same problem that I suffer from? I'm a fairly normal nineteen-year-old woman, who has had – and is still having, thank God – her share of men. I've met all sorts.

I've given as good as I've got, and I've got – up until now – as good as I've given. I don't have too many hang-ups. I'm not into water sports. That's a bit too specialist for my tastes. I'm not overly keen on being fucked up the arse, although your letters pages tell me that I'm missing a lot of fun there. I'm not against it in principle. It's just that in my limited experience, I've found it painful. I don't believe that sex of any kind should hurt. But perhaps I've been unlucky. I'm willing to try again, with any man who loves me enough to take it gently. But that's by the by. My complaint is that I love to suck cock. I'm really into oral sex. I can come with a beautiful, preferably large, cock in my mouth. I don't even have to touch my pussy. But my Jewish boyfriend of the moment tells me that he isn't into oral sex. Either way. He says it's dirty.

I've read a lot of letters in your columns, over the years, putting forward the thought that sucking pussy is disgusting. Sadly. But I've never before come across a man who doesn't want his cock sucked. I mean, in my book, that makes my boyfriend a real cocksucker, if you'll forgive the expression. I started off, as most young girls do, before we are ready to experience real sex, by giving my very young boyfriends a slow, loving wank at the end of a pleasant evening. I was a virgin in those days, as were most of my girlfriends, and although I didn't want to lose my virginity, I wasn't against giving as much sexual pleasure as I was able, within those limiting circumstances.

From there on, over a period of time, I progressed from what eventually became mutual masturbation (when the boys eventually got to the stage where they realized, however reluctantly, that girls like to have orgasms too) to mutual oral sex. And finally, of course, to adult sex. I have no sexual inhibitions whatsoever, apart from those I've already mentioned. But I was left at the end of the day, with an all-consuming desire to suck cock. I would almost pay money for the privilege of taking a swollen, gorgeously erect penis in my mouth, and tonguing and licking and sucking it until it spurts its owner's come down my throat. Fantastic!

So why on earth doesn't my present boyfriend enjoy that which (again from your letters columns) I read that a small percentage of women refuse to do, on the grounds that they think it's dirty? Or degrading. Or using them like prostitutes. I gather that the world is much fuller of men who would like a nice girl like me to – what do you want to call it – give them head, go down on them, suck them off, French them? You can call it what you like, as far as I'm concerned. Just show me a man who wants his cock sucked. And if he wants to suck my pussy in return, who am I to stop him?

K. O'G. Newton Abbot, Devon.

We'll forward your mail on to you.

THANKS FOR THE MAMMARIES

Years ago, when I was younger, men standing around in pubs over a pint or so of beer would ask each other whether they were tit men, leg men, or arse men. The answer indicated which of those three delightful sectors of female anatomy appealed most to the person being questioned. It implied, I always understood, a question of aesthetic beauty, rather than specifically of sex, although I may be wrong here. Nowadays, one never hears the question. Have we become so blasé about our relationships that we no longer categorize our chosen area of admiration? It would seem so.

I have always been a breast man, ever since working in Africa as a youngster. Before my arrival out there at the age of twenty, the number of ladies that I had seen close to *sans* vests was very few. Suddenly – and joyously – I was thrust into a society where women wore little other than a row or two of beads around their loins. It seemed, after a while, the most natural thing in the world. When walking through the bush and passing some local beauty on a jungle path, one would murmur 'Good morning' or 'Good afternoon' in the local language (usually Mende) whilst assessing her exposed bust for entry into the office competition on return to base. The categories, as I remember them, were (not necessarily in order of merit) bee stings, pears, spaniels' ears, super-duper droopers, and block-busters. If it were possible to take a photograph without causing embarrassment, one did. This was usually a clincher in the competition – or not, as the case might be – but, regrettably, it was not often possible. I remember that the rainy season was a particularly happy time. I submit that there is no more stimulating sight than a fine pair of young, black, firm, well-shaped breasts with pointed nipples, running with rainwater, the nipples dripping like miniature drainpipes. A secondary consideration (bearing in mind that one was also oneself wet through in these circumstances, if better dressed) was the fact that the rain was warm.

The years that I spent in Africa were extraordinarily happy ones. The people were charming, the countryside beautiful. It also gave me the experience necessary to enable me to give the lie to an oft-repeated rumour, back here in the United Kingdom, that black males are better endowed sexually than their white brothers. From years of walking along riverbanks in Africa in the mornings and seeing both African males and females at their ablutions, I am pleased to be able to report that, in that respect, black males are exactly the same as white males. They come equipped with every variation of male organ size, from the impressive to the insignificant. Just as we whites do.

C. L. H. Bournemouth, Dorset.

But do they play a better tune?

HAIR OF THE DOG

Am I unusual in loving hairy women? I just adore women with a plethora of hair. I love unshaven armpits, unshaven and/or untrimmed pudendas, hairy arseholes. The whole bit. There are only two exceptions; I am not fond of women with moustaches, nor women with hairy legs. But give me a girl with a luxuriant pubic growth, and you'll see a happy man. Nuzzling my nose into a nest of hirsute pubic locks brings muff diving into real perspective for me. I love to lick a bushy armpit, suck a bewhiskered rectum, kiss a nipple surrounded by soft, wispy hairs. Am I alone in this pursuit of the hirsute?

S. St. P. G. Andover, Hants.

You sound like any normal eager beaver to me.

BROTHEL CREEPER

I've never actually been to a brothel. In fact, although I live in England's capital city, I've never been able to discover such an establishment. Maybe they are but figments of overworked, feverish imaginations? Relics from Victorian memories? Or superseded, perhaps, by the individual ladies advertised on the cards stuck to the insides of telephone boxes throughout the city?

But the thought of brothels dominates my fantasies to such an extent that I am moved to write to you and relate my feelings to your readers. In every fantasy of mine, the door is always opened by a pretty girl in a French maid's uniform. The classic bit. You know: short black skirt. White apron. White blouse. Black stockings, black suspenders, black knickers. White mob cap. Black high-heeled shoes in patent leather. She smiles at me, and opens the door. I walk into the passageway, and feel up underneath her skirt as I pass her by. The crotch of her knickers is wet, and I finger her cunt through the moist material. She says, 'Ooh, that's naughty. But I like it.' And she shows me into a waiting room. On the walls are pornographic photographs and paintings of pretty girls performing every possible kind of sexual act you can think of, and one or two that may not have occurred to you. There is always one of a girl who has a cock up every orifice. One up her pussy, one up her anus, and one in her mouth. In addition, she has two more cocks – one in each hand – which she is masturbating. Then there is one of a girl who is simply the filling in a sexual sandwich.

She is being fucked and buggered at the same time.

There are always lots of pictures of girls bound into sexually receptive, or painful – or both – positions. Hands are usually bound or manacled behind the back, and the girls are usually bent over a variety of whipping posts, offering access to their so-called private parts, although anything less private than what is represented in some of these pictures is difficult to imagine. Mouths are frequently tightly gagged. Then there are explicit photographs of girls masturbating themselves. Sometimes simply with long, carefully manicured fingers. Sometimes with huge over-sized dildoes. And then there are the illustrations of girls sucking girls. You know what I mean. Cunt sucking. And fucking each other with strap-on dildoes. Or double-ended ones, so that they both get off at the same time.

And then there are the flagellation pictures. Girls being beaten. Whipped. Thrashed. Spanked. Slippered. The girls are often pictured with raised weals criss-crossing their thighs and buttocks. If not naked, they are inevitably pictured with tight, silky knickers pulled tautly over full bottoms. There are girls being whipped by men, and girls being whipped by girls. Very thin girls, being raped by men with very fat cocks. Girls being raped by brutal, phallic monsters. The girls' mouths are open in long, silent screams, and any men in these pictures always have enormous, swollen erections. Then there are the one-on-one oral sex scenes. Men with their cocks forced all the way down girls' throats, with the girls patently gagging at the exercise. There are always a few shots of girls sucking two men off at the same time. That doesn't appeal to me at all, but I know a few chaps who support this approach. And of course there are photographs of men sucking girls' cunts. The girls lie back, their eyes closed in utter sexual gratification, their legs spread wide, their hairy pussies (or bald pussies, depending upon the artist's or the photographer's predilection) open wetly under the ministrations of attentive male tongues.

And don't forget the fetish pictures. Some of them real photographs. But more often the work of imaginative artists. There are women wearing every kind of rubber, latex, leather and patent leather items of clothing that you can think of. Skirts. Dresses. Brassieres. Knickers. Gloves. Stockings. Women wearing latex gloves, masturbating men. Women bound with intricate ropes and knots. There are women wearing every possible kind of lingerie, from the frankly sexual to the femininely sweet. From the virginal, simple, plain white, to the tartish, open-crotched, open-nippled, fantasy brothel wear. It's either very exciting, or it's very boring, depending upon what your sexual proclivities are. But, being brothels, there is something for everyone. Variety, as they say, is the spice of life. Just then, the door to the room that I am in opens and an attractive woman of around thirty comes in and introduces herself. She is French, she is called Jeanne, and she is, of course, the madam. We talk of payments. I produce a credit card and hand it over, and Jeanne leads the way out of the room and down a corridor, where she opens another door which turns out to open on a large room full of gorgeous girls.

'Take your time, m'sieur,' Jeanne says to me. 'There is no hurry. Have a good look around, and choose the woman that you fancy. She will ask you what sexual act or acts you wish her to perform, or which you wish to perform upon her, and she will tell you whether or not they are within her repertoire. Not all the girls do everything. Some girls specialize. Others do not like, for example, being physically beaten. Some do not perform oral sex. Some prefer not to have anal sex. But they will all tell you, quite plainly, what they are prepared – or not prepared – to do with you.' She handed me a printed card. 'Here is a list of your prices. They are fixed. They are not negotiable. Do not let any of the girls hustle you into doing something that you do not want to do, or into choosing them if you are not sure that they are what you are looking for. Call me if you need me. Otherwise I will be back in a while, to see how you are getting on. Au 'voir, m'sieur.' She left me there, surrounded by pretty girls.

Some were naked. Some were fully dressed. Very elegantly so. Others wore varying degrees of undress. All were fantastic. There were blondes, redheads, girls with black hair, girls with brown hair. Amongst the naked girls, I could see that there were girls with shaven pubes. I particularly fancied a redhead with a bald pussy. I made a mental note. She had beautiful, pointed, firm breasts, an arse that would have given the Pope a hard-on, and the loveliest green eyes. She saw me looking at her, and she came over and spoke to me. 'Hi,' she said. 'My name's Monica. What's yours?' 'Hallo, Monica,' I said. 'I'm George.' 'Well, George,' she said. 'Look no further. I'm the greatest fuck you've ever had in your life. Are you looking for anything special. You know, kinky? I'm into pretty straight sex, myself.' I looked at her. 'No, nothing kinky,' I told her. 'A little fellatio. A good fuck. Maybe a wank.' 'Here I am, George,' she said. 'I give terrific head, and my hand-jobs are sensational. And I fuck like a dream. A dirty dream,' She laughed. 'Let me think about it, Monica,' I said. I moved away. She smiled at me as I left. I gave her full marks for that.

I was also attracted to a tall, black-haired girl, who looked foreign to me. Italian, maybe. She had a slightly olive-coloured complexion, and her hair was thick and lustrous. She was wearing a figure-hugging leotard. You know the things. Almost a one-piece bathing suit. This girl was tall, long-legged, with a fabulous figure and a lovely smile. I went over to her. 'Hallo,' I said. 'I'm George.' 'Hallo, George,' she said, in the softest of Irish accents. 'I'm Bridget.' How wrong can you be, I asked myself? 'Are you looking for anything special?' Bridget asked. 'I saw you talking to Monica over there. She's a lovely girl. She's a friend of mine.' I suddenly had this wondrous idea. I looked deep into Bridget's beautiful blue eyes. I told her what I'd told Monica. About fellatio. And fucking. And being tossed off. And then I said, 'But do you and Monica do a lezzie act? I mean, you know, a show? An exhibition? Just for me? I know Monica said she was pretty straight, but don't most of you lovely girls put on little pretend-lezzie shows for people like me?' She looked at me for a while, without saying anything. Then she smiled and said, 'We do that. In fact, Monica and I were rehearsing ours only yesterday. Let's go over and talk to Monica together.' We walked back across the room to where Monica was standing. She smiled at Bridget.

'So you've picked Bridget, then?' she said. 'And a very good choice too. She's a lovely girl.' 'No, no, shhh,' said Bridget. 'Listen. He hasn't picked me at all. Or, rather, not *just* me. He's picked both of us. He wants us to put on a girly show for him. Do you fancy that? You know? Like yesterday?' Monica giggled. I didn't see anything particularly amusing about what had been said, but patently Monica had. 'Well, does he now?' replied Monica. 'Well, now. I think we could manage that,' she said. 'Leave it to me. I'll go and find Jeanne, and set it up. You stay here and talk to George.' At which she left, naked as she was, through the main entrance door. 'Is this your first visit here?' Bridget asked me. I suppose it was fractionally better than, 'Do you come here often?' To which, had she asked me, I would have said 'I hope to.' Ha ha. Ah, well.

Just then Monica came back through the door. 'We're in Suite Seven,' she told Bridget and me. 'If you'll take George up there and show him what's what, I'll go backstage and start to get things ready. Will you join me there?' 'I will that,' said Bridget. Monica stood on tiptoe and gave me a kiss on the cheek. 'Thank you for choosing Bridget and me,' she said. 'You won't be sorry.' She left, once more, and Bridget turned to me and took my hand. 'Follow me,' she said. She guided me out of the room, along a short passage, and up some broad, well-carpeted stairs. At the top, the corridor led off in two directions. We took the corridor to the left. It was rather like walking down the corridor in an expensive block of flats. The walls were painted cream. The carpet was a dark green, and thick. The lights were bright. Every twenty yards or so there was a door, and each door had a number. Otherwise, there was no character. No ambience. No sound. We stopped outside a door bearing the number seven. Bridget pressed a button, and the door swung open. Silently. She entered, and beckoned me to follow her. We were in a smallish hallway, with two doors leading off. One of them was open. As we passed the shut door, Bridget said, 'That's the bathroom, when you need it.' 'Thank you,' I said.

The room we entered was nicely, expensively, comfortably furnished. It was a wide, long room. In the centre of the space there were two large sofas, facing each other, whilst the floor in between them was padded and covered with what looked like a silken sheet. It was, to all intents and purposes, a large bed, but one obviously intended for people to perform upon. There was a large, traditional double bed up at the other end of the room. There were side tables, easy chairs, and a small, well-stocked bar, with a sink and a refrigerator. The entire ceiling was mirrored. There were spotlights trained onto the padded area.

'This is where Monica and I will do our thing for you,' said Bridget. 'If you feel like joining in at any time, feel free.' As she spoke, she was peeling off her leotard, and in seconds she was naked. Her breasts were beautiful. She had huge teats. I looked at them, completely mesmerized. She stepped right up close to me, and took my right hand in hers.

Her naked breasts pressed hard against me. She put her lips up against my ear, put my hand between her legs, and said, 'And speaking of feeling free, feel *this*, darling.' I did. I thrust two fingers deep into her moist slit. She wriggled appreciatively. She was wet. She was tight. She was warm. And she was raring to go.

Her other hand found my swelling cock and she began to massage it through my trousers. She put her lips on mine and thrust her tongue into my mouth. After a few moments of heavenly sexual anticipation, I pulled my mouth away from hers. 'Hold on, sweetheart,' I said. 'If you go on doing that, it will all be over before you've even started.' I pulled my body away from hers as I spoke. She grinned at me. She looked as if she was about to say something, but right then Monica came in through the door. 'Getting to know each other, I see,' she said. She was still naked, but this time she was carrying a largish holdall. She dumped it in a corner of the room, away from the 'stage'.

'OK, boys and girls,' she said. 'Let's get George here comfortable, and then the show will commence. What can I get you to drink, George?' 'Scotch and water, please, Monica,' I said. 'No ice.' She went over to the bar, and came back a couple of minutes later with an unopened bottle of The Famous Grouse, a cut-crystal tumbler, and a carafe of water. 'Here you go, George,' she said. 'Help yourself. Cheers.' She and Bridget went over into the corner where the holdall had been dumped. Monica picked it up, and the two girls went through to the bathroom. I kept my eyes on Bridget as she walked past me. Her pubic hair was indeed thick and luxuriant, as I had guessed. I remembered that it was only a few moments since I had been standing there with her naked, my two fingers up inside her cunt, her tongue in my mouth. My penis swelled at the memory. I poured myself a large drink, and settled back on the sofa. Bridget popped her head around the door.

'Are you ready, sweetheart?' she asked. 'Ready as I'll ever be,' I replied. 'Hey, why don't you get your clothes off, darling?' Bridget said. 'First of all, you'll be more comfortable.' She grinned at me. 'And secondly, you'll be ready for anything,' she said. 'OK?' 'OK,' I said, and I stood up and quickly undressed. I felt faintly embarrassed, sitting there with half a hard-on. But then I thought what the hell? And I relaxed. Some music suddenly began from somewhere. Softly at first, and then building slowly. It was very sensual.

The two girls appeared out of the bathroom. They were wearing crotchless black satin knickers, which revealed Monica's shaven pussy and Bridget's hirsute one. They also were wearing black satin bras, with holes which allowed their nipples to jut through. Bridget's giant teats looked eminently suckable. As did both their pussies. Monica had the holdall in her hand, and she put it down at the edge of the padded arena.

Bridget lay down on her back on the area, her legs apart, her knees drawn up. Monica lay beside her, and began to massage Bridget's pudenda through her thick growth of black, curly, pubic hair. Soon – as I had – she found Bridget's pink, wet slit and she thrust just one finger deeply into it. Bridget made a noise somewhere between a moan and a deep, rich purr, and opened her legs even wider. Monica stopped her fingering, pulled her fingers out of Bridget's honeypot, and, kneeling up for a moment, she pulled Bridget's black satin knickers down her long legs and off. Bridget sat up for a moment, reached behind herself to undo her bra, and took that off. Whilst she did this, Monica put a hand out, pulled the holdall nearer to her and looked for, and found, a large vibrator. She kept this in her hand, and I assumed – wrongly, it transpired – that she was going to use it up Bridget's vaginal orifice. But no.

Still holding the vibrator in her right hand, Monica

positioned herself so that she could lower her head between Bridget's legs. She started by kissing her cunt, then licking and sucking it, and finally she treated her colleague's sex to an enthusiastic combination of all three. Clear liquid soon started running down Bridget's thighs. After a little while, Monica let go of the vibrator, and I assumed that she had changed her mind about using it. As I watched, she slid a hand beneath Bridget's buttocks. Bridget obligingly raised them slightly, to permit Monica's hand free access, and I was surprised to see Monica's middle finger ease its way through Bridget's thick growth of anal hair, and into her tightly clenched anus.

Bridget let out a gasp, as if this intrusion was as much of a surprise to her as it was to me. However, Monica continued with her cunnilingus as she finger-fucked Bridget's anus, and Bridget soon began to pant, after which she started to move her hips up and down in an extremely explicit fucking motion. Then, almost before I realized it, she was screaming and moaning, and tossing her head from side to side, her hips working double time, as she succumbed totally to Monica's ministrations, and underwent an enormous, almost continual, series of orgasms. I thought that might be the end of at least that part of the show, but neither girl showed any sign of getting up. Instead, Monica reached out for the vibrator and, pulling Bridget's legs wider apart, she started to ease it up the other girl's rectum. I could see that Bridget was thrusting her hips and buttocks downwards, endeavouring, it seemed, to help the vibrator all the way in, and quite quickly it was fully in position. Only the tip of the very end – the end incorporating the on/off switch – could be seen, sticking obscenely out of Bridget's arsehole.

At that point, Monica switched the device on. 'Oh, God,' screamed Bridget, almost immediately. 'Oh, Jesus. Oh, fuck. Somebody fuck me. Please. Oh, God. Please, God.' Monica raised her head, looked at me, and then raised a quizzical eyebrow. 'The lady wants a fuck,' she said. 'Do you fancy a fuck, right now? She's good and wet, I can guarantee.' My prick stood to full attention at the very thought. The idea of fucking this gorgeous, nubile, randy young woman with a live vibrator buzzing away up her anus was too much. I practically leapt up off the sofa and stood there, looking down at Bridget's lewdly spread legs, her magnificent pubic growth, and her wet, pink slit running down the centre, immediately over the humming vibrator. I was not entirely sure what to do next.

Monica came to my assistance. 'Here,' she said, standing up. 'Let me help you.' She took a hand, and pulled me over towards Bridget until I was standing between her open legs. 'Now kneel down,' she suggested. I did as I was told. She took hold of my tumescent cock and guided it down to the outside of Bridget's saturated cunt. 'Now push forward. Slowly,' she said. Again, I did as I was told. She was still grasping my erect cock and, as I pressed forwards and downwards, she fed it into Bridget's hot, wet sex. Then I was literally sucked in. It was as if Bridget had switched on some kind of suction pipe in her pussy. And over all, over and above the noise of the vibrator stuck up Bridget's arse, I could feel its actual vibrations, transferring themselves through Bridget's rectal passage to her pussy, and through her pussy to my cock. Fantastic!

Despite the temptation to just lie there and let it all happen to me, I began to move my hips in the classic fucking motions. It felt fabulous. I was in no hurry, and I fucked away slowly, wanting these wonderful sensations to last forever. But there was more to come. As I fucked Bridget, Monica had stripped off her bra and knickers, and she now came and lay beside Bridget, naked, her open legs on a level with my face, her shaven pussy right beside my mouth, its lovely gash shining wetly from within her pinkly open labia. 'Why don't you suck my beautiful bald pussy while you fuck Bridget?' she asked. I couldn't think of a single reason why not so, without in any way interrupting my rhythm, I leaned down to my left and began to suck at Monica's smooth-lipped cunt. She smelt of clean, sexually excited young pussy.

It was open, and wet, and it tasted delightful. It was as smooth as the proverbial grape skin, and I sucked and licked at it with wholehearted erotic pleasure. As I fucked and sucked, I reached up with my right hand and began to knead Bridget's enormous left-hand teat. It swelled and grew in my hand, and Bridget began moaning again. Monica turned her head to the left, where it was more or less on a level with Bridget's head, and she reached over and pulled Bridget's face towards hers. She then started kissing Bridget on the lips, which favour Bridget returned with enthusiasm. I wondered if Bridget could taste her own vaginal juices on Monica's lips, remembering how Monica had been busying herself down at Bridget's sex, and I wondered whether, if she could, she found the thought of that as sexy as I did.

The sight of the two girls French kissing each other, their tongues deep in each other's mouths, their eyes shut, their breath impassioned, whilst I fucked the one and sucked the other's cunt, was almost too much, sexually, to bear. I thought that I might explode from sheer sexual fulfillment. And all the time, the soft buzz of the vibrator in Bridget's anus sent a sexual message to all our brains. As well as to my cock.

Bridget pulled away from Monica's mouth. 'Oh, God,' she moaned. 'I'm going to come again. Oh, God. Oh, yes. Oh, I'm coming. I'm coming now. I'm being fucked, and I'm coming now. Oh, Jesus. Oh, yes.' And with her final shout, she writhed and twisted as her orgasms took over her whole body, and she moaned and cried out and then, as the orgasms died away, she fell silent. Monica leaned up, reached down, found the end of the vibrator, and switched it off. She withdrew it carefully, and placed it on the edge of the padded area. 'Well, that's one lady well serviced,' she said. 'Now, how about me? I haven't been fucked yet, you know.' She lay down, a few feet away from Bridget, and opened her legs. She looked over at me. 'And you haven't had your cock sucked, and you haven't had your hand job yet. What an idle couple of tarts we are. Whatever next, I wonder?' she said, smiling at me. 'Get yourself over here at once.' She looked fantastic. Her long, auburn hair was lying spread around beneath her head and shoulders like the aura around an angel's head. Her green eyes looked somehow translucent. Her lips were wet, and she kept licking them. Slowly. One finger of one hand was idly playing with her shaved pussy. It had disappeared up to the first knuckle of her finger and, as I watched, she slowly pulled it almost out, and then thrust it down deep inside herself again.

'Mmmm,' she said. 'Reminds me of something. I'm not sure what.' She grinned a lazy grin. 'What do you want first?' she asked. 'Or, perhaps I should say, what would you *like* first? A slow wank? A quick fuck? Or perhaps you'd prefer a quick wank and a slow fuck? Or would you like to suck me while I fellate you? I told you that I give great head, didn't I? And I do. You don't have to suck me, of course. But I've been watching you. You like girls with shaved pussies, don't you? And you love to suck shaved pussies, don't you?' I nodded. 'I knew you did,' she said. 'I can always tell. Come over here, for God's sake.' She patted the padded carpet beside her.

'Am I allowed to change my mind?' I asked her, getting up and walking over to her, and then kneeling down beside her. She reached out and took my throbbing cock in her hand. She sat up, leaned forward, took my knobhead into her mouth and began to masturbate me. She smiled at me over the top of my cock. She gave wondrous head, as she herself said. She was the best fellatrice that I had ever had the pleasure of, as they say. She must have spent her childhood blowing eggs. When I had asked her if I might change my mind, I was playing with the idea of anal sex with her. But her expert fellatio completely distracted me – in the nicest possible way – and the added invitation to suck her delightful, smoothly shaven cunt was too much to resist. 'Let's use the bed, Monica,' I suggested. 'It'll be more comfortable.'

I pulled out of her mouth, albeit reluctantly and, taking her by the hand, I led her over to the bed. I lay down on it, my cock standing proudly erect up between my thighs. 'Kneel over me, Monica,' I suggested, 'so that you can sit back on my face, and suck my cock in comfort.' She did as I asked and threw a leg across me, grasping the base of my cock and taking it in her mouth again as she slowly settled herself comfortably down on my mouth. I looked up as her bald sex lowered itself down towards me. And then her sex was upon my mouth, and I thrust my tongue inside her as my lips closed over her labia. As I sucked her, I had a close-up view of her shaven anal cleft and her tight little anus. Someone must shave that for her, I thought, as I sucked happily away. Probably Bridget. I would have loved to shave it for her. Her cunt was running wet with her juices, and she tasted strongly of sex. She had that extra, tangy, slightly musty odour that redheads always have, giving them a subtle, underlying, marginally acrid flavour. I always find it particularly erotic, and sexually very stimulating.

As I kissed and licked and sucked, Monica began to wriggle her hips, thrusting strongly down onto my hard-working mouth, and I guessed that she was building up towards an orgasm. I began to pump my cock up and down, relishing the sensations she was giving me through the obviously practised use of her lips, mouth and tongue, and I felt my own ejaculation starting somewhere deep down. Her buttocks were smooth and soft, and I clasped them in my hands, squeezing them sensually. As I did so, the thumb of my right hand brushed over her puckered rectum, and I watched it clench, then relax as it reacted to this encounter. Fascinated by its almost automatic response, I drew my forefinger gently down across its brownish-pink diameter, and saw the same instant reaction. I next pressed my finger gently into its centre, and found it dry to the touch, and resistant to my attempted entry.

I spat a gob of saliva onto my finger, then rubbed it over her anal circumference, spat another gob, and pressed into her again. This time my finger slid inside her on the saliva, and once I was inside, she seemed wet, as if from her own internal anal lubricant. 'Mmmm,' she said. 'That's *naughty*.' I was still busy sucking at her sex with my mouth, so I didn't reply to her. It didn't seem necessary, somehow. I insinuated my finger slowly farther and farther inside her anus. She felt hot up there, and the deeper I got into her, the wetter she seemed to be. She was gloriously tight and I shut my eyes, imagining my cock where my finger was. I wished I *had* changed my mind, earlier on.

My cock spasmed in Monica's mouth at the very thought, and my anal fantasies brought my ejaculation spurting down Monica's throat, rather like a miniature geyser. She used her hand to masturbate me as she sucked and swallowed my semen, and I finger-fucked her briskly anally, while carrying on sucking her off, as I continued to shoot my come into her mouth. And then, finally, it was all over. She had literally sucked me dry, and she had a series of increasingly shuddering orgasms as I concentrated on my cunnilingus. When we were both finished, she rolled off me and kissed me, wetly, on my mouth. 'Oh, God,' she said. 'That was fantastic. Terrific. Thank you. Truly. Thank you.' 'My pleasure, darling,' I said. And I meant it. Bridget was still lying on the floor where we had left her, but she was turned on her side, watching us and smiling. 'Well,' she said. 'You two certainly looked as if you were enjoying yourselves.' 'We were,' we said, together. And then we all three of us laughed. I never did get my hand job in that particular fantasy, but I'm sure it will happen sooner or later.

J. L. Maida Vale, London.

Brothels certainly exist, that's for sure. But it doesn't sound to me as if you seriously need one.

GYM WILL FIX IT

I recently joined a mixed health club. Unlike a number of these clubs, mine is open all day, every day, to whoever wishes to use it. Provided, of course, that they are members. There is no question of the male and female members being separated, or of each sex having set hours. There are also both male and female instructors, and every member can choose the instructor of his or her choice. These facts have brought a new sexual pleasure into my life. First of all, I have suddenly become aware of the sexual attraction of a woman's body as it is working out. I now am almost hypnotized by the sight of a woman *in extremis* in a gymnasium. In a sweat-stained, clinging top, her nipples standing out brazenly against the moist cotton. With perspiration running down her trim thighs, from beneath her skimpy, athletic shorts, or from under the elasticated edge of a tightly-fitting leotard. I get stimulated by the scent of a woman who is sweating after exercise. I can smell the sweet, liquid effusions from her armpits, her thighs, and her groin, and the mixture of these is extremely sexually exciting to me. I love to look at girls' crotches as they strain at the various machines in the gym, the thin cotton of their exercise clothes drawn tightly into them, often outlining the shape of their vaginal lips, so tautly are they pulled into the womens' groins. On extra-special days, I may be fortunate enough to see a moisture stain darkening this private area. I often get a hard-on, watching a girl on an exercise bike, imagining what the hard leather bicycle saddle is doing to her clitoris as she pedals frantically away, her eyes on the mileometer, measuring her efforts.

Having spent some days when I first joined simply sitting around and watching the action, I selected a female instructor to work out an exercise programme for me. One whose lush body particularly appealed. She is short – about five-two – but has a fabulous figure. Large, firm, well-shaped breasts, with nipples that stand out beneath her T-shirts or work-out tops like erect thimbles. Her thighs are generous and the space between her legs, emphasized by the tautness of the thin material at her crotch, hints at a generous pudenda and large pussy lips.

I love to watch her on one of the gym's rowing machines, for as she comes forward after the end of each of her 'draws', with her legs fully splayed and with her hands fully forward on the 'oar', I like to imagine that in this position her labia are firmly outlined against the gusset of her skimpy shorts. I also enjoy standing beside her, whichever of the machines she is demonstrating for me, and watching the sweat gather and then trickle down the cleavage which separates her thrusting breasts. My instructor is called Melanie and recently it became fairly obvious that she was beginning to fancy me, a situation that brought me much anticipatory pleasure. The indications included leaning against me when demonstrating particular items of equipment, thrusting her gorgeous heavy breasts into me at every possible opportunity, and leaning down over me when I am seated on some piece of equipment so that I am blessed with a view of her breasts in free fall, unencumbered as they are by any kind of brassiere.

On one particular evening, I booked a session with her at the last possible time in the evening – eight-thirty until ten-thirty, as a matter of interest – and was delighted to discover, as we finished, that we were the only two people left in the gymnasium. There were others – members and instructors – in the showers, the changing rooms, and the bar, but we were alone in the actual gymnasium area. When we finished, we were both wet through with perspiration and physically exhausted. As I got up from one of the rowing machines, Melanie grabbed me, put her arms about me, and gave me a big hug. 'I don't know about you, Peter,' she said, 'but I'm knackered. What I need is to go and lie down somewhere.' She looked up at me, a smile on her face.

'What a good idea, Melanie,' I agreed. 'That's exactly what I need too.' She detached herself from me. 'Follow me,' she said. I followed her through a door at the side of the gym marked 'Private Staff Only', and we went through into a corridor, off which were a number of doors. Melanie took a bunch of keys out of the pocket of her shorts and unlocked one of the doors. Once inside, she locked it behind us, and then she grabbed me again. This time, she had one hand between my legs, stroking my cock. 'Oh, God, Peter,' she said, breathing hard. 'I've been lusting after you for weeks. I thought you didn't fancy me. I want you to fuck me. Now. Feel me. Suck my tits. Suck my cunt. Fuck me with your huge tool. Take me. Rape me. Do anything you want with me. Please.' She pulled my head down and kissed me fiercely, her tongue working away in my mouth, whilst she started to massage my cock through the thin material of my shorts. It stood politely to attention for her.

Suddenly she let go of me, pulled away, and tore off her shorts and T-shirt. 'Take me now,' she said. There was a small pile of exercise mats stacked over on one side of the room which was plainly a storeroom. Melanie lay down on the mats and opened her legs. 'Now, Peter darling,' she said. 'Fuck me now. Please.' What can a chap do? In any case, my erection was so hard, it was becoming painful. I tore my own clothes off and lay down between her legs. She took my cock and guided it into her cunt. She was very wet. And as tight as the proverbial duck's arse. I slid in, and she began using her vaginal muscles on me. 'Oh, darling,' she said. 'Suck my tits while you fuck me.' I did as I was bidden, and as I sucked her nipples fully erect, she worked her hips, her cunt muscles and her buttocks as I fucked her.

In what seemed like moments, she was coming all over the place, shouting out her pleasure, and bucking like a horse that's just trodden on a snake. I was concerned that someone might hear her and wonder where the riot was. As she lay there, shuddering with yet another orgasm, I came into her, jetting my semen up her in long, strong spurts. 'Oh, yes,' she groaned, bucking yet more wildly. 'Oh, Jesus, yes. Oh, God. You're shooting your spunk up me. Oh, God, God, God.'

It was tremendous stuff, and we subsequently spent some hours doing all the things that Melanie had initially suggested, and one or two that she hadn't originally thought of. My sexual excitement was kept on the boil by the all-pervading aura of fresh sweat that surrounded us both, as well as by her nubile enthusiasm and her seemingly boundless sexual energy. When I finally called pax, we spent a further jolly time together in the women's showers (the entire club was, by then, completely deserted) and by the time we had finished carefully soaping each other's orifices and protrusions, we must have been the cleanest two people in town. We have, since then, carried on with our mutually satisfying affair, but we now work ourselves up sexually as we work out together. We then shower and take ourselves off to either Melanie's place or to mine, where we work off our sexual fantasies on each other until we fall asleep, exhausted, in each other's arms.

P. W. Bromley, Kent.

Seems like you've worked it out for yourself. Congratulations.

THE BOTTOM LINE

I am a young woman who first started butt-fucking when I was still in college in New York State. I was introduced to this pleasure by one of the members of the college football team, and I've never looked back. I admit that I was nervous at first, but with loving care, and a generous amount of K-Y jelly, I quickly became an enthusiast. Harry was a gentle, patient teacher who took me through the various stages, one at a time. Maybe it would interest those of your readers who have not yet explored this satisfying aspect of sexual relations if I took them through the whys and wherefores?

First of all, both parties should be sure that they want to try anal sex. If one partner is forcing the issue, or if one partner is agreeing for all the wrong reasons, then it will almost certainly not work well. Rule one: be familiar with each other's anal parts. Look. Touch. Feel. Explore. Familiarize yourselves beyond any possible embarrassment, until each other's rectum is as exciting, and as enticing, as each other's penis and vagina. Two: always, *always* use plenty of sexual lubricant. K-Y jelly is ideal. Failing that, anything greasy is better than nothing at all. Butter, margarine, olive oil, lard are usually around in most people's kitchens. Cold cream, Vaseline, any kind of greasy unguent. Soap, as a last resort. But if you haven't got a lubricant of any kind, forget it until the next time. Trying to fuck a dry arsehole will cause pain to both parties.

Three: begin anal penetration first of all with something small. A finger. A vibrator with a small anal probe. Lead up slowly to full penile penetration. Four: be certain that both parties are comfortable with the actuality, before commencing penile penetration. Five: do it very gently. Six: if your girl says stop, stop immediately. Seven: be sure you know whether anal sex with a female is legal in your state. Despite relaxed homosexual laws in most states these days, anal intercourse with a female isn't legal everywhere. Hank was a gentle teacher, like I said. He encouraged me to plan my introduction to butt-fucking carefully. When the agreed evening arrived, we dined out at a favourite neighbourhood restaurant. Afterwards, when we got home, we opened a good bottle of wine and went to bed in the normal way that we did as the culmination of any pleasant evening. Hank spent time on foreplay, as he always did, but for obvious reasons, this night he concentrated on my anus. Touching me there. Stroking. Kissing. Licking. Until I felt fully relaxed. He then greased me thoroughly with K-Y jelly, after which I greased the full length of his penis, and then, finally, we were ready.

I was quite well worked up by this time, and was aching to be fucked. Hank got me on the bed on my hands and knees, my legs well spread, and began by inserting his finger up my anus. I was by now well accustomed to him doing this and it excited me, made me even randier than I was already. Then came the moment of truth. I could feel the head of his penis against my rectum, at which point he suggested that I reach behind me and hold his penis around its base. This was intended to give me confidence that I was in complete control.

Looking back, I don't now believe that I was, but it was a very reassuring gesture at the time. All the time this was going on, Hank was talking me through it. Slowly bolstering my confidence, reminding me that all I had to say at any time was 'Stop' and he would do exactly that. Having checked that I was finally ready, he began to press the head of his penis carefully up my arse. I had been practising dilating my anus for about a month before this evening, and I now used my muscles to dilate my back entrance as he pressed slowly against it. Suddenly, with minimal effort (and no discomfort at all) he was inside me. It felt very exciting. Very sexually stimulating. 'Oh, terrific, Hank,' I almost shouted. 'Now fuck me. Fuck my asshole. Do it to me. Now. Please.' He needed no second bidding, and began to thrust further into me, until I could feel his balls against my cunt, and I knew he was in me up to the hilt.

'OK, sweetheart?' he asked. 'Are we ready for take-off?' 'OK, honeybun,' I told him. 'Have your evil way with me.' He began to move in and out of me, increasing his tempo rapidly, until he was fucking my butt seriously. It felt good. Really. I could feel an orgasm building, although there was absolutely no contact, of course, between Hank's cock and my clitoris. It was more a mental thing, in that the feelings that his penis was producing in my anal passage were sexually both exciting and stimulating, I think it was the *thought* of what he was doing to me, rather than any direct result of the presence of his penis in my anus, which finally brought me to orgasm. These days, I either masturbate myself to orgasm as I'm being fucked in the arse, or I get my partner to do it for me. Either way, I'm guaranteed a truly satisfying sexual experience. Men love it, after they've got over the initial shock of a woman suggesting that they bugger her, because of the enjoyable tightness of any girl's asshole.

Since that delightful introduction to butt-fucking, it has become an essential part of all my subsequent sexual relationships, and I have had the intense pleasure of introducing a number of men to their very first experience of butt-fucking. I thoroughly recommend it to all my sisters under the skin. Have fun!

P. I. New York, New York.

David Jones

It certainly sounds fun. I only hope your enthusiasm doesn't bottom out.

PARTY GAMES

I was lucky enough to meet a really pretty girl at a party given by friends recently. Things started off fairly light-heartedly with her. I happened to be wearing a rather tight pair of jeans, since girls tell me that they find my bum attractive in tight denim and I've never been one to ignore a possible edge over the competition. Tight jeans also allow me to bulge at the front a bit, you know where. I'd just arrived, I'd greeted my host and hostess, and I was sipping my first drink and looking at the talent when this lovely girl comes up to me and says, 'However do you get into those jeans?'

I've been asked that question before and I'm well prepared so, quick as a flash, I say, 'Well, you could always offer to buy me a drink, for a start.' Some girls take a while to get there, but this little doll saw it straight away. She loved it, and fell about laughing, after which we got chatting and it wasn't too long before she'd accepted my invitation to find somewhere to eat together after we left the party. After a while, we agreed that it was time to go and eat. I think we both wanted to sit down somewhere on our own and find out more about each other. There was a definite, very positive, mutual attraction.

The party was in Chelsea, and we found a pleasant little restaurant in a quietish back street, just off Flood Street. One where we could take our time, enjoy our food and each other's company, and not be rushed to make room for another tableful of customers. The girl's name was Jenny. She told me that she was twenty-three, single, uninvolved with anyone right now, and lonely. She smiled at me as she said the bit about being lonely, and I thought, hallo. Play your cards right, and you could be onto something really nice here, my boy. So I played my ace card. I told her where I lived. It almost never fails. At the end of the meal, I said to Jenny, 'Do you fancy coming back to my place for a drink? It's not far. I live on one of those houseboats off Cheyne Walk. Just around the corner.'

Looking back, I think she would have come back with me wherever I lived. But it's amazing the number of girls who would normally turn down that kind of an invitation the first time you meet them who'll almost take their knickers off before they get there once you tell them that you live on a houseboat.

I don't know how many of your readers know London's Cheyne Walk, but there are two groups of houseboats moored there alongside the road: a largish group of smaller boats, and a smaller group of larger boats. Mine is one of eight larger boats. It's actually a tank landing craft converted into three flats and mine is the stern flat, meaning that I am in the back end of the boat, away from the road, sticking out into the River Thames. It's a lovely place to be. This was a summer evening, and it's totally restful and relaxing, after the hustle and bustle that commences the moment you set foot ashore. Well, Jenny happily dropped her drawers, as most girls do in those circumstances. It's got nothing to do with me, and everything to do with the romance of the river. And, of course, actually being on board a ship which is moving up and down gently on the water as other craft go by. At low tide, she settles down on the mud, but when the tide is in, you can shut your eyes and imagine yourself at sea anywhere in the world that you would like to be. I poured us both a glass of wine, put some romantic music on the hi-fi, and sat next to Jenny on the one sofa. The slight disadvantage of houseboats (apart, of course, from the large, modern, floating caravan kind) is that they are not exactly spacious. But in this instance, I was delighted to be as close to Jenny as I could get. And she seemed similarly inclined.

In no time at all, we were off the sofa and down on the soft fitted carpet of the main cabin, easing each other's clothes off. Jenny had short, medium brown hair, cut like a little close-fitting hat, surrounding a diminutive face. It suited her. It made her look like a little cherub. She had brown eyes, long brown lashes, and she wore dark red lipstick. As I unbuttoned her blouse, to reveal small, pretty braless breasts, she was unzipping my jeans and reaching down inside for my cock. Her short brown leather skirt took no time at all to remove, leaving her in transparent brown seamed hold-up stockings, and a pair of pale-green satin knickers, embroidered with beige lace, that only just covered the subject. I let go of Jenny for a moment, and stood up and peeled off my jeans myself. There was no way, tight as they were, that she was going to be able to get them off me on the floor. But they had certainly served their purpose.

My prick was jutting out like a small truncheon as I slipped the jeans off over my ankles, and as I divested myself of my boxer shorts Jenny reached up and took hold of it. She then pulled me gently towards her and took its throbbing helmet into her mouth. Her lips were soft and wet, and her tongue was warm. I almost came then, as she began to work at me, but I managed to control myself. I eased myself down onto the floor beside her, without needing to pull out of her mouth, and I began slowly to pull her knickers down. I noticed, as they came down her thighs, that their cotton gusset was damp with her juices, which I took as an indication that she was wanting to be fucked. And soon.

I got her knickers properly down and off over her ankles, and she lay back and spread her legs while still fellating me.

Open, her legs revealed her inner feminine secrets. She had a neatly clipped small bush of quite luxuriant pubic hair, the same medium brown colour as that on her head. Down below this trimmed area, she was completely shaved, revealing her plump pink fleshy labia running down the centre of her pale soft white pudenda. It seemed something of a sexual compromise. A sort of half-woman, half-girl approach to sex. But there was nothing girlish about her actions. Jenny liked her sex, and she didn't mind who knew it. She was obviously very experienced, and she took enormous pleasure from everything that she did.

She sucked cock like an angel. Or at least how I imagined an angel would suck cock. Which was slowly, imaginatively, and with great enjoyment. She fucked like the proverbial stoat, giving as good as she got, and she enjoyed her seemingly endless orgasms both loudly and strongly. I can't remember how many times I came before I had to call a halt to our endeavours, but it was certainly a world record for me. She had ways of getting my cock back up again that I'd never even thought about. She stayed for a memorable night, sharing with me my rather narrow bunk. We had no sleep at all, and I strongly suspect that we kept most of our quasi-nautical neighbours awake too. That night was the beginning of possibly the best sexual relationship I ever had in my life. And it wasn't only the sex. Jenny was amusing, intelligent, good company, understanding, and loving. She was even a fabulous cook. She was everything that a normal male could wish. After three weeks, I was seriously beginning to think of marriage. Me, the original confirmed bachelor. And then, one evening on the houseboat, it all fell apart.

Jenny and I had pretty much avoided any kind of discussion about previous lovers. I think we both agreed, without needing to discuss it, that there wasn't any future in that kind of a conversation. At our reasonably young age – I'm twenty-seven – we're bound to have had a number of previous sexual adventures. Everyone does. So I didn't know at that time that my immediate predecessor had been a rock-band drummer who was seriously into S&M. And drugs. And booze. So he'd get drunk, down the tablets, get out a leather strap, and beat the shit out of Jenny. When you looked at her back and buttocks, you could actually see the faded scars. Bastard. But until she told me what they were, I just assumed that her skin on those areas wasn't quite as perfect as it was everywhere else. Why should I ever think that they were scars from beatings? But the saddest thing of all was that Jenny had come to like it. She'd finally given up the drummer, thank God, because the drugs and the booze had made him impossible to live with. She was eventually frightened for her life, she told me. But she'd come to enjoy the beatings.

We were lying on my bunk on the houseboat one summer evening. We were naked and we'd been necking happily like a couple of teenagers, when Jenny had rolled over onto her side, looked me straight in the eye, and said, 'Will you beat me, please, David?' I thought I'd misheard her. 'Will I what, darling?' I said. 'Beat me,' she said. 'You know. With your belt. On my bottom. Beat me. Please?' 'Don't be silly, sweetheart,' I told her. 'I can't do that. I'm not into it. I've never beaten anyone in my life.' I thought for a moment. 'Well, no. Make that, I've never beaten a *woman* in my life. I've never physically hurt a woman in my life. Ever. I'm just not into it,' I said. 'Well, I am,' Jenny said. 'Why?' I asked. She was silent for a long time. And then she told me about the drummer.

'At first, I just used to cry,' she told me. 'But after a while, I really got into it. It made me feel sexy. It might simply have been the association of ideas. I mean, it turned him on. And after a while, like Pavlov's dogs, I came to associate being beaten with being fucked. And eventually, I got to expect it. Then to accept it. Then to like it. And finally, to *need* it. I need it now. Beat me, darling, and you'll see what it will do for me. I'll get wetter than you've ever known me. And randier than ever. And I'll fuck you like there's no tomorrow, as they say in the bad jokes. Except that this happens to be true.'

I lay there for a while thinking about what she had just said. Closing my eyes, I tried to imagine her lying there, getting a wet pussy while the drummer beat her. Trying to envisage the blood. Because, to get scars, you've got to draw blood. While I was thinking, she put out a hand and held mine. 'It'll hurt me more than it'll hurt you,' she said, trying to make light of it. I think she knew, as I did, that suddenly it was all over. That the idyll had become an embarrassment. To be fair to myself, I did try. I got up off the bunk and went and found a good, strong, wide leather belt. Jenny turned over onto her stomach. I looked at her beautiful bottom, and I thought of all the things that I had already done to it, and some of the things that I had fantasized about doing it. And I'd never even considered beating it! I raised up the belt in my hand and gave it an exploratory *swish* through the air. It didn't do anything for me at all. But if this was what Jenny wanted, then so be it.

I laid the belt across her naked buttocks, and then I took a rather half-hearted swipe at her. It echoed throughout the small cabin with an awful *thwack*. Jenny shuddered as the belt hit her. 'Harder,' she said. I tried again. This time, I think it probably did hurt her. I kept going, but I couldn't get any kind of enthusiasm for what I was doing. As I kept at it, Jenny's bottom began to turn pink, and then red. But there was no question of blood. Indeed, there was no question even of the odd weal. I simply wasn't hitting her hard enough to produce those kinds of injury. Suddenly, Jenny rolled over onto her back, and then stood up. 'For God's sake, David,' she said. 'It's not too much to ask. Give me the belt.' I gave it to her, wondering if perhaps *she* was going to hit *me* with it. But no. She turned around, and started beating the bed. Viciously. With all her strength. After half a dozen strokes at full force, she handed the belt back to me. '*That's* what I'm after,' she said. 'Do you think you can manage that?' Her voice shook with emotion. Whether it was anger or passion or what, I wasn't sure.

I looked at her and shook my head. Sadly. 'No, Jenny, darling,' I told her. 'I'm sorry, but I can't manage that. It just isn't my scene. It actually turns me right off. I'm sorry.' We both spent the rest of the evening in sulky silence, and we didn't make love when we finally went to bed. After that, I didn't call Jenny, and Jenny didn't call me. Three months later, a girlfriend of hers rang to ask if she could come and pick up the few things of Jenny's that were still with me on the houseboat. I said yes, naturally. When she came, she was pleasant enough. She said that Jenny had taken a job in Italy, and that she was leaving London at the end of the month. I never saw or heard from her again. Have any of your readers managed to overcome an initial, genuine dislike of flagellation, and come to enjoy it? I feel I may have thrown away my one real chance of happiness.

D. T. A. Chelsea, London.

Like the song says, the party's over. I don't believe that there was any real alternative. I'll pass on any letters that I get on the subject.

FLASH OF INSPIRATION

I work in a bank, but not as a bank clerk. I'm not in contact with the general public who come into the bank. I sit in a general office with a number of other people – men and women – at desks arranged around the edges of the room, leaving the centre of the room empty. I sit opposite a young girl whom I rather fancy, except that she's in her early twenties and I'm well into my forties. She started work here about six weeks ago now. She seems a perfectly normal girl, and is always pleasant. But never more than that. She doesn't seem to show any serious interest in any of the other men, even the younger ones, and never speaks of a boyfriend, or boyfriends. But to the point.

After she had been there a few days, I noticed that her desk was missing the usual 'vanity' panel across its front, offering me a splendid view of this young girl's pretty legs. She wears rather shorter skirts than do the other women in the bank. From my position directly opposite her, I can hold up a piece of paper – a letter, or anything, really – and pretend to be reading it, whilst actually enjoying looking at the girl's shapely legs. This has become something of an obsession. But the really interesting thing is that whilst the girl – Jane is her name – shows absolutely no indication of being aware of my interest, I think you will agree that the following details prove that she is not only aware of but also actually enjoys my attention.

At first, all I could see were her legs with her short skirt coming down to perhaps three or four inches above the knee, thus revealing a few inches of lower thigh. Fun, but nothing to get overly excited about. Then one day I noticed that she had crossed her legs beneath the desk. Something she had never done before, to my knowledge. The interesting thing about this was that this position afforded me a brief glimpse of underskirt, or petticoat. And then, only a couple of days later, whilst I was holding up a document in order to look at what was becoming a daily pleasure, Jane simply opened her legs. Another first.

I swear she never looked up herself from her work, and couldn't have known that she was affording me such joy with her (as I thought then) involuntary exhibition. For with her legs apart, I could see a glimpse of white knicker. The bit stretched tautly between her legs, down the front of her crotch. I have to admit that I sat there with a throbbing erection, praying to God that I wouldn't need, for any reason, to stand up whilst thus embarrassed. Since then, I now have the daily pleasure of being shown what colour knickers young Jane is wearing. She has an extensive lingerie wardrobe, in every colour that you can imagine.

My own particular favourite is white, after which I think black comes second. Beige is nice too, for I can almost imagine that she isn't wearing any knickers at all. But yesterday! Ah, yesterday. She opened her legs to me first thing yesterday, and I could see that she was wearing white knickers. My firm favourites. Shortly after having spread her legs so generously, Jane received a telephone call. There is too much noise in the room for any of us to hear what any of the others may be talking about on the telephone, what with phones ringing, computer printers buzzing and clicking, and the general hum of conversation. So I have no idea whether her conversation was about business or pleasure. But I could hardly believe my eyes when, as I watched, she slipped her right hand down below the desk, up under her skirt, on underneath the elastic of her knicker leg and there, in full view, she began to masturbate herself!

She continued to look down at her desk as she spoke into the telephone, and no one walking past her or looking at her desk from anywhere in the room other than directly opposite her, would have had the faintest idea what she was doing. But as I watched, both amazed and fascinated, I could see the increasing rhythm of her fingers moving under her knickers and then, finally, the sudden slump of her shoulders as she – presumably – came. I almost came myself as she withdrew her fingers from her pussy and then put them in her mouth and sucked them. After which she looked directly across at me, and smiled. Do you think that, if I invite Jane out for a drink after work one day, she will accept? I don't want to spoil what has become a daily delectation. But then, if the girl is willing to put on a sexual display especially for my benefit (or so it would seem), surely she wants to take this situation to its logical conclusion?

P. W. Wellingborough, Northampton.

I wouldn't bank on it. Maybe you should wait until she does a Sharon Stone for you? On the other hand, faint heart never won fair lady. Let us know what happens.

A TOUCH OF EASTERN PROMISE

My fantasies centre entirely around Eastern and Oriental women. I've never had the pleasure, as they say, but in my dreams I always begin by entering a brothel somewhere in the Far East. I sit down at the bar, where I am served by pretty Thai girls, stripped to the waist, their tiny pointed breasts brushing against my hand as they lean over my table to give me my drink. They are very young, and heavily made up, which I find sexually exciting. They smell delightfully of heavy perfume, and they simply exude sex. I am not in a hurry, and I lean back in my seat and enjoy my drink as I look around me. Oriental music is playing softly and as I sit there I notice that there is a stage at the far end of the room. I get up from my chair, and go and sit nearer the stage. If there is a show, I want to be as close to it as possible. As I watch, the music rises to a crescendo, the curtains part, and a master of ceremonies announces that the show is about to begin. Apart from the MC, the girls behind the bar and me, there is no one else in the room. It doesn't seem to matter. The Oriental music changes dramatically to a European rock beat, and a chorus line of six girls runs onto the stage. They begin a sort of Asian Radio City Music Hall ensemble number, the main difference (apart from the number of girls involved) being that these girls are wearing shoes, stockings, gloves, hats, and nothing else. As they high kick, they split their beavers, as our American cousins say, showing off pretty little pink-lipped cunts, surrounded by black, wispy pubic hair. As they finish their number, I applaud loudly, along with the MC and the bar girls, and they dance off.

One of them comes back almost immediately, and begins to do all sorts of conjuring tricks, mostly of the kind in which she makes things disappear up her pussy. She even smokes a cigarette and blows smoke rings out of her cunt. Honestly. After a while, realizing that I am the only customer, the girl comes and kneels on the stage right in front of me. She is maybe a foot away from me. She leans back on her heels, and pulls her outer labia apart with her fingers, showing me the pale pink interior of her shiny, wet little pussy. It is, like all of her, very small, and I begin to get a hard-on, thinking how tightly it would fit around my swelling cock. 'You like?' she asks me. 'I like,' I tell her. 'You want to lick it?' she asks. 'Sure, baby,' I say.

I lean forward, and as she continues to hold her pussy lips apart I lick and tongue her pink inner hole. It tastes of a combination of pussy and urine, a blend which I find strangely erotic. 'You like to jig-a-jig me?' the girl asks. 'Up here on stage. No charge.' 'You're kidding me,' I say. 'No. No kid you. You come up here, fuck me. No charge. No money. Buy me drink after, if you like.' 'You're on, baby,' I said. I got up out of my seat, and climbed up a small ladder that I could see at the side of the stage. The girl walked towards me.

She was even smaller, standing up in front of me, than she had appeared as I looked up at her on the stage. She smiled at me, and then reached out and unzipped my fly. She stood close to me, and pulled my cock out of my trousers. 'Hmmm,' she said. 'Not bad. Better than Japanese man.' She massaged my cock. Wanked it, really, is a better description. Not unreasonably, it quickly became fully erect. 'Usually now,' she said, 'at this stage in show, I ask audience how they like you to fuck me. Then take vote. You know? Fuck mouth? Fuck cunt? Fuck arsehole? Fuck hand? Anything. Doggy fashion. Straight up and down, like mum an' dad. Anything.

No audience, so you choose. How you like fuck me? I looked at her. She was gorgeous. 'Very, very slowly,' I said. She doubled up with laughter. She patently hadn't heard it before. 'Oh, yes,' she said. 'Very good. OK. You fuck me very slowly. But where?' I reached down, and insinuated my forefinger slowly up her pussy. 'Here, darling,' I said. She really *was* tight. Like a mouse's earhole. She was still wanking my cock. Frankly, I would have been more than happy to stand there, my finger up her pussy, her small, cool hand wanking me expertly, until the inevitable happened, and I came in her hand. But it was not to be.

She let go of my cock, to my chagrin, and slowly pulled my finger out of her pussy. Then she said, 'Lie down on floor now, please. Is clean. No make clothes dirty. Then I fuck you. You like? OK?' 'No problem, baby,' I said. I lay down on the stage, my erection thrusting upwards stiffly through my open fly. The pretty little Thai girl straddled me and then took hold of my cock again. She slowly let herself down onto me, guiding my prick up into her as she did so. She was delightfully soft, and warm, and wet. And yes, you've guessed, she *was* very, very tight.

I nevertheless slid into her all the way, without the slightest hindrance, and she began to fuck me. She moved her body up and down the length of my shaft, and at the same time she used muscles in her cunt that I didn't know women had. She literally massaged me with them. I swear that she used her pussy like a hand, grasping me, pulling my foreskin up and down, squeezing me, masturbating me into her with her expert, well trained, very practised pussy muscles. In no time at all, I was pulsing my semen up into her, and groaning aloud at the pleasure which she was giving me. She leaned down and kissed me on the mouth, her small tongue wet between my lips. 'Good?' she whispered in my ear. 'Good, baby,' I groaned, overcome with unspeakable, exquisite sexual pleasure. 'You buy me cold beer after show,' she whispered. 'Then, afterwards, I fuck you properly. Slowly. Make you come many times. You like that?' 'Oh, baby,' I said. 'Yes. Yes, please. I'd like that.'

She kissed me once more, and slowly pulled herself off me. My cock came out of her with a sort of sucking noise, so strong was the suction from her pussy. 'Go back to your seat, now,' she said. 'The show must go on.' We laughed together, and I did as I was told. Once seated, I remembered to tuck away my now flaccid cock, and zip up my open fly. The rest of the show passes pleasantly, but the only thing that I am thinking about is that I am waiting to fuck this delightful young girl, in the privacy of her own room, and that I will be able to take as long as I like, and to take her any way that I like. And that is exactly what I do, all night, in my fantasy. I hope, one day, to turn it into a reality.

T. K. A. Wrexham, Clwyd.

We wish you well to wear it.

OH, MISTRESS MINE

I got into an interesting conversation recently with a male friend of mine on the subject of choosing the ideal mistress. As a woman, I take the view that an ideal mistress would be young, beautiful, sexy, and always available. To which one could add such ideal things as not being jealous (of a wife, perhaps), not greedy, financially (for any proper mistress has to be paid, if only in the sense of supported, i.e. rent, utility bills, clothes, food, holidays, etc.) and – most importantly – she has to be satisfied with the amount of time that her lord and master is prepared (or able) to devote to her.

My friend agreed with all of these attributes bar the first two: that she should be young and beautiful. Nubile, yes, he said. Sexy, certainly. Available, of course. But neither too young, nor too beautiful, for the reason that he would very soon find that he had unwanted competition for her hand (metaphorically speaking). Anyone young and beautiful, with time on their hands, was bound, he said, to become involved with other men, even if it were only one man. A lover, of (perhaps) her own age. What my friend didn't know was that I *am* a mistress, and have been now for over three years. I am kept by a married man, who tells me that he loves his wife and children (two boys and a girl), but that the fun has gone out of his sex life. His wife is pushing fifty, as is he, and no longer, he says, enjoys sex.

But he loves her, and likes her, and finds her a charming, amusing, and happy companion. I'm twenty-five, and I love sex. He says I go like the nine-ten from Paddington. I know that I am simply here for fucking. I accept that. At least for now. My man is very up-front about our relationship, and he doesn't pretend that his wife doesn't love him any more, or that he has any plans for leaving her. Ours is a business relationship which we both enjoy. It's not a hard life. I live in a nice flat in W1. I don't want for anything, and I don't need to work. All I have to do is to keep Wednesday evenings free for him, and occasionally other times by arrangement. And then I do the sexual things which his wife no longer finds fun, like suck his cock, let him fuck me anally (which I love) and so on.

For the record, I do not have any other lovers – either privately or professionally – although I have had offers. What do your readers think? Which view do they take? I expect that your male readers may agree with my male friend, and your female readers with me. I'd love to know.

P. De C. London, W1.

We invite readers of both sexes to write in with their ideal choice of either (a) a young and beautiful mistress, or (b) a not so young and not so beautiful mistress. We'll keep the score, and let you know, Miss P. De C. Personally, we're with you. In our opinion, a man who isn't confident that he can keep the competition away from his mistress doesn't deserve to have one. (Editor's note: for the record, the votes came in fifty-four per cent for a young and beautiful mistress, and forty-six per cent for the alternative.)

KEEPING HER HAND IN

I was moaning a few weeks back to my friend Jean, in the office, about being a cricket widow, what with the summer county games, the Test Matches, and then the World Cup, and I was telling her how I get my husband's attention by giving him hand jobs in front of our television set. She seemed greatly amused by this confession at the time and at the end of the week, when Friday came, she invited me to join her in our office local for a drink before going home. By the time we got to our second drink, she brought up the discussion of earlier in the week, about my giving my husband a wank in front of the TV, and pleaded with me to give her more details. This surprised me, since we have never discussed sex of any kind ever before.

In fact, to be honest, I have always seen Jean as being rather strait-laced. But she wanted to know absolutely everything about these events. How, specifically, did I grip my husband's cock with my fingers? Could I demonstrate my grip on her thumb? (I did!) Was he circumcised, or not? How long did it take him to come? Did he go on watching the cricket while I was wanking him? Did I do it quickly, or slowly? (Meaning the speed of my strokes up and down his member.) Was talking dirty part of the session, or did I wank him in silence? She seemed obsessed with the subject of my masturbating my husband, but I nevertheless gave her as much information as I was able.

Over the next few weeks, every time that there had been cricket on TV the previous day Jean would ask me how my masturbatory sessions had gone with my husband and I would tell her that all had gone well. About two weeks later – again on a Friday – Jean invited me for a drink after we finished work, and when I agreed she almost immediately got onto the same old subject. Eventually – more to tease Jean than in all seriousness – I said that perhaps my husband and I should invite her over one weekend when there was a cricket match on, and she could watch us. She said yes, she'd love to do that, and then we changed the subject.

That Friday night I told my husband, Frank, about the conversation, and he was greatly amused by it. He also said, however, that if I seriously wanted to bring Jean over to watch us at our indoor sports, he didn't mind in the least bit. In fact, I think he got quite excited by the idea. So the following Monday, I invited Jean to supper with us the next Saturday, reminding her that there was a whole day of Test cricket on the box that day. I invited her for a drink at about six, which meant that there should be at least an hour of cricket before the end of the programme. When Saturday came, we all three of us sat on a sofa in front of our TV set, watching the cricket and drinking. I sat with Frank on my right, and he had Jean on his right. After a little while, I put my drink down and casually unzipped Frank's fly. Jean watched as I pulled his rapidly expanding cock out of his trousers and began slowly to masturbate him. She was absolutely fascinated and she leaned over towards Frank so that she might have a really close view of me pulling his pud. I talked her through what I was doing and then I took my hand away from Frank's cock, suggesting to Jean that she try her hand at it, as it were. Her eyes nearly popped out of her head, but she nevertheless took hold of him and began to wank him. Bearing in mind that she told me later that this was the first time she had ever given a man one off the wrist, she did pretty well, and it wasn't too long before Frank was shooting his spunk in the air as she wanked him to a climax. I think the excitement of a different woman's hand on his dick may have had something to do with it!

Fortunately I'd had the sense to have a box of tissues to hand, and I caught his ejaculate before it stained anything or anyone. Frank went off to wash himself, and then we all sat down to supper. After supper, I suggested to Jean that Frank was probably now back in a state where she could practice some more, if she so wished, and she said that yes, she'd like to, so we all repaired back to the sofa. The cricket by this time was finished, of course, but no one seemed too bothered by it.

Frank pulled his cock out with great enthusiasm and Jean began her ministrations again. Not to be left out, I slipped my hand up my skirt and began to rub myself off through my knickers, as I watched Frank being jacked off by Jean. I brought myself off very quickly, and, almost without thinking about what I was doing, I moved over to kneel in front of Jean. Then I slid my fingers up under her skirt and up inside her knicker leg. I quickly found her wet gash. She spread her legs for me, without saying anything. I immediately found her clit and began wanking her off while I did myself again with my other hand in my own knickers. We all more or less orgasmed at approximately the same time, and a great time was had by everyone. You won't be surprised to hear that we have already set a date for the next session.

P. W. St Albans, Herts.

So, eventually, everything came to hand . . .

GETTING INTO GEAR

I'm the only chauffeuse that I know, although people tell me that there are other girls driving limousines about in Bristol. I own and drive my own car, and I've built up a good business in the three years that I've been at it. I drive a beautifully maintained old Daimler, and I do a lot of weddings, as you can probably imagine. I do, of course, get propositioned a lot. Perhaps I should say here that I'm twenty-six, five foot seven, slim, with a good figure, and I love sex. I can also say no when I want to, and that's most of the time actually. But let me tell you of a rather special occasion recently when I was more than happy to say yes!

I was booked by the manager of one of the city's larger hotels to collect two of his guests arriving at Bristol Airport. I was given their names, and a card to hold up at the arrivals gate, to identify myself to them when they arrived. They were both in their early thirties, I would guess, and they were both pretty good-looking. They seemed as pleased to see me as I was to see them, and when I delivered them at their hotel, they took one of my business cards and promised that they would use me for any journeys that they made during their stay in Bristol. I didn't have long to wait, for they telephoned me late that afternoon, and hired me for what they described as an 'open-ended evening'. I was free, so I was delighted. When I picked them up at seven p.m., they said that they would first of all like to go to a decent restaurant. One that I would recommend. I took them to one of Bristol's better restaurants – one owned and run by one of the famous, original, old Bristol sherry shippers – and they insisted that I joined them for their meal. It was a great success, in that they were delighted with the food on offer, and I enjoyed both my meal and their company.

They both turned out to be Londoners. They worked for the same company, a firm of auctioneers, and were friends as well as colleagues. They didn't discuss their marital status, but I would guess that they were both married. The more particularly so from the way that the evening developed. They spared nothing over dinner, buying fabulous wine, and they were as generous with their hospitality as anyone I have ever known. After dinner, when we got back to the limo, they announced that they wanted to go to Bristol's best strip club. Driving business people around, you get to know where everything is in your own city, and, having translated 'best' as 'horniest', I took them to a club down by the docks that was infamous for the explicit sexuality of its show.

They again insisted that I accompany them, and so I got to sit through a strip show that met their every requirement. The girls were young and pretty. It was raunchy. Not to say, frankly, disgusting. Girls were sticking vibrators up their pussies, and switching them on. Openly masturbating themselves. (And I do mean openly. You could see the pink.) Taking off their knickers and holding the moist crotches under their clients' noses, for them to sniff the aroma of wet pussy. The audience – including my two punters – loved every minute of it. When we finally left, the two of them could hardly walk for the size of their hard-ons, and I guessed that the next request would be for high-quality, immediately available women.

I was right, but I didn't exactly reckon on what that could mean. 'How much will you charge us to fuck you?' asked Jimmy, the more vocal of the two. 'I know we could have got laid back at the strip club, but there was nothing there to compare with you. How much? For both of us?' I looked at them. They seemed in control of themselves, and they looked as if they could accept a no, if that was what I was going to say. But to my surprise, the strippers had turned me on too, and I fancied both of these men.

'Let's not fuck about, chaps,' I said. 'Let's say five hundred pounds. Cash. For that, you can have me any way you want me, for as long as you like.' 'Done,' said Jimmy. He reached into his pocket, pulled out a wad of fifty-pound notes, and counted off ten. 'There'll be a good tip, of course,' he said, 'for work well done.' He got into the back of the limo, undid his fly, pulled out his rampant cock and said, 'Suck that.' I love being dominated and I knelt on the floor in front of him and began to fellate him. He was circumcised, and the purple helmet of his swollen cock stretched my mouth. As I was sucking him, I felt the other guy's hands underneath my jacket, clutching at my breasts. He felt them, squeezing my nipples hard. They obligingly became erectile beneath his fingers, after which he released them and slid his right hand up under my skirt and into my knickers, feeling for my snatch. He found it quickly, and immediately discovered how wet it was. 'Oh, baby,' he said. 'You're good and ready for me. Here comes Old One-Eye.'

I felt him unbuckling his trousers and then suddenly he was right up me, fucking me from behind. His tool felt enormous and it was doing delicious things to me. After a little while, I took Jimmy's cock out of my mouth just long enough to look over my shoulder and say, 'Play with my clitty. Please.' He did as he was told and put a finger down between his cock and my pussy wall. He immediately found my clitoris, which he began to manipulate. He'd done it before, I could tell. I like a man who knows his way around a girl's pussy. It shows that he cares. I managed a few small, sneaky orgasms before he realized, and then I felt the biggy building.

Then he began to fuck me harder, more urgently, and I knew that his ejaculation was beginning too. I began to wank Jimmy's cock into my mouth with my expert fingers, in addition to sucking it, and he very quickly came, his cock pulsing and throbbing, spurting his thick, creamy seed into my mouth. I swallowed it all. I love the taste of come, and as he ejaculated it brought on my own orgasm, which was transmitted through my pussy muscles to the other guy's cock, instantly bringing him off too, so that all three of us were bucking and moaning as we erupted into each other. It was terrific.

That, of course, was just the beginning. By the time the two of them had finished, both Jimmy and the other guy – whose name, I discovered, was Lionel – had fucked me, and they had taken it in turns to suck my appreciative pussy. Jimmy had also fucked me anally. It took him forever, since he'd come twice before that, and I loved every long, slow, lingering, gorgeous minute of it. I just adore the feeling of hot come spurting up my rectum. It's *so* sexy. If any of you girls out there haven't tried it yet, you should. I guarantee that you'll love it. And, finally, I sucked Lionel off. When we had eventually all recovered, we got ourselves together, dressed ourselves, and I got back behind the wheel of the limo, with the two guys sitting in the back. When I dropped them off back at the hotel, each of them gave me a hundred pounds tip, and a big kiss. I took them both to the airport the following morning, and they swore that they would be back again just as soon as they could arrange it. I can't wait. They can auction me any time they like.

D. H. Bristol, Avon.

Sounds as if you drove them wild with excitement!

MOUTHING OFF

I would much appreciate the opportunity to be able to tell your readers about my new girlfriend. Annette is eighteen, and that singular sort of woman – in my experience – who just loves oral sex. She can't give me head often enough. Every male's fantasy! But it didn't start like that. We met in a local pub here in Gloucester. I was with three other male colleagues, from work, and she was with a group of girls from her office. She seemed quite shy at first, but she reacted very naturally and pleasantly when I singled her out and devoted my whole attention to her. One thing led to another, and we started going out. I didn't rush things and eventually, after about a month of visits to the movies, meals in restaurants and visits to the pub, we started having sex together. Looking back now, it seems strange to remember that she was actually shy about undressing in front of me. She was fine once she was naked – she had few inhibitions about her body – it was simply that she was embarrassed to be watched whilst she undressed. The first time that I sucked her pretty little pussy, she loved it. She was entranced. She came almost continuously, and while she was certainly not a virgin when I met her, no one had ever sucked her pussy for her before.

But when I first suggested that she might suck my cock, she was literally horrified. She was, admittedly, young, and she wasn't *that* sexually experienced. But her distaste at the thought of performing fellatio was a surprise to me. I didn't press the issue, and the rest of our sex was so good that it wasn't a big problem. As we grew to know each other better,

Annette's enthusiasm for sex grew too. I continued to suck her pussy, and she continued to enjoy it. Then I began to masturbate her. I would deliberately choose to do this during daylight hours, for at night Annette was happier with the lights off when we fucked.

Then, one day, I asked her to masturbate me. Again in daylight. This too was something that she had never done before. (To my surprise. I thought all girls started off their sex lives by masturbating boys, and being masturbated by them.) She seemed to enjoy doing this for me, and she giggled with surprise and delight when I shot my semen all over her agile little fingers. It excited her so much that she masturbated me back to full erection as quickly as possible, and then she leaped upon me and fucked me – and herself – to rapid orgasm. The next time that we had sex, Annette started off by playing with my cock and, leaning down over it, she examined it, very closely. I was happy to explain the rudiments of how a cock works. I showed her where it was sensitive to friction, and then I pulled back the foreskin, and displayed my swollen purple helmet to her. I then encouraged her to masturbate me again, slowly, until once more I spurted my come over her fingers. For the first time, she looked at me, grinned, and put her fingers in her mouth. 'Mmmm,' she said, after a moment's consideration. 'That tastes rather nice. It's not actually nasty at all. What a nice surprise.'

She then bent down and, taking my now flaccid cock in her mouth, she slowly sucked all the come off it, and from out of it, which she swallowed with evident enjoyment. Naturally enough, the feel of her soft mouth and lips around my prick for the first time ever, having been wanting her to do exactly that for so long, soon had it fully erect again, and in no time at all I came once more, this time in her mouth. I did nothing but lie back and enjoy what was being done to me. I didn't take her head in my hands, or begin to fuck her mouth, or do any of the many things that a more experienced fellatrice might reasonably expect.

Her enthusiasm for oral sex stems from that day. Now we almost always start our sex with her fellating me. She prefers that, she tells me, to our *soixante-neuf*ing each other. She loves me to suck her pussy, and she now loves to suck my cock, but she likes to separate these two activities. Her favourite way of fellating me is to have me sit on one of the two easy chairs that we have in our bedroom, naked, my legs spread wide for her. She then kneels – also naked – on the floor in front of me, and takes my cock in her fingers, wrapping them around the base of it, and pulling down my foreskin, so that my cock-head is fully exposed to her oral ministrations. It excites me as I sit there, with my swollen prick just inches away from her innocent lips. She smiles at me, and licks her lips in anticipation of what she is about to do. My cock throbs in her hand. She squeezes it.

Then she slowly exposes her wet tongue and, looking up at me all the time, she takes my full length deep into her mouth, closes her lips about me, and begins to suck. She tongues me, and pulls me in and out of her mouth, her head bobbing faster and faster as she gains momentum. And then, after a while, she will deliberately stop and slowly pull my cock, wet now with her saliva, out of her mouth, and blow upon it. A delightful sensation, but every single nerve in my blood-rich, throbbing penis is screaming for her to put it back in her mouth again.

As I watch, she pushes two fingers up her pussy, wiggles them about, and withdraws them. She holds them up and shows me how wet they are. 'Would you like to suck the pussy juice off my fingers, darling?' she asks me, all innocently. 'Yes, please, darling,' I say, and she puts her fingers in my mouth and waits while I suck every last vestige of her love juices off her fingers. 'Now I'm going to wank us both off together,' she tells me. 'Or, more accurately, I'm going to suck you off until you come in my mouth, and I'm going to wank my pussy with my other hand. With any luck, we'll come together.' She grins up at me. 'Here we go, sweetheart.' She takes hold of my cock again, this time with her left hand, and takes it into her soft, warm, wet mouth. She starts sucking and licking immediately. As I watch, she puts her right hand down between her open legs and begins to play with her pussy. At first, she simply thrusts two fingers in and out of herself, but quite soon she has isolated her clitoris and is massaging that for all she is worth. Then she takes my prick out of her mouth, looks up at me once more, and says, 'I want you to come in my mouth. I want to feel your hot spunk spurting down my throat. And then I'll come with you. OK?'

'OK, baby,' I said, trying not to show my surprise. Here was this young girl, who not so long ago was horrified at the suggestion that she take my cock in her mouth, kneeling naked in front of me, my erect prick deep in her mouth, having just said that she wanted me to shoot my ejaculate down her throat and make her come. She sucked, and licked, and wanked me at the same time with her hand, while her other hand was mightily busy between her legs. It was an enormously sexually stimulating sight, watching my rigid prick, wet with her saliva, disappearing in and out of her lips. Saliva was running out of the corners of her mouth, and she was becoming really worked up as she began to feel her orgasm building somewhere deep down near her womb. She began a sort of strangulated moaning, the sound distorted by the fact that her mouth was full of my cock, and I could see and feel that her orgasm was about to start. I knew that the very moment I began to ejaculate, she would orgasm. I took her head in between my hands, and she looked up at me. I began, very gently, to move my hips in the smallest possible fucking movements, and as I did so, I ejaculated deep into her mouth.

She moaned as I spurted into her mouth, and she immediately came herself, her body shuddering, her shoulders shaking, her mouth trembling. After that occasion, there was no holding her. Patently, the thing that had been putting her off oral sex was the thought of my ejaculating into her mouth. Now that this phenomenon held no fears for her, the problem disappeared. She simply couldn't suck cock often enough. Many evenings, she now prefers to spend the entire time giving head, without any thought of actually getting fucked. She has gradually improved her technique, until today I would enter her into any oral sex contest, and be more than surprised if she didn't win outright.

These days, when she is in the mood, she asks me to fuck her mouth. She loves to lie on her back, her legs wide apart, and have me kneel over her and literally fuck her mouth. She has become accustomed to the fact that I like to suck her pussy whilst I do what she wants, and now allows me to do so. I always ask her to keep her knickers on at the beginning of one of our mutual oral sex sessions, since it has always turned me on to suck pussy through girls' knickers. For me, there is something tremendously sexually exciting about sucking pussy through thin silk or nylon material. The feeling of warm, wet, fleshy, swollen vaginal lips beneath the coolness of wet fabric, is a guaranteed turn-on, and Annette has become accustomed to my fetish.

Nowadays, she takes my prick in her hand and feeds it into her mouth. I then start to move my hips, slowly at first, and then faster and faster, until I am seriously fucking her mouth. As I get more and more aroused, she starts to jack me off into her mouth, until finally I spurt my come into her in great long pulsating gouts. At the same time, I will masturbate her clitoris as I suck her pussy, and she too will come, bucking her wet, swollen pussy up against my mouth as she orgasms wetly. Long gone now are the days when she thought oral sex was disgusting.

J. T. L. Gosport, Hants.

It sounds as if she's seriously paying lip service to your needs.

TWO'S COMPANY

It's always been a fantasy of mine to be fucked by two men at the same time. My husband has always known this, but I never thought that he would actually do anything about it. How wrong could I be! On my birthday recently, he took me to one of New York's few surviving swinging sex clubs. We had both eaten a sumptuous dinner previously, at the Cirque de France, and had consumed sufficient beautiful wine, followed by liqueurs, to be in the mood for anything. On arrival at the club, over on the West Side, we sat at the bar for a while, and watched the dancing.

It wasn't long before an attractive young man came over and asked my husband if he might ask me to dance. My husband told him that he would be only too pleased, since he himself wasn't one of the world's great dancers. That was a lie, in fact. My hubby dances like a dream. However, so did the young man I was now dancing with, and it wasn't long before I could feel his erection thrusting stiffly between my legs as he guided me around the floor. My immediate reaction was to get very wet myself. It was the first time in years that I had felt a cock other than my husband's between my legs. After the young man returned me to my husband at the bar, he – my husband – suggested that we perhaps move on, to see what amusement we might find somewhere else, and asked the young man – Joe was his name – if he would care to join us. To my surprise, Fred, my husband, then drove us back to our apartment. We live on the East Side, in the low eighties, in a modern high-rise apartment on the twenty-eighth floor. When we got home, my husband told me that if I fancied Joe, he was happy for me to get fucked by the two of them, thus fulfilling my long-held fantasy. It was to be a birthday present. I looked at Joe, and Joe looked at me, and we both said, more or less at the same time, 'No problem!' We moved into the bedroom, and undressed in what must have been – for me – world record time.

I'm twenty-four, and have a good body. I'm dark-haired, with long legs (which I love to spread for my hubby), a great ass, and good tits with over-sized nipples. Fred is twenty-nine, and he's pretty fit. He's six foot tall, slim, and has a giant schlong. It was one of the things that most attracted me to him when we first met. Getting fucked by Fred is like being fucked by a stallion. My wanting to be fucked by two men at the same time in no way reflects on Fred's ability in the sack. Not to my mind.

Once naked, I lay on the bed and watched the two men undressing with some interest. Both had full erections, and Joe's cock was every bit as large as Fred's. Joe turned out to be twenty-seven and single. And then, suddenly, I had two pairs of hands all over me, feeling me up, squeezing my tits, massaging my butt. The men soon settled down to sucking my now fully erect nipples and someone – I didn't know who – had a finger up my ass. The fingers up my pussy, I soon discovered, belonged to Joe. I was wetter than I had ever been in my life before, as I took Joe's circumcised cock into my mouth and began to suck it, whilst I took Fred's uncircumcised cock in my right hand and began to jerk him off. Joe found my clit with consummate ease, and in no time I was writhing on the bed and moaning with ecstasy at my first orgasm of the evening. Joe had his tongue halfway down my throat by now, and I could feel Fred applying K-Y jelly to my asshole, so I knew what I was in for there. And then, as Fred spread my ass cheeks and began slowly to ease his huge schlong up my asshole, Joe swivelled around, his cock once more in my mouth, and got himself into a position where he could eat my pussy whilst I sucked him off.

Since Fred's cock by this time was all the way up my asshole, my right hand was free, and I began to jerk off Joe's cock at the same time as I sucked him. In no time at all, he exploded into my mouth, and I had the truly sensual pleasure, for the first time ever, of swallowing the hot come of someone other than my husband. This excitement, plus Joe's expertise at eating me out, brought on my second orgasm of the evening. Seconds later, Fred spurted his hot seed violently up my asshole, increasing the intensity of my orgasm tenfold, and then all three of us were, for the moment, sexually replete. We all disentangled ourselves, the one from the other, and took time out for a short break. Fred went off to the bathroom to wash his cock. I got up and went through to the sitting room, where I freshened up our drinks and took them through to the bedroom. Quite soon, the men finished their drinks and turned their attention back to me.

Fred seemed in a generous frame of mind, and was obviously allowing Joe, as our mutual guest, the first choice of whichever orifice in my body appealed the most to him. He chose my pussy, and decided that he would like to fuck me doggy fashion. I consequently knelt on all fours, thrusting my ass up in the air and offering it to him. He grabbed me around my waist, thrust himself into me, and began to fuck me enthusiastically. This particular position didn't leave a lot of opportunities available for Fred, so I suggested that he lay on his back, his cock stiffly erect beneath my face, and allowed me to suck him and jerk him off. This he seemed happy enough to succumb to, and for a while I maintained that position, one very large schlong fucking my pussy from the rear, whilst I masturbated the other one into my mouth, and sucked and licked it in my best fellatrice manner.

Your women readers will know that it is not easy to blow a large cock. Smaller ones are much easier. A cock that stretches your mouth to its limits doesn't leave a great deal of room for subtle use of your lips or tongue. Which is why, with both Fred and Joe, I used my fingers as well. It is, in my opinion, the only occasion in sexual games where a girl would prefer to work on a smaller cock. Joe was doing a great job fucking me from the rear, but this isn't the best position for any woman to be fucked from, simply because, in that position, contact between the man's cock and the woman's clitoris is minimal. Consequently – since my own right hand was busy with Fred's cock – I looked over my shoulder at Joe and said, 'Play with my clit, baby, please.'

I'm pleased to be able to tell you that it was no sooner said than done. He knew exactly where my clit was, and precisely what to do with it, and within seconds I was enjoying yet another orgasm. My vaginal contractions brought on Joe's ejaculation, and whilst all this was happening, I increased my masturbation of Fred to such a speed that he immediately shot his hot semen into my mouth and, once more, all three of us were satisfied. We went on for some time after that. The novelty of the situation for all three of us excited and stimulated our sexual responses far beyond what was normal, and the man kept changing places and orifices, until I finally fell asleep, exhausted but happy. When I awoke the following morning, Joe had gone, and we haven't tried to contact him since (nor he us). But I continue to thank Fred – nightly – for the greatest birthday present ever. And I have made up my mind that when his birthday arrives, in approximately three months' time, I shall return the compliment and have a threesome set up for him, this time with me and another girl! The youngest, prettiest girl I can find.

R. C. New York, New York.

Wish him 'Happy' Birthday from us.

TYING ONE ON

Although I'm a one hundred per cent dyed-in-the-wool male submissive, bondage and humiliation are not exactly my wife's favourite bag. She's frankly a straight-up-and-down, like-mum-and-dad girl. But, happily, she loves me enough, and is broad-minded enough, to indulge me on occasions. I particularly enjoy it when, to punish me, she forces me to eat her pussy for long periods. Last weekend, she told me that she was pretty pissed off with my behaviour generally, and that she was going to punish me. She ordered me into our bedroom and ordered me to strip. She then ordered me to lie on the bed on my back. When I had obeyed, she blindfolded me and then bound my wrists and ankles to the four corners of the bed frame. For a while, I could see and hear nothing, and the next thing that I knew was when she started pinching my nipples into nipple clamps. She screwed them down hard, and they were quite seriously painful so I soon had a rock-hard erection. Then I felt her undo the bindings on my wrists and ankles: she ordered me to turn over and lie on my stomach, after which she tied me up again. There was silence again for a while, and then I heard a *swish*, and almost at the same time I felt the burning sting of a cane across my buttocks. Then she began to cane me properly, *thwack* after *thwack* landing on my backside until I was crying out in pain. But I loved every minute of it. My wife asked me if I wanted her to stop, but I said 'No', and she continued thrashing me until I was pleading for mercy. Finally she stopped and undid my blindfold. She then took my painfully erect penis in her hand

and quickly masturbated me to the best climax I can remember having. When it was all over, I thanked her, humbly, and she told me to watch my step in future, or she'd have to punish me again very soon.

J. T. H. Limerick, Republic of Ireland.

You're bound to be pleased, you might say.

NAUGHTY KNICKERS

As I grew up, all the way through boarding school (Cheltenham Ladies' College) and university (London University) I thought that I was a fairly normal young woman. I started having sex when I was nineteen, which was about when most of my contemporaries started doing the same thing. And up until then, I had worn the kind of underclothes that were practical, rather than sexy. You know the kind of thing? I mean, plain cotton Sloggis. Practical. Comfortable. Plain colours. Reasonably priced. Easy to launder. All of those things. And then, one evening, in a pub off Gower Street much used by university students, I met David. David is a university lecturer, and is thirty-four and married, with three children. He is also cock-happy (perhaps *cunt*-happy is a more accurate description) and fucks everything in sight, given half a chance. I was delighted to give him all the chances he needed, for I found him amusing company, great in bed, and his wife and family were his problem, not mine.

He was teaching European Politics, which I wasn't taking, so we didn't have a problem there. He was – to me – innovative in bed and quite an appreciative, gentle lover. On about our third week together, we got back to my furnished room in Belsize Park after a few at the Haverstock Arms, down the road, and he produced a small parcel. He was stripping off as I unwrapped it, and he got into my bed preceded by the most enormous erection. I was dying to follow him and take it in my mouth, but I felt duty bound to open the present. Which I did, to find inside two pairs of what looked like extremely expensive, pure silk, very lacy, beautifully embroidered knickers. The kind rich men buy in Harvey Nichols, in Knightsbridge, for their mistresses (which, I have always believed, is why everyone calls them Harvey Knicks). One pair was primrose yellow, the other a bright royal blue.

'Darling,' I said. 'They're really beautiful. Thank you.' 'Put them on, sweetheart,' he said, 'and come to bed. My pleasure is in taking them off. Eventually.' I didn't know what he meant by that 'eventually', but I very soon found out. I put the pale yellow pair on. They felt fantastic, and the rub of the soft silk against my pussy was highly erotic. I was very touched. In more ways than one! As I got into bed with David, he threw back the covers, the better to get at that which he wanted to get at. Spreading my legs, he buried his face between them, and began to suck my pussy through the soft silk of the knickers. It was a delightfully sexy feeling, and as he sucked me I took hold of that magnificent erection and returned the compliment. David sucked and licked and tongued as if he had never put his head between my legs before. (He had. Often!) The sensation seemed that much improved by being strained, as it were, through the expensively silky material.

He next gripped my buttocks, one in each hand, and pulled my whole groin up that much harder against his mouth, until I came in an enormous, almighty orgasm that racked my whole body, down to my very toes. It was, for me, the best oral sex ever.

Finally, he started to ease the new knickers down my legs, very slowly, obviously enjoying what it was doing for his libido. He finally pulled them off over my ankles and, instead of dropping them on the floor, as I expected, he pressed the crotch of them – where they were now quite sodden, by a mixture of his saliva and my pussy juices – against his nose. He then breathed in an enormously deep breath which he held for a while and then let out, very slowly. 'Mmmm,' he said. 'My favourite perfume. Wet pussy. Do you mind if I take these away with me when I go?' I thought for a moment. Why on earth would he want to take away a pair of knickers that he had just given me? I couldn't think of an answer. 'Sure, baby, if that's what you would like to do,' I told him. 'But why?' He grinned at me. 'So I can keep them in a drawer in my office and, when I'm on my own, I can take them out and sniff the scent of your wet little pussy and toss myself off while I think about you,' he said. 'OK?' I had to laugh. He was so up front. 'That's quite a compliment, if I think about it,' I told him. 'Now fuck me. Please.' Looking back, I now know that David was particularly well endowed, but after the oral session through the crotch of my new knickers, he seemed even larger than usual, and he fucked me to a standstill.

I did my best for him too, his excitement creating excitement in me. I wrapped my legs around his back and crossed them, and then I locked them together, pulling him down hard onto me as he fucked me into oblivion. I fell asleep after this excellent performance and when I awoke, David had gone. Back to his wife and family, presumably. The pale yellow knickers had gone too. But I still had the royal blue pair.

David rang me the following evening and arranged to meet me at the Haverstock Arms once more. He arrived breathing heavily and couldn't get his drink down quickly enough before he asked me, 'Are you wearing the blue knickers?' 'No, darling,' I told him. And then, when his face dissolved into what I can only describe as a caricature of disappointment, I said, 'I'm not wearing any knickers at all. And my pussy is so wet that the liquid is running down my thighs. Does that make you feel happier?' I swear he walked the short distance from the pub to my rooming house on three legs. When we got there, I stripped off at high speed and lay on my back, my legs apart, and then I waited, patiently, while he took his clothes off. 'I'm so wet, baby,' I told him. 'Why don't you lick me dry? I'd like that.' He buried his head between my legs once more and sucked and licked until I think I was even wetter than when he started, but we both enjoyed what he was doing. He loved the taste and smell of pussy juice and was always telling me that he couldn't get enough of it. I was feeling lazy that evening, and enjoying just lying there being sucked, so I didn't suck him, I just took hold of his erect cock and wanked it slowly as he sucked me. I had a number of orgasms before David stopped sucking me and, kneeling up, urgently thrust his stiff cock up my pussy and gave me a very serious seeing-to. All this, and I've still got the royal blue knickers in reserve. Aren't I the lucky one?

K. G. Belsize Village, London.

Sounds like you're taking him for a sucker... No, seriously, yes, you are a lucky girl. And David is a lucky guy.

GOING PUBLIC

My particular bag has always been sex in public places. Not always necessarily out in the open. Last week, for example, I was with my boyfriend in a Mexican restaurant in Soho. I guess we'll never be able to go *there* again. We were enjoying our food, and our conversation, which was getting more and more blatantly sexy until we were both about as horny as could be, and I said to my boyfriend, why not? Moments later, we were locked into the restaurant's only lavatory – it served both men and women – fucking like rabbits. There wasn't a lot of room, but it *was* a lot of fun. The thought of being caught by a member of the restaurant staff added spice to the occasion. It was all over almost as soon as it started, we were so hot when we began, but we both came long and strong, and together. It was the best fuck all week. What we didn't know was that all four of the restaurant's waiters were lined up in the passage outside, listening to the urgent sounds of our sex. As we opened the door, intending to sneak back to our table, they all four gave us a round of applause.

We have fucked on the landings of the emergency stairs at Underground stations. The excitement of wondering whether or not we'll get caught by someone who uses the stairs, rather than the lifts, makes up for the discomfort of what inevitably has to be a knee-trembler.

We *have* been passed by other people. Twice. On both occasions, they pretended that we weren't there. We've never fucked in a public telephone box, considering them far too obvious. Everyone and anyone who has nowhere to go uses telephone boxes. We try to be more creative. Museums and art galleries are fun, although you have to keep an ear cocked for the attendants who tend to creep about, looking for people who are misbehaving. We haven't actually been caught (yet!) but I *have* been in a situation where I've had to hold my handkerchief over my boyfriend's ejaculating penis at the moment of truth and pretend to be kissing him in order to disguise what we were really doing, due to the unexpected arrival of an attendant in one of the galleries at the Victoria and Albert Museum. The National Portrait Gallery is a favourite place. It has a myriad smaller rooms – particularly on its upper floors – where members of the public seldom seem to venture. Even the attendants rarely patrol up there.

Hyde Park, Kensington Gardens, and the gardens in various inner London squares are all good places in the summer, except for the facts that, one, they tend to become rather overcrowded with other couples doing the same thing, and two, these days, they get very full of vagrants, alcoholics, the homeless, and other unfortunates. Some of the upper floors of the Festival Hall, in the mornings, are good places for public copulation, but they're obviously non-starters in the evenings. Women's changing rooms in West End stores are both exciting and challenging, but you need to be extremely careful. The basement of C&A at Marble Arch is an excellent and less challenging venue than many of the grander stores. Big, expensive hotels, like the Savoy, for example, or the Ritz, offer excellent opportunities, if you know your way around. After years of arranging private functions in West End hotels, I know where all the smaller function rooms are. It's easy enough to see whether or not they are in use, since this fact is always displayed publicly, usually in the reception area. The older hotels are the best, because of their old-fashioned buildings. Places like the London Hilton, in Park Lane, are useless, due to their contemporary design.

The Serpentine, in Hyde Park, is an excellent place, again in the summer, provided that you enjoy underwater sex. The girl has to wear a bikini, enabling her to stand in the water up to her waist, and pull her bikini bottom down. The man, of course, simply pulls down his trunks, and *voilà*, you're in business. (It always reminds me of Fatty Arbuckle, the old Hollywood silent-movie actor, who ruined his career by allegedly raping a teenage girl with a champagne bottle. As an alcoholic, he was vehemently against drinking water. 'Fish fuck in it,' was his loudly proclaimed objection to its assimilation.) Come summertime, I now feel a common bond with the Serpentine's fishy inhabitants.

I've heard tales about sex on aeroplanes. Who hasn't? The Mile High Club, and all that. But despite a considerable amount of flying, both within the UK and overseas, with and without partners on the flights, I have never made out on a plane. I've been masturbated to a climax, beneath the cover of a blanket, and have returned the compliment. I have given blow jobs, on more than one occasion, in similar circumstances. But I have never enjoyed cunnilingus or full sex on an aeroplane, ever. Sadly.

But my favourite venue of all is almost any box at the Royal Albert Hall. During a concert, of course. One can indulge in sex of most kinds in most theatre boxes. From mutual masturbation whilst apparently sitting up, paying attention to whatever is going on upon the stage, to abandoning the performance and giving one of one's own on the floor of the box. I have done both, and everything in between. I have knelt between the open knees of my lover as he sits up at the front of the box and given him a fine blow job. I have then changed places with him and been handsomely sucked off as I sit there, my long, evening skirt bunched around my waist, my knickers around my ankles, and my lover's tongue up my pussy. Delightful! One does need to be very careful about not making the kind of noises that one usually makes when achieving orgasm. It can be very distracting for the actors upon the stage. I know. I've moaned out loud whilst being sucked off at the theatre. All I could do was to try and turn it into an apologetic cough. I think I succeeded.

One needs to be careful too with one's timing when indulging sexually in theatre boxes. One has to be certain that the lights aren't going to come up for an interval, to reveal to those seated in the circle, and in boxes in higher tiers, oneself with one's legs spread wide, one's skirts about one's waist, and one's lover shafting away enthusiastically. I did that once, to my intense embarrassment. But I *did* get a round of applause from those able to see what was going on!

P. V. Battersea, London.

Are you offering shares?

NOTHING BARRED

Bars are probably more popular today than at any time in our history. They are even more popular now – and there are more of them now – than in the so-called Swinging Sixties. Since I'm a professional barman, that's got to be good for me. I wonder if I've ever served you? If I have, all you would remember is that you got your drink – or drinks – quickly, efficiently, and with polite pleasure. I love my job. But one thing you probably don't know about barmen is that, by and large, we get more pussy than our male customers. Does that surprise you? It happens to be true. How? It's simple, really. When you work behind a bar, you can't get away from it. So you're at the beck and call of anyone who cares to pull up a barstool and engage you in conversation. Male or female. And you would be amazed to know how many pretty girls are stood up in any bar on a given evening.

When they first come in, they won't even talk to you. They order a drink, and keep themselves to themselves. When they start looking at their watches, you know that their partner is late. When they start checking the time with you, you know that they're *very* late. And many of them stick it out to the bitter end. They can't actually believe that they've been stood up. So, by the time the bar closes, the chances are that they've absorbed far more booze than is their normal custom. They're angry. And they're maybe a little drunk. And they're feeling a combination of disappointed and randy. Over the course of the evening, the barman – provided that he's polite and sympathetic – becomes more and more attractive to them.

If not physically, at least emotionally, in terms of being pleasant. A friend in need. And then, at the end of the evening, if handled carefully, these girls are anybody's.

I'm the head barman in a bar just off Curzon Street, in the West End of London. Being head barman gives me priority over any of the other bar staff with any spare crumpet that may be around. It's an expensive bar, and the male customers are mostly well-to-do businessmen, with a sprinkling of show-business people. Actors and actresses. TV people. Publishers. That sort of thing. And the young, single girls who meet their dates there are mostly what we used to call good-time girls. They're not on the game. Not really. But they like money, and luxury, and being taken to expensive restaurants, and then on to a casino, maybe. Or to a fashionable nightclub or discotheque. After which, they're usually more than ready to drop their panties.

One or two of them are probably actual mistresses, and I exclude them from this conversation. They are, at the very least, having their rent paid, and are almost certainly given a living allowance. If they're stood up, they know that it's part of the arrangement. Perhaps their boyfriend's wife arrived unexpectedly at the office, just as he was about to leave to meet his mistress. They aren't going to fuck any barman, anywhere. It would be more than their job's worth. But the rest of them, by the time they've downed half a dozen champagne cocktails, or gin-and-tonics, they're probably raring to go. You have to approach them carefully. 'I'm afraid we're going to close in ten minutes, miss. May I order you a taxi?' One last look at their watch, and a cross little voice, covered up quickly by a painfully forced smile, says, 'Yes, please.' You wait until the bar is actually closed and then, 'Where shall I ask the taxi to take you, miss?' They usually say somewhere or other in the West End or nearby. Living close to the action is vital with these girls. Wherever it is, (provided that it isn't a million miles away) you say, 'Actually, miss, I've got my car outside, and I'm passing through X on my way home. May I offer you a lift?' The thought of saving the cab fare, plus having some company on the drive home, usually appeals.

Along the way to Bayswater, or Maida Vale, or the Edgware Road, or wherever, the chances are that they'll lean against you, and put their head on your shoulder, and tell you how unhappy they are. You're full of sympathy, of course. When you get to the block of flats (it's always a block of flats: it's the anonymity that appeals) you say, 'Hang on a minute, miss. I'll just see you to your door. It's much too late for you to be out on the streets by yourself at this time of night.'

You say this even if all she's got to do is cross the pavement from the car. They always accept. Who wouldn't? And you make certain that you accompany them all the way up to whatever floor it is that their flat is on and stand there while they unlock the front door. After which, they will always turn round to give you a thank-you kiss. This is where you take the only chance that you take all evening. You grab them and kiss them back. Hard. What the hell. You've got nothing to lose. They're never going to tell their boyfriend, your customer, back at the bar. It's almost guaranteed, I tell you. And the moment they start kissing you back, you slide them inside the door, close it behind you, and slip your fingers up their skirts and into their panties. Some of them have strange ideas about sexual loyalty. 'I've never been unfaithful to X,' they say. 'I love him. So you can't fuck me. But you can suck my pussy while I suck you off/give you a wank.' None of which I ever refuse. Would you?

Last night's was called Caroline. I've seen her in the bar a good few times, and she's always been nice to me. She seems to be in there usually with different men each time, rather than with the same one all the while. Last night was the first time that I've known her to be stood up. I've always fancied her, so I kept refilling her glass – she was drinking white-wine spritzers – without charging her. It's easy enough to do in a largely cash bar, if you know your way around. Which, of course, I do. Caroline chatted to me all evening, and so I didn't bother with the taxi spiel. I simply offered her a lift, which she accepted with alacrity. As soon as we drew away from the pavement outside the bar, she had one arm around my neck and the other one was unzipping my trousers. She put her hand inside and began to squeeze and pull my dick. She didn't actually take it out of my trousers, but she said, 'Are you going to come in for a drink, when we get there?'

Not fucking half, I thought. 'Thank you, miss,' I said, all respectful-like. I had to concentrate so as not to come in her hand as I was driving her home. It's not that often that I have a twenty-year-old girl playing with my cock as I drive along. She lived in Ennismore Gardens, just off Kensington Gore, so we were there in no time. What with Caroline's hand on my dick and the sight of her short little skirt, which had ridden up, exposing her shapely thighs encased in shiny, nylon, flesh-coloured stockings – or tights, perhaps, I couldn't see *that* far up her legs – it was just as well it wasn't too far to drive. I found a parking space and as I locked up the car she opened the front door to one of those enormous old Edwardian houses that so elegantly grace that part of London. Inside, I could see that it had been divided up into flats – one flat per floor – and there was, thank God, a lift, since it turned out that Caroline lived on the top – the fifth – floor.

Caroline began stripping off as she got out of the lift. By the time she had unlocked the door to her flat and closed it behind us, she was down to what were now apparent as self-supporting, flesh-coloured shiny nylon stockings, a tiny pair of crimson bikini panties and that was it. Everything about her said, 'Fuck me.' My erection said, 'Any time.' As she disrobed, she simply dropped each item of clothing where she stood. 'Drink, darling?' she asked. I said 'Yes, thank you. I'd love a Scotch.' 'Ice?' she asked. 'No, thanks,' I said. 'I'm so wet,' she said, in the same tone of voice that she might have said, 'I'm so tired' or 'I'm so bored'. I couldn't think of anything to say.

'Do you like to suck pussy?' she asked, as she poured a generous scotch into a crystal tumbler. 'Do I,' I said, as she handed me the glass. She went out of the room, presumably into the kitchen, and came back with a matching crystal jug of water. 'Say when,' she said, as she poured water into my glass. 'When,' I said. She poured one for herself. 'Cheers,' she said, raising her glass. I raised mine back. 'Cheers,' I said. She might have been standing there fully dressed, such was the aplomb with which she was carrying on. 'So,' she said, having taken a long pull at her glass. I hoped that it wouldn't react badly with all the white-wine spritzers she'd been drinking. 'You like to suck pussy, mmmm? But how about sucking *wet* pussy? Does that bother you? Mine's extremely wet, and getting wetter. It's telling me that it needs some of that lovely big cock I was playing with in the car on the way home shoved up it. But it needs sucking first. What do you say?' 'The wetter, the better,' I told her, sincerely. 'I love the taste of pussy. It's like nectar to me.'

'Oh, great,' she said. 'Then we can start straightaway.' She put her glass down on a nearby table, selected a large easy chair with a moderately high seat, and said to me, 'Shall I take my knickers off, or is that something you would like to do? Some men get a great rush out of taking girls' knickers off.' 'I'd love to,' I said. 'It always excites me.'

She stood there, smiling at me, as I knelt in front of her, my nose just inches away from her scarlet-silk-covered snatch. I could see her wetness staining the crotch of her knickers, and I could see the shape of her outer labia moulded in the silken material. I reached out a finger and felt her between her legs. She felt fleshy and moist, even through the material. 'Mmmm,' she said, wriggling as I touched her up. 'Don't stop. I like it.' I love girls with big, fleshy pussies. The kind that fill your mouth when you suck them. 'Hang on a second,' I said, and I stood up and almost literally tore my clothes off. She looked at my rampant cock. 'Oooh,' she said. 'Naughty. I like that too.' I knelt in front of her again, and, putting a hand on each side of the waistband of her knickers, I began to ease them down over her hips and buttocks, and then down her long thighs. I did it slowly, exposing first of all a thick expanse of soft, curly blonde pubic hair, obviously dyed to the same tint as that which crowned her head. Then, because I had been pressing my fingers into her snatch earlier on, through her knickers, I saw that the cotton-lined crotch was caught up inside her pussy, so that, although I was pulling them down, the gusset was reluctant to follow the rest of the garment. A truly sexual sight.

Reluctantly, I pulled a little harder, and the gusset slid out of her wet quim with a tiny sucking noise. I then slid her panties all the way down her long legs and held them as she stepped out of them. I caught a glimpse of elongated wet pussy lips, their interior aspect shining pinkly, and then she stepped back and sat down on the armchair that she had chosen. She spread her legs and lay back. 'It's all yours, baby,' she said. She put her fingers down and opened up her pussy, pulling her long outer lips apart. 'Feel free,' she said, and laughed. 'And kiss free, lick free, and suck free. And then we'll fuck free.'

It was only then that I realized that Caroline was just the littlest bit drunk. I hoped that she wouldn't have any regrets in the morning, but this wasn't my night for playing Goody Two-Shoes, putting her to bed and tucking her up carefully without taking advantage of her. I began to take advantage of her immediately. She smelled and tasted divine. She was patently no stranger to cunnilingus, and she obviously enjoyed it, from the writhing about and moaning and groaning noises that she was making. She began to orgasm almost immediately, and I don't believe that she stopped all the time that I was tonguing and sucking her. We both had a ball, for sucking pussy is seriously one of my favourite things. She was noisy with it too, shouting out from time to time things like 'Oh, my God, I'm coming again', and 'Oh, yes, baby. Oh, yes. I'm coming now. Oh, God', and then, finally, 'Oh, Jesus, fuck me, fuck me, fuck me'.

Jesus Himself not being to hand, I decided to stand in for Him. I rose, pulled Caroline up out of her chair, picked her up in my arms and carried her out of the lounge, looking for the bedroom. It wasn't far. The first door on the right, down the passageway. The only thing I noticed about the room as I entered was the king-size bed against the opposite wall as I went in. I laid her down on it. She opened her legs immediately and began playing with her pussy.

I always think that's one of the more stimulating sights, and I stood there for a little while, just enjoying watching her playing with herself. Caroline was a beautiful girl. She had full, firm young breasts, with small, dark pink nipples which right now were standing out, fully erect. Her stomach was flat, her hips narrow, her pudenda surprisingly generous, bearing in mind how slim she was everywhere else. I couldn't see her buttocks, since she was lying on them, but I had noticed, whilst she was walking about in the sitting room, that they were firm, taut and well-shaped. I wondered, for a moment, if she liked being fucked in the arse. She was clad only in her shiny nylon stockings . . .

I remembered why I was there. Because Caroline wanted to be fucked. Her fingers were still busy as I knelt between her legs. I watched her diligent digits for a few moments, whilst I could still keep my hands off her. She had her forefinger deep down inside herself, massaging her clitoris. Her eyes were closed and her mouth was open. Saliva was seeping from the corners of her mouth, in small trickles. She was breathing heavily, and she looked the epitome of fuckable female pleasure.

I took my cock in my right hand, used my left hand to pull her fingers away from her pussy, and thrust myself into her. 'Oh, my God,' Caroline said, opening her eyes in what looked like disbelief. 'That's what I've been waiting for. Cock. Seriously hard, rigid, beautiful, lovely cock. Hot cock.' She began to move her hips, slowly at first. She closed her eyes again. She sucked me into her vagina, and then she began to do wondrous things to me with her vaginal muscles. You've heard of pumping iron? This lady was pumping another kind of iron. My cock. I nearly died. From pleasure.

I began to try and return some of what she was doing for me. I thrust and withdrew. Thrust and withdrew. My cock really was hard, thanks to her, and it swelled even more within her tight, moist cunt, filling it completely. I grew inside her, distending her vagina, filling it, making it contract around my shaft, until, very quickly, she began to orgasm, her vagina contractions bringing on my ejaculation. And then we were both shouting, and gripping each other, and coming into each other, with loud, animal-like noises. 'Oh, yes,' she said. 'Oh, Jesus, yes. You're fucking me. You've got your huge cock up my cunt. You're fucking me. And I'm going to come. Now. Now. I'm going to come. Oh, JESUS. I'M COMING. NOW. YES. NOW. OH, GOD. YES. NOW. OH, FUCK. OH, JESUS. GOD, HELP ME. OH, YES. YES. YEEEEEEESSS.' After that we went on all night. She couldn't get enough, and I was sufficiently excited and more than happy to try and fulfil her needs. Happily, there were no regrets in the morning. Caroline is now on my regular fuck list. Maybe that will make some of you think before you jilt another young lady in a bar? But please don't change your habits.

P. W. Camden Town, London.

No holds barred, eh? Good luck.

TIGHT FIT

At the age of twenty-eight, I have – for some few years now – been secretly pleased that I'm the proud possessor of a large cock. I've never actually measured it, but all the girls whom I fuck tell me that it's the largest that they have ever had the pleasure of, if you follow me. They can't all be telling fibs. But recently, I have discovered that a large cock isn't always a good thing. You see, I've recently become a devotee of anal sex. And the one thing that most girls don't like up their tight little arseholes is a large cock. A lot of girls don't like *any* size of cock up their arse. But even those who *do* welcome a rear entry tend to be disapproving of a *very* large cock up there.

For me, the first time I was invited to ram my penis up a young lady's rectal passage I knew that this, sexually, was for me. I was in seventh heaven. But the young lady concerned spent most of the time that I was anally fucking her screaming, and she has never allowed me to repeat the event. So you can imagine my intense pleasure when, after work one day, I picked up a young Welsh girl in a bar near my office. She was what anyone would normally call petite. She was about five foot three or four, and with a small – but nicely shaped body. We got on well from my first approach and she happily accepted my invitation, at the end of the evening, to accompany me back to my place. All went as expected, but the interesting thing was that she began to show me some things about anal sex that were quite new to me. As is my wont, I began with a loving, caring, and quite intense session of pussy sucking. I love oral sex, and I find that, if one has brought about enough orgasms in a woman earlier on, then she is much more likely, later in the evening, to agree to anal sex. That's my experience, anyway.

This turned out to be the case on this particular evening, and Annabel (as was her name) was no exception to the general rule. When I gently suggested a little rear-entry sex, she was not only agreeable, she was actually ready, willing, and able. She had a gorgeously tiny, puckered, hairy little arsehole, and as I entered it, it seemed – to me – to be unusually pliable. As I looked at it, before I had even touched it, never mind attempted to enter it, she began to dilate it and then contract it. As I continued to watch, she went on with these exercises: each time she dilated it, her entry hole expanded and got larger, until she said, looking over her shoulder, 'OK, honey. It's ready for you now. It's all yours. Fuck me up my arsehole.'

As I slid into her, with the ease and pleasure of entering a well-lubricated cunt (none of the screaming and angst of my previous anal shafting experience) she began to open and close her sphincter muscle around my rampant cock until – it seemed like only seconds later but actually it was much longer than that – I shot my load up her beautifully tight little anus. We continued to fuck all that night, alternating between her cunt and her arsehole. At one stage, I was slipping in and out of the one, and then in and out of the other, switching backwards and forwards, until finally I spurted my come up her bottom. Her ability to open and close her anal sphincter was the most exciting thing, sexually, to happen to me in my entire lifetime.

S. P. A. Inverness, Scotland.

Sounds like you got to the bottom of the problem.

SHADOWS BETWEEN HER LEGS

I've always wanted to be a bondage girl. You know the kind of thing? Like the photo sets you see in girlie magazines sometimes. Tall girl (that's me) with long legs in black silk stockings. Held up by a black silk suspender belt. Very sexy. Patent leather 'fuck me' high-heeled pumps. Black knickers. Very *small* black knickers. And a studded leather collar around my neck. In the early pictures, my hands are bound behind my back, and there are shackles on my ankles, connected by a short length of chain. There are close-ups of my naked breasts. Close-ups of me peeling my knickers down, showing off my pubic hair. And in the final picture, on that page, I'm dropping my crumpled knickers on the floor by my feet. No cunt shots yet. Only pubes. Over the page, you get a terrific close-up of my arse. It's a lovely arse, if I say so myself. The kind where you want to pull my bum cheeks apart and ram your stiff cock up my darling anus. And then there's a tit shot, showing my erect nipples. Dead sexy. Next come close-ups of the crotch of my knickers, drawn tightly into my pussy, so that you can see the shape of my pussy lips beneath the silk. Then the camera pulls back and you see my crotch from further away, framed by the tops of my black silk stockings at the bottom of the picture, by my black suspender belt at the top, and by the long, thin, black suspenders running down my thighs at each side. Centrally, the photograph features (yes, you've got it!) my knicker-clad crotch.

In the next shot, I'm peeling the top of my tiny knickers down, revealing my pubic hair, and the final picture on that page is taken from my crotch looking up, with my breasts jutting out above, capped by my erect nipples, and my face smiling down from over the top of my breasts. There is no real continuity to these shots. For example, in twenty-four photographs spread over six pages there are pictures of me naked but for my stockings and suspender belt on the first page and pictures of me wearing my knickers on the final page. The only real interrelationship between the shots is the fact that each one is carefully chosen to raise your lust factor to the maximum. To make you want to reach out and touch me. Feel me. Lick me. Sniff me. Fuck me. Beat me, maybe. Subject me forcefully to your most degrading sexual needs. (I wish you were here with me right now.)

Over the page, I'm squatting on the floor on one knee, my legs apart, my other foot beneath my buttock. You can *almost* see my snatch, but not quite, because my pubic hair is long and thick. It needs parting to find that wet, pink gash that you want so badly. In the next shot – it's the first full-length shot of me since the opening picture – I'm shown standing, facing the camera. I'm naked from the waist up. My pretty breasts are thrust forward, and my hands are still bound behind my back, and the shackles and chain between my ankles are prominent in the photograph. I've got my knickers on again. The new thing in this shot is that there is a rope, running from somewhere unseen behind my back – presumably my wrists – down to the chain that is around my ankles. The effect of this rather short rope is that I am forced into a rather bent-over position.

It's all change in the next shot. This is of me from the waist up, and this time my wrists are bound up beside my face, by tight cords, tying me to some kind of crossbar behind me. The studded leather collar around my neck is very much in evidence in this picture, as is a peacock feather, the end of which is brushing against one of my nipples. My eyes are closed, as if in ecstasy. The adjoining picture is a close-up of the same feather. This time it is teasing my pussy.

And then, suddenly, everything comes together. The following shot is a whole-page picture of me sitting on the floor, my arms raised and bound behind my neck, my legs spread. My knicker-crotch has been pulled to one side, fully exposing my naked cunt for the first time. Standing behind me is a beautiful dominatrice, dressed much as I am but without the bondage gear. She is leaning over me, tickling my exposed cunt with the peacock's feather. I'm not certain, from the expression on my face, whether I'm showing pain or pleasure. Perhaps both. There are two smaller prints inset over the main photograph, one of which shows my hands handcuffed rather than bound with ropes, and a second one, which is a close-up of the dominatrice woman standing over my head, which is thrown back. I have my rigid tongue poking out of my mouth, just millimetres away from the woman's knicker-covered pussy. I am obviously about to lick her snatch through her panties. In the next shot, I am kneeling down, my buttocks to the camera and with my face buried between the dominatrice's legs. You can't actually see what I am doing, but I don't think I need to spell it out. You can see the top of my head, over my naked buttocks.

The rest of the shot is cropped tightly around my bottom, the centre of which features my extremely hairy anal cleft and my nakedly exposed anus. My tightly clenched dark-skinned anus is puckered, and shining wetly in the studio lighting. If the camera were a man, it would bugger me forthwith. In the final picture, I have a dog-lead attached to the studded collar around my neck, and I am being led off camera by the dominatrice, who is now fully dressed in an elegant, full-length evening dress. In my fantasy, she leads me off to a luxurious bedroom, next door to the studio, where she assists a handsome young dark-haired stranger to rape me in each orifice, a number of times over. She guides his huge weapon into me, masturbating him back to full erection when he has jetted his hot sperm up one or other of my entrances. She greases my rectum prior to his raping me anally and coats his huge tool for him slowly, with the same lubricant.

She makes up my face carefully, paying much attention to the colour and thickness of the lipstick that she uses on me, before he fucks my mouth, and she holds my head for him as he ejaculates his flood of semen down my throat. When it is finally all over, she performs cunnilingus upon me until I orgasm, and then she forces me to do it to her. I enjoy her sucking my pussy, but initially I resist doing the same to her and she whips me. It is extremely painful. She thrashes me and she goes on whipping me long after I have screamed out that yes, yes, I'll suck her pussy, just stop, please stop hurting me. She seems to enjoy causing me pain. When I finally get to suck her, I actually enjoy it. She tastes delicious. It's difficult to describe, but she tastes so *feminine*. And she smells so nice. A gentle fragrance, reminding me of some exotic tropical fruit.

When I make her come, I come myself, partly from sexual excitement at what I've done to her, partly because I want her to love me as much as I now love her. I wish I could turn these fantasies into reality. Are there any attractive young dominatrices out there who would take a willing, submissive female bondage freak and teach her what S&M is all about? But one thing is vital in any such arrangement: I have to get fucked at the end of it all. Up where, I don't mind. Preferably everywhere. Will somebody help me, please?

K. R. Belgravia, London.

Any offers? Sounds like a willing servant.

AMERICAN PIE

I'm from Miami. I was born and bred there. Florida may be known as the Sunshine State, but we don't really have that good a reputation any more, sadly. The state has been taken over by immigrants in recent years, that's for sure. But it still isn't a bad place to live, if you know your way around. The weather's mostly good. Why else do all you New Yorkers come down here in December/January? Not to mention retiring down here. But it's still a great place to pick up women. Let me tell you about it.

I was in one of the resort bars the other evening, and this archetypal hippy-type girl comes in. I mean, maybe she was a few years out of place, but she looked pretty good to me. I was sitting at a table when she came in and sat down at the bar. I was instantly attracted to her. I think it was her smile. And so I went and asked her if she minded if I sat next to her. 'No, honey,' she said. 'Why should I? Tell me your name.' I told her it was Vince, and she told me hers was Jessie. Lovely old-fashioned name, isn't it? Biblical, almost. At first she told me that she was a dancer. It turned out, in fact, that she was a stripper, on her day off. She had a small apartment near by, and she felt like a little company, she said, So here she was. My good fortune, I told her. She laughed.

To cut a long story short, we ended up back at her place. She got out this sensational grass and we both got pretty ripped. Then, after a while, she asked me if I would like her to strip for me, and of course I said yes. Please. So she disappeared into the bedroom and came back about ten minutes later, wearing this amazing tasselled silver-and-white bikini. It put a whole different aspect on her body, which had looked pretty good to me before. Now it looked sensational. Then she put on a record. You know the kind of thing. The sort of music that strippers strip to. And she did a strip for me. My own show. Fantastic. She did some real dirty bits, too. Like she came up to me, just after she'd taken her panties off, stood right in front of me, stuck her fingers up her pussy, waggled them around – and then stuck her fingers in my mouth. To my intense pleasure, I have to tell you. And then she did that bit that all strippers do, where they turn their backs on you, and bend down, and stick their ass up in the air in your direction, and wriggle it about. Only when Jessie did it, she did it about two feet in front of me, allowing me to peer up (or maybe that should be down) the crack in her ass, including her asshole. I'll swear it winked at me. I sat there with the biggest hard-on I think I've ever had. I had to control myself, not to start jerking off while I was watching her. I only just managed not to.

She was a big girl. Bit tits. Big ass. Big pussy. All in proportion, but *big*. Lovely. When she finished, she was sitting on the floor, her legs spread wide, holding her ankles up above her head. Her hairy beaver was split, and I could see the pink of her cunt. It looked very wet. She held that pose for a few moments, and then she relaxed. 'Well, that's the audition, honey,' she said. 'Do I get the position?' I told her that she could have any position she wanted with me, and which one would she like to start with?

'On my back, baby,' she said. 'I love an old-fashioned fuck. I so rarely get one these days. Everybody wants you to be an acrobat, or a contortionist.' She stood up, stark naked as she was, and came over to where I was sitting on a sofa. She leaned forward and unzipped my fly. She then pulled out my cock. 'Mmmm,' she said. 'I think it's got something on its mind.' It was standing up, fully erect, doing me proud.

'Perhaps this will help it,' she said. She knelt on the floor in front of me and took me into her mouth. She gave sensational head. The best I've ever had. When I came, she kept me in her mouth and swallowed everything I could shoot into her. When I'd finished, she took me out of her mouth and said, 'I always like to start off like that because, first of all, I love to suck cock. And secondly, it guarantees me a better fuck. No one's in any kind of a hurry.' There was no way I could argue with that.

We went into the bedroom, got onto the bed, and I began to suck her vulva. It was really big and fleshy. She started moaning and groaning and came very quickly, after which I simply pushed her down onto her back and fucked her as hard as I knew how. She shouted out loud as she came again, and she kept on coming, more and more strongly, until eventually I came with her and shot my jism into her once more. But this time up her pussy, rather than down her throat. 'Oh, baby,' she said, as I shot my load up her. 'I can feel your hot spunk shooting up me. Oh, God, that's good.' And so on. We spent the night fucking and sucking, interspersed with smoking grass, and by the morning, we were both fucked out. Finished. I mean, *out* of it.

By that time I had fucked her, sucked her, had anal sex with her, and masturbated her. She had fucked me, fellated me, and masturbated me. We'd both had a great time. I left at midday the next day. We exchanged telephone numbers, and since then I've been round to her three times, and she's been to my place twice, in about three weeks. As far as I'm concerned, Florida is the place to be. And Jessie is the lady to be with. Who needs New York?

R. H. L. Fort Lauderdale, Florida.

Who indeed? It sounds as if you've asset-stripped parts of Florida pretty thoroughly. But it's a big state. Enjoy.

HOT TO TROT

I'm single, female, and twenty-three. I love to look at the girl sets in your raunchy magazine, and I get really hot looking at some of them. Since I have no man about the house at the moment, I'm left to handle my own sex these days, if you follow me. I dreamed last night that I was one of the girls in your magazine, and I don't ever remember being so sexually excited. Would you like to hear about it? You would? Good. At the beginning of my dream, I was stopped in the street here in Chichester by an attractive young man, who introduced himself as a photographer (although he didn't, at that stage, say what *kind* of photographer). He asked me if I had ever considered being a model, and, quite frankly, I thought it was all simply down to an attempted pick-up. However, he gave me his card, with your editorial number on it, and – to my surprise – he checked out. I telephoned him back after a few days, and he invited me round to his studio for a glass of wine and a chat. With no commitment on either side. When I got there, I was pleasantly surprised at both the amount of equipment in his studio and the sophistication of some of it, when he explained to me what one or two of the items did. (All this before I'd even *thought* about *his* equipment!) After a pleasant conversation I came away, having agreed to go back a couple of days later to do some test shots. It had been agreed that we would both make up our minds about progressing further – or not – when we saw the results of this photographic shoot. I dreamed that I arrived feeling good on the morning of the day arranged for the shoot. I'd had my hair cut and set, and had a massage, which had made me feel relaxed. At home, first thing, before I left, I'd wallowed in a long, luxurious bath, and after that I had shaved my pubic hair, as I normally do. (This is true in real life, as well as in my dream. I find that men like girls with shaven pudenda. It excites them sexually, although I'm not certain exactly why).

Tony (that was the photographer's name) seemed pleased to see me, and gave me coffee and biscuits when I had taken off my coat. He pointed to a screen over at the far end of the studio. 'Will you go and undress, please, sweetheart?' he said. 'We need to allow the elastic marks on your thighs and bottom to wear off before we can take any photographs. So if you'll strip off now . . . You'll find a robe hanging up behind the screen to put on.' I'd never thought about elastic marks on my flesh, but he was right, of course. I don't wear a bra, so marks on my breasts weren't a problem.

When I got back to where Tony was, he was looking at a selection of underwear. A lot of it was very exotic. Tart's knickers, I'd call them. But he held up a pair of plain grey cotton knickers for me to look at. Made by Benetton, as I remember. They had just a hint of cotton lace around the edges. 'Do you like these, sweetie?' he asked me. 'I think the grey will go nicely with your tan, and this ribbed cotton clings well. Fits around all the interesting places.' He grinned at me, and I laughed with him, thinking about the only place where knickers can cling. 'Yes, they're neat,' I said. 'I like them. I like simple underwear.' Tony next produced a pair of white stockings. 'I think just the knicks and the stockings,' he said. 'That's all we need. Slip the robe off for a moment, sweetie, and let's see if there's anything we need to cover up.' I took off the robe, and Tony walked around me, examining me closely. 'Mmmm,' he said. 'Pretty tits.' 'Thank you, kind sir,' I said, and bobbed a pretend curtsey. 'Oh, don't mind me,' he said. 'I don't mean to be rude. It's just how I react.

It's my job, you see.' He smiled at me again. 'No,' he said, finally. 'Not a blemish in sight.' Just then the doorbell rang, and Tony went and let in a young woman who smiled at me when she saw me. 'This is Angie,' said Tony. We shook hands. 'Angie will do your hair and make-up,' Tony told me. 'After which we should be ready to go.' Angie pointed to a chair in front of a mirror over in a corner of the studio. 'Shall we go over there?' she suggested.

I went and sat myself down, and Angie began to do my make-up. She did my face first, and then surprised me by asking me to take off my robe. It makes sense, of course, if you think about it, that if you're taking pictures of a nude body, then the body needs making-up too. She powdered me thoroughly, all over, and then surprised me again by anointing my nipples and areolae with a brownish-pink lip colour. I was faintly embarrassed to see my nipples stiffen up under her attentions, but neither of us said anything. I guess she was accustomed to it.

Then she did my hair, in a fairly loose, casual style, and just before she finished she picked up my hand and looked at my nails. I stood up while she did that, and she looked at me and smiled. 'They're fine,' she said. 'Is this your first nude modelling session?' I had to admit that it was. 'Good luck, then,' she said. 'I'll be off now. That should last you through the session all right.' 'Thanks,' I said. 'Good to meet you.' Angie called over to Tony: 'She's all yours now, Tony. I'm off. See you Tuesday.' 'Thank you, darling,' he called back. 'See you then.' He looked over at me. 'OK, sweetie,' he said, 'let's go.' I walked over to him. He had constructed a fairly simple set, consisting of a rather pretty Victorian *chaise longue* covered in a pale-yellow, patterned, heavy silk material, standing in front of a plain, dark red velvet wall hanging.

'We'll do the nude shots first, now that your knicker lines have disappeared,' he said. 'And then we'll do the knicker-

and-stocking shots after that. OK?' 'Fine,' I said. 'Just tell me what you want me to do.' 'Sure,' he said. 'First of all, just sit on the *chaise longue* and think pretty thoughts.' I did as he asked and he moved about me, using a hand-held Pentax camera. After a while he said, 'Now, sweetie, if you'll just move around a bit. You know, change your position. Just keep moving. I'll tell you when to hold it.' Again I did as I was asked, and as the time passed, I began to relax, and then, eventually, to actually enjoy it.

Tony kept saying things like 'That's good, sweetie', 'Hold it right there,' 'Just move your head a tiny bit to the right', 'Smile now, darling', 'Open your legs a bit more', 'Can you take a deep breath, and hold it?' and so on. From time to time he would rearrange me completely, like having me kneel over the *chaise longue* rather than sit on it, and when that happened, I was conscious that he was taking close-ups of my anus. 'Just put your hands behind you, and hold onto your buttocks,' he said, at one stage. And then, 'Now pull your cheeks apart. Yes, that's it. Lovely. Oh, yes. Terrific.' I was embarrassed because, although I shave my pubes, I've got a very hairy anal area. It's simply that I can't get at it myself. Not with a razor, anyway. And because my pussy is so smooth, it makes my entire anal area look even more coarsely hirsute. But Tony didn't say anything, so I guess that was OK with him.

And speaking of being embarrassed, I spent most of the shoot being embarrassed, one way or another. For example, after Tony had told me to take a deep breath, and hold it, he said, 'Hang on there a second, will you?' and went away into the kitchen, off the far end of the studio. When he came back, he had some ice cubes on a saucer. 'Just rub your nipples with these, darling,' he said. 'The ice will make them nice and erect.'

I remembered how erect they had been when Angie had

been putting lip colour on them, and I had to admit that they certainly weren't erect now. I felt a real failure. But the ice cubes did the trick. Instantly. And from then on, Tony just handed me the saucer of ice cubes whenever he wanted my nipples to stand out. But my main embarrassment was that when Tony started doing close-ups of my pussy, he used a different camera from the Pentax. He used a rather bigger camera, on a tripod. I could see the name Hasselblad across the top of it. It wasn't the camera that embarrassed me, it was the fact that the more he focused on my pussy, the wetter I could feel myself getting. Eventually I could feel my sexual lubrication beginning to trickle down my thighs and, blushing madly, I said to Tony, 'Can you hang on a second, while I just go to the bathroom and wipe myself? I don't know why, but I'm getting rather wet.' 'Wipe yourself, darling?' he said. 'Don't be silly. It's gorgeous. The punters'll love it. They'll all be wanking themselves silly at the sight of it. Get as wet as you like. It's good for business.' So I stayed where I was. Eventually, Tony decided that he had run the gamut of nude shots, and he asked me to put on the gray cotton knickers and the white cotton stockings with the lacy tops.

This time, I *did* go off and mop myself up. I wasn't just wet. I was horny. Seriously horny. Well, think about it. I'd been lying around stark naked in front of an attractive young man who had spent the entire time we'd been together focusing his cameras on my tits, my arse and my cunt. Now what would *you* think about, whilst you were doing that? That's right. And so did I. When I'd dried myself off and put on the knickers and stockings – which were of the self-supporting kind – I made my way back to the set and we started off again.

We repeated pretty much what we had been doing up until now, with the difference that, this time, in each picture I was either putting on or taking off the knickers and stockings.

There were what I now began to realize were the inevitable open-leg shots, with Tony homing in on my crotch, now covered with grey ribbed cotton. As he had quite correctly put it at the start of the day, the ribbed cotton clung beautifully. To my pussy. I couldn't see myself down there, of course, but putting my fingers down to feel the material stretched so tautly across my pussy, I could feel the lips of my outer labia clearly outlined in the thin fabric. And to continue my almost non-stop embarrassment, I could also feel how wet the material had become. 'Oh, great,' said Tony, cutting across my reverie. Startled, I pulled my hand away from my crotch. 'Oh, no,' said Tony. 'That's what I was appreciating. Your hand on your twat. Put it back. Please.' *Twat*, I thought. *How delicate. How feminine. How intensely romantic*. But I did as I was told, and put my fingers back down there. 'Oh, yes,' said Tony. 'Put your forefinger down, as if you were playing with yourself.'

I wasn't at all sure that I wanted to have pictures of me taken looking as if I was playing with myself, but who was I to argue? And as far as I knew, I had the right of veto if I didn't like what I saw when the pictures were developed. I put my forefinger down, found my outer lips, and pressed my finger firmly between them so that the outline of what I was doing would show clearly through the ribbed cotton. 'Oh, yes,' said Tony. 'I like it. Keep still. Don't move. Oh, yes.' As he was speaking, he was moving around me, once more with the hand-held camera. He was using the motor, and the camera was going *click, buzz, click, buzz, click, buzz* as he worked. At one stage he got me into quite a complicated position. I was sitting down on the *chaise longue*, with stockings on but no knickers. My legs were together and I had my arms around my knees as if I was hugging them, and my thighs were raised off the seat.

If you can imagine that position, then you will instantly

see that my naked pussy was completely exposed and, as you will have realized before I spell it out to you, that was where Tony's camera was duly focused. After a while, I began to look at his crotch, to see if any of my more raunchy poses – the ones where he was shooting close-ups of my pussy, or my anus – were having any effect at all upon his cock. But no. There wasn't – as far as I could see – the slightest suggestion of an erection.

I began to worry about whether or not I was going to get laid before I went home. It was becoming a matter of some urgency. I didn't fancy going home and getting out my bloody vibrator yet again. Here I was with a real live male only inches away. He could see absolutely everything that was on offer. Didn't he find me attractive? He must have done, or he wouldn't have asked me to model for him in the first place. He didn't *look* gay. But you never can tell. But even that was all right. If he wanted to bugger me, I was more than happy to offer him my bottom. I looked at him, trying hard to read what was going on in his mind.

Right at that moment, he stood back from both me and his cameras. 'I guess that's about it, baby,' he said. 'Thank you. I reckon we've got some pretty good stuff here. I find it difficult to believe that you've never been photographed before. You're a natural. An absolute natural. I think you'll love these shots when you see them. Do you want to come around about the same time tomorrow? They should be back from the lab overnight. I would expect to see them delivered here by about ten o'clock tomorrow morning.' At least it would appear that I had *something* going for me. 'Thank you,' I said. 'And yes, I'd love to come and look at the pictures. Thank you again. I'll be here.' I got up and stood beside him. 'Is that it?' I asked him. He looked at me. 'Yes, darling,' he said. 'Unless you'd like some tea or coffee. Or a drink. What do you feel like?' 'I feel like a fuck,' I told him. 'What do *you* feel like?' He looked somewhat surprised. 'Jesus,' he said. 'Thank God for that. Normally, I'd have been trying my luck hours ago. I haven't seen a body like yours in years. Literally. Years. But, this being your first photographic session, I didn't want to risk putting you off for life. Frankly, I can't think of anything I'd enjoy more.' I reached out a hand and carefully unzipped his fly, and then I reached inside and pulled out his dick. It swelled in my hand as I stood there. It was big, and getting bigger. I knelt down in front of him, and took it into my mouth.

As I sucked him, he put out his hands, one on each side of my head, and held it while he started to fuck my mouth. I began to wank him as well as suck him, and seconds later he came in my mouth, a great *swoosh* of creamy, warm come. 'Mmmm,' I said, it being about all I could manage, what with my mouth being full of cock and come. I swallowed rapidly. He kept coming for a little while, and I kept sucking, until everything was finished. Then I took his flaccid cock out of my mouth and stood up. 'How would you like to suck my wet pussy now?' I asked him. 'One good turn deserves another. And which way is the bedroom?'

'Love to,' he said. 'And through the kitchen, and up the spiral staircase.' I walked through the kitchen and went first up the iron staircase, enjoying the feel of the finger he was sticking up my arse as we climbed the stairs. I looked down at him over my shoulder. 'That's *naughty*,' I told him. 'Isn't it?' he said. 'But if you were me, this is exactly what you would be doing in my position.' The spiral staircase led directly into the huge bedroom. It was almost the size of the studio beneath. He had the largest bed I think I've ever seen. We had ended the photographic session with me wearing the grey cotton panties and the white stockings. I now divested myself of the panties. Suddenly they seemed superfluous. Their white cotton gusset was indeed very wet. I dropped them on the floor. But I kept the stockings on. They made a nice frame for my pussy. I lay back on the huge bed and opened my legs. 'At your service, kind sir,' I said.

Tony had by this time taken off the trousers, sweatshirt and underpants that he was wearing, kicked off his shoes, pulled off his socks, and, as I spoke, he buried his head between my legs, and began to return my oral compliment to him of earlier. He was both an enthusiast and an expert, and I came very quickly. I continued to come, almost non-stop, as he worked away at me. I didn't even stop coming for very long when he pulled away from my pussy, turned me over onto my tunny, pulled me up into a kneeling position, and started to fuck me doggy fashion. It was months since I had been properly fucked, but Tony certainly made up for the absence. By the time he had finished with me, I was all fucked out. He was almost literally unstoppable. He fucked me in every possible position. When he finally practically fell off me, after the umpteenth copulatory act, I was about to call *pax*. I put my arms around him, and we fell asleep in moments.

The photographs were, of course, perfect. They made me look terrific, and the fee that Tony paid me for my modelling was only exceeded by my excitement at eventually seeing them published in the pages of your wonderful magazine. All good things, they say, come to an end, and, sadly, so did my fantasy. I woke up! But I can dream, can't I?

G. H. L. Chichester, Hants.

Yes, of course you can. If you would like to send us some nude photographs of yourself, we'll tell you, honestly, by return, what we think the chances are of turning your dream into reality. At least as far as the photography goes. (Editor's note: Ms G. H. L. did send us some photographs. Three months later, we featured her in a six-page girl set in the magazine. Since then, she has become an internationally famous nude model. She tells us that she no longer has any complaints about her sex life).

SUBMISSIVE MISS

I have been a submissive ever since I can remember. I try and explain this to my girlfriends sometimes, but they simply don't understand. I wonder if I might describe a recent day that I spent with my husband during one weekend recently, and then enquire of your female readers whether they can see how this could bring me such sexual pleasure? I'm curious to know if others are like me.

My husband and I both work and I'd had a particularly bad week at the office, which made for a pretty short temper by the time the weekend came around. On Saturday morning I went out and did the weekend food shopping at the supermarket, and so on, and when I came back my husband was cutting the grass in our largish back garden. Shopping hadn't improved my temper any, and I guess that when I criticized the fact that he had missed a couple of places on the lawn with the mower it was probably the proverbial last straw. He stopped the mower, got off it, and attacked me, in the sense that he began tearing my clothes off. I got very excited.

This was something entirely new. He was obviously really angry with me, and at first I fought back as hard as I knew how. However, Hugh is a big man, and my resistance was useless. He very quickly had me completely naked, and to my amazement he produced a length of cord from his jacket pocket and bound my hands behind my back with it. I couldn't believe it when, as I was lying there, he kicked my ankles apart, effectively spreading my legs. Then, as he stood there, his feet keeping my legs open in that position, he undid his flies, pulled out his cock, and wanked all over me. He deliberately aimed at my cunt.

He then left me there, his spunk running down all over my body, and went into the house. When he came back, I saw that he had brought a couple of the nipple clamps that we normally keep in a bedside drawer in our bedroom. This particular pair is joined by a chain. He bent down and fixed first one, then the other, to my nipples. The difference between his usual use of these clamps and now was that this time he screwed them up so tightly that I was screaming with pain and pleading with him to loosen them off, at least a little. He ignored both my screams and my pleading. He next knelt over my face, and started to fuck my mouth. There was no question of my fellating him. He was simply fucking my mouth and throat. When he came, flooding my throat with his come, I nearly choked. He took very little notice of my problem, other than to make sure that I *didn't* actually choke. He then left me where I was.

During the whole of the rest of the day, he left me where I was. Naked, bound, lying on my back on the back lawn. Thank God that it was summer, or I could have frozen. And thank God, too, that our back garden isn't overlooked by anybody. From time to time, during the day, Hugh would come and perform some sexual act or other upon me. At different times, he fucked me, he frigged my clit with his fingers until I came, he had anal sex with me – something normally reserved as punishment for some really serious marital infringement, since I am not greatly fond of being fucked up my arse – and he fucked my mouth again. He didn't piss on me, though, for which I was grateful.

Throughout the day, he repeated all the sexual acts, whilst totally ignoring my attempts to talk to him, to reason with him, to plead with him to release me. But here is the extraordinary thing. Despite the pain and the discomfort, despite the humiliation and the degradation of what he was doing to me, every time he sexually assaulted me – for that was what he was doing: making love he wasn't – my orgasms were the greatest that I have ever experienced in my entire life. They were fantastic. Can anyone explain that to me? At the end of what became a very long day – it must have been early evening – Hugh came out and stood and looked down at me. He then told me that his actions of the day had been intentionally and deliberately to punish me for being a real bitch for the entire week. He'd had enough, he said. If I either wanted, or needed to be released, it would only be on my sincere promise never to behave like a bitch again. *Ever*. If I didn't promise, then I would stay where I was until I did.

I couldn't get my promise out quickly enough. I promised, tearfully, to be a better wife and partner. And I meant every word that I said. Hugh unbound me, and helped me up. I spent some hours in the bathroom, soaking off the despair and humiliation – and the stink – of the day. That night, we neither of us referred to the day's events. Nor at any time since. But we had the best sex since our marriage.

P. B. Tonbridge, Kent.

What can I say? It has always been a firm rule with me that whatever two (or more) people do together sexually is fine, provided that (i) everyone is in agreement about what is being done and (ii) no one is injured.

HER SUIT

I read many letters in your columns saluting the joys of shaven pussy, and to a certain extent I can understand the appeal of a well-trimmed pudenda. The sheer smoothness against one's face when performing cunnilingus, for one thing. The clarity with which the female sex organs are exposed when clean-shaven, for another. But when I get down to it (and I do, as often as possible!) for my money you can't beat a really hairy snatch. A totally untrimmed, thick, coarse-haired, black, curly snatch. Not for me the inconsequential frivolity of dyed blonde pubes. Give me a girl who lets it grow long. A real bush. A feminine bird's nest, within which nestles that lovely pink gash that we males so ardently favour with our full attention. My ideal woman wears a black wool short-skirted suit, to meet me for a drink before dinner. She will probably wear a plain white or cream silk shirt beneath her suit, and her short skirt will reveal the fact (when she sits down and her skirt rides up) that she is wearing old-fashioned black silk stockings, with (unseen, but absolutely essential) black silk knickers and a matching black silk suspender belt. If her skirt is *really* short, it will reveal, as she sits down, the beginning of that wondrous gap of naked thigh exposed between stocking top and knicker leg.

Not to be seen until later is the fact that her delightfully hirsute cuntal tresses extend from where they begin just below her navel, all the way down, through between her legs and back up through her anal cleft – surrounding her rectal opening with a particularly spectacular growth – until they fade away just beneath the small of her back. Hidden by the neat black suit, as we enjoy our meal, is the black silk underwear I have already described. Other parts of the same essential woman are the full lips, painted a deep crimson, and the dark brown, almost black nipples, areolae, and pussy lips. She will have full, fleshy, oversize outer labia, hanging down when at rest, swollen when sexually aroused. Lips that you can take between your lips as you suck at her altar of desire. She will exude her love juices copiously before, during, and after the varying acts of sex, and she will accept you into all and every orifice her body offers, with welcoming warmth. She will have no inhibitions whatsoever, and will expect you to be as completely devoid of them as is she. She will not want protected sex. She will want to trust you. Completely. Her underarms will be unshaven.

Almost the sexiest view of her shock of pubic hair will be as she drops her short skirt and steps out of it, exposing herself to you in only the briefest of black silk bikini knickers. They will be so thin as to be totally transparent and will permit you to ogle her tumescent labia, glistening wetly at you through the silk from within the centre of her pubic bush. This sight is only slightly exceeded in its carnality, its sheer, prurient sensuality, by the same view of her naked, as she pulls those tiny knickers down her legs, steps out of them, lies down and spreads her legs, waiting for you to do that which she has been wanting all evening. She will probably reach down with her long, slim fingers, with their manicured talons – painted the same crimson as her lips – and pull her vaginal lips apart for you, that you may see, feel, taste, scent her wanton sex.

Similarly, as you enfold those luscious, moist labia between your eager lips, she will take your engorged penis and suck it between her own full, lascivious, wet crimson lips. She will do things to your sex with her mouth and tongue and fingers that you never before thought possible, and as you suck and lick and kiss her hirsute cunt, your fingers will stray through her thicket, tantalizing you with the feel of its unexpected silkiness. When you have had your fill of cunnilingus and move to thrust your painfully erect pole between her legs, she will fold her arms behind her neck and allow you to lick and suck at the soft hair in her armpits, relishing the tart, exhilarating scent which emanates from there.

As your manhood pierces her sacred entrance, she will bring into play muscles that you didn't know existed, and she will grasp you and massage you, clenching your rigidity, stroking your maleness, until you succumb to her entrancing mystery, shooting your seed up into her in almost painful spurts, and she will scream and call out your name, and orgasm over and over again herself as you spend yourself in her. Here's to happy, hairy handmaidens. Long may they last.

T. O. Northallerton, North Yorkshire.

She'll obviously always be true to you, in her fashion.

STRINGING ALONG

It's always been my fantasy to be a stripper in a small strip club. Small, so that the strippers have to get out there, in amongst the paying customers. There's no stage as such. The girls do their acts in between the tables – and sometimes *on* the tables. I start off with just a G-string – black, of course, and very small – black self-supporting stockings, black gloves, and a black top hat. I dance about to really raunchy music, and my particular thing – the thing that makes me different from the other girls – is that I'll stand in front of you and let you feel inside my G-string, provided that you tuck a note down it before you start. The value of the note dictates the amount of time you get to feel my pussy (because that's what all the men do, in my fantasy). I'm rather over made-up to perform my act and I move from table to table, bumping and grinding, thrusting my pubis out in front of me, putting my own fingers down inside my G-string and very obviously playing with my pussy. It isn't long before the first punter waves a ten-pound note at me, and I go over, climb up onto his table, and kneel in front of him. I very slowly pull down the front of my G-string, exposing my hairy pussy and my wet slit to him. To cheers from his companions, and from the rest of the audience, the man puts his fingers down into the crotch of my G-string, and his fingers find my – by now – soaking wet pussy. He pushes his fingers inside me, and I thrust hard against them, enjoying the feelings that they deliver. As he touches me up, I have a huge orgasm, and I wriggle about and blow kisses at him to indicate my grateful pleasure.

David Jones

I forget about the time, and the fact that a tenner isn't supposed to get him all that much, and I just go on kneeling there on the table in front of him, letting him feel me up, until the MC, on the club's microphone, suggests that there are other customers waiting. Embarrassed, I pull the man's hand out of my G-string and, with a great show of enjoyment, he puts his fingers into his mouth and slowly sucks and licks them. I usually dream up this fantasy while I am in bed, and you won't be surprised to hear that it always ends with my frigging myself violently to orgasm as I imagine that member of the audience coming into my little room backstage after the show, unzipping his fly and taking out his huge, swollen member which he then forces me to suck off before he rapes me with it, over and over again. In my fantasy, cocks stay hard for ever.

S. L. Montreal, Canada.

Sweet dreams!

ROUGH STUFF

I'm a male who is into discipline and domination, and while I read avidly the occasional feature that you devote to those topics, in my limited experience the real thing is difficult to come by, if you'll forgive the pun. For that reason, maybe you'll allow me to indulge my favourite B&D fantasy? In it, I'm a famous Hollywood film producer, and as with all Hollywood film producers, I am constantly pestered by amazingly available, incredibly beautiful young women, all of whom are anxious to submit to my every sexual desire, in order to help them, they believe, along the road to certain movie stardom. The names, hair colours and styles vary as the girls come and go, but they all have certain specific qualities in common. They all have long legs with muscular thighs, and heavy breasts with huge, oversize areolae and long, thick, teat-like nipples. They have full, fleshy buttocks, and they have either extravagantly hairy cunts, with thick, coarse, long tangles of pubic hair, or they are completely clean-shaven, with their fleshy cunt-lips thus nakedly, blatantly displayed. There is nothing, in terms of pubic decoration, in between the two extremes.

As I pursue my business week around the various offices of Hollywood agents and those of the film studio executives, I meet hundreds of these big-bosomed aspiring young actresses in the waiting rooms, and I hand out my business cards to them without any thought of expense. When they telephone me, I ask them to come to my offices to audition where, naturally enough, I ask them to strip off. This is, of course, to see if they fulfil my private requirements, but I tell them that there is a nude scene in the movie I am casting and so I need to see them naked.

If they are close – for example, they may be perfect, bar the need to shave their pubic hair – then I will tell them that, provided they shave their pudenda, I will then audition them properly. It never fails. Then I arrange the audition at my home, a typical Hollywood mansion, up in the hills behind Hollywood, looking out over the city, with a pool, and a view of the sea in the distance. When the aspiring young actress arrives – let us call her Olivia – I tell her that the film is about a depraved movie director, and that her audition is a scene from an orgy which takes place as the grand finale of the movie. She may, I warn her, find parts of it quite shocking. She smiles at me, rather nervously, but she doesn't say anything. I take her to my punishment room, which I tell Olivia has been built as a set for the audition, and I tell her to strip.

I watch, lustfully, as she releases pendulous breasts from her straining white lace brassiere. Next she peels down her white lace panties. This particular girl has auburn hair, and a particularly thick mane of auburn growth around and in between her heavy thighs, virtually covering her pudenda. I feel my cock swelling as I look at this intensely erotic display. She next pulls down her tights, and then she is completely naked. She smiles at me, and I smile back. I then give her a pair of leather anklets, joined together by a chain, and I tell her to put them on. I help her to pull the straps tight. I next show her a leather thong, and explain that this is to bind her wrists together, behind her back. She turns away from me, and I bind her wrists for her. I find it difficult to keep my hands off her full, naked buttocks. I can see a fuzz of auburn anal hair rising out of the cleft between them. Then, when her wrists are tied to my satisfaction, I explain that I am going to attach a rope to the chain around her ankles. The rope, I tell her, is attached to a pulley in the ceiling which, when I pull on it, will haul her up, feet first, so that she is hanging head down.

Olivia looks somewhat startled, but she doesn't say anything in reply. I pull her up, and secure the end of the rope to a bracket on the wall that is there for the purpose. Olivia is now hanging upside down, with her head on a level with my groin. Yes, you've guessed. I undo my trousers, take out my now rampant cock, and say to Olivia, 'Here, suck this. And suck it good. If you don't suck it to my complete satisfaction, I will thrash your bare ass until it is raw and bleeding. Oh, and yes,' I say, grinning to myself, 'make it as realistic as you know how.' I feed my cock into Olivia's mouth. She takes me between her full lips, and starts to suck. At the same time, she puts her tongue to work. She has obviously sucked cock before. Haven't they all?

I stand there, being orally serviced rather well. Immediately in front of me, upside down, is Olivia's hairy cunt. I reach out, part her thatch with my fingers, and find her cunt lips. I spread them with my fingers, and discover – to my surprise – that she is very wet inside. I lean forward, and give her sticky gash a long, slow lick, from top to bottom (actually, from bottom to top). She tastes good. Gamey and strong-tasting, as red-heads usually do. I love it. She smells strongly too. Of sex. Of cunt (reasonably enough). I hold her by her bare buttocks, and pull her towards my mouth, and then I begin to suck her cunt. She moans. Or, at least, she moans as well as she can, with her mouth full of my cock. I think she is trying to tell me that she is enjoying what I am doing to her.

I thrust my tongue deeply into her cunt, and she moans again. I start to lick her clitoris, and she begins to move her ass, at least as best as she can in her predicament. She is doing magnificent things to my cock, and I start to feel my ejaculation building. I too begin to move my hips, and I start fucking her mouth. I let go of her buttocks and reach down and hold her head as I fuck her mouth. In moments I am jetting my sperm down her throat in huge, throbbing spurts. She begins to choke, so I withdraw, and she coughs and splutters, my sperm dribbling out of her mouth. I thought this clumsiness of hers unnecessary, so I selected a cane from an assortment hanging along a rail on the wall, and, standing behind her, I thrashed her naked buttocks for ten minutes or so, until her sobs and screams had died away into a kind of bubbling, throaty mumble. Her skin reddened under the cane's assault, and her arse became criss-crossed with raised weals.

This titillating interval quite restored my erection, and I lowered the rope by which she was suspended until her still-wet cunt was on a level with my newly rigid cock. 'Oh, please,' she said, through her tears. 'Please fuck me. Please do what you want with me, but please don't cane me any more. I can't stand that much pain. I don't care if I don't get the part, but please don't cane me any more.' Since she *had* done a pretty good job of fellating me, and I had enjoyed thrashing her bare bottom, I took pity on her and let her down from the hook in the ceiling. This left her lying on the floor, with her hands still bound behind her back, and her legs still bound together by the chain and the ankle shackles. But at least she could now spread her legs, a difficult thing to do when suspended upside down.

I picked her up off the floor and threw her, face down, over the padded top of a whipping block. I then kicked her legs apart and, without any kind of preamble – least of all any kind of lubricant – I forced my aching cock up her arsehole, and began to fuck her. She screamed as I thrust my way up her tightly clenched anus, but very soon the anal mucus in her secret flesh-depths lubricated her rectum, and I began to slide in and out of her asshole rather more comfortably. For me, anyway. Her screams subsided quite quickly, and she began moving with me as I humped her up her fundament. When I spurted my semen into her once more, she cried out. Whether with pain or pleasure I shall never know, but it didn't feel to me as if she had any kind of an orgasm.

I pulled out of her, and left her where she was while I went off to my bathroom to clean myself up. I showered and dressed, and then went back to my punishment room, to find her still bent over the whipping block, sobbing. I lifted her up, undid her various bonds and shackles, picked up her clothes from where she had dropped them earlier, and led her through to my bathroom. I left her there. When she emerged, she was more or less back to normal, at least from what I could see. Whilst she had been freshening up I had taken the tape from the two video cameras that had been running all the while through our 'audition', and I now asked her if she would like me to run through them with her. She looked horrified, made her excuses, and left. Hurriedly.

I never heard from her again. In my fantasy, I put a different girl through this and similar (sometimes rather more painful) kinds of S&M experiences, regularly. I'm into whipping girls' breasts and cunts, the use of clamps on nipples and labia, and the whole gamut of sadomasochistic fun and games. I appreciate that these are not everyone's ideas of amusing sex, but we S&M enthusiasts find them both exciting and satisfying. Does anyone know where I can turn my fantasies into realities? Are there any women out there who would like to explore the pleasures of pain with me? Please write.

W. A. A. Chelsea, London.

You've got me beat there, I'm afraid. But we'll forward any letters. (Editor's note: we actually forwarded over twenty letters to W. A. A. We don't, of course, know what the contents were.)

CAVEMAN

I like to believe that I'm as sophisticated as the next man. I think that I understand most of what women are about, and I have reason to believe that I understand at least the basics of what the average woman desires in bed. They like – not in any particular order of priority – a good, large, hard cock. This thing about size not being important is codswallop. The bigger the better. Ask your girlfriend! They like cleanliness. It's not so much next to godliness as next to a big, hard cock! They like men who are gentle, and thoughtful. Men who consider their bed partners. Men who spend time on foreplay. Most women – if they're honest – adore oral sex. Having cunnilingus performed upon them, that is. A number cry off oral sex altogether, simply because they don't want to have to fellate their partner. Here again, cleanliness is relevant. And perhaps most importantly of all, women adore men who have good sexual manners. Me? After years of practice, I get by. I don't get too many complaints. (Nobody's perfect!) But by choice, from preference, given the opportunity, I'm a caveman. Give me a club, let me knock them unconscious, and drag them back to my cave by their hair, and I'm happy! Sadly, my preference only happens in my wildest fantasies. Which is why I'm writing this letter to you today...

It excites me to think of living in some kind of primitive landscape, where everything in sight – including other human beings (men and women), animals, birds even – are potentially my enemy. And the women, of course, are also potential prizes.

I imagine being out of my home cave, hunting, with my stout bow made of fine yew and my arrows tipped with pointed, sharpened flint. I also have a flint knife, and a flint axe. As I tread warily through the forest looking, essentially, for something to kill to eat, I see in the distance another young tribal warrior, accompanied by his woman. I watch carefully for a while, following them silently, and as far as I can see, they are alone. Both have woad tattoos stencilled upon their faces. The man is black-haired, the woman also. He wears a sort of fur sarong, with a single shoulder strap. She has only a fur skirt. Her breasts are bare, and as I look at them, I realize that this woman is of fuckable age. Certainly under twenty. Her breasts are firm and pointed. Her stomach – as much I can see of it – is flat. Her face is unlined, and she smiles at her companion often. He smiles back. They are obviously lovers.

I try and imagine that other little furry animal between her legs, with its soft, wet centre like raw meat. I wonder if it is still reasonably unused, and therefore fairly tight and pleasant to dip into, or whether the woman has been much used, and has borne many children, and has a slack, loose centre to her furry muff. But there are no children with them, and her breasts do not look as if they have been over-sucked. There is only one way to find out for certain. My penis is stiff as I creep up upon the couple. I do not have a woman, and I do not get to dip my penis in a woman's place very often. Maybe I can capture this one, and keep her for my own. As I gain upon them, they both suddenly stop. It looks as if they are going to rest for a while. Good.

I hope the woman isn't menstruating. The gods strike down any man who fucks a woman who is menstruating. Or so they say. I imagine that I can see her little pink mouth, open at the centre of the fur in her groin, but this may be wishful thinking.

The man starts to collect wood to make a fire, and soon he has collected a small pile of dry twigs. He strikes flints together, and soon his fire is crackling away. He is watching the fire so intently that he is careless, and I creep up on him and fell him with a blow from the blunt end of my axe. The woman attacks me, screaming and clawing, but one carefully aimed blow to her chin renders her unconscious too.

While the man is still out, I bind his arms and legs together, and then I tie him, very carefully, to a tree. I go over to the woman, who is still unconscious. I pull her through the undergrowth out of the sight of the man when he regains consciousness. I lift up her fur skirt and spread her legs, exploring with my fingers. At close sight, her furry muff is thick and black. I part this heavy pussy beard and find her pink lips. I press them apart and put a finger inside her. She is not menstruating. She is gloriously tight: I kneel in between her legs, and feed my rampant tool up her. I hold her arms by the wrists and, while she is still unconscious, I begin to fuck her. Her pointed breasts are quivering as I move her body beneath me with the intensity of my fucking, and as I watch, her nipples stiffen. I lean down, and take one in my mouth. It tastes sweet, and I feel it thicken and grow in my mouth. After a while, I take the other one in my mouth, and do the same to that. Suddenly, after I have sucked both her tits, I am looking at her woad-stained face as I fuck her, and she opens her eyes.

Three moods pass across her face in rapid sequence. At first, the only thing she realizes as she becomes conscious again is that she is being fucked, and she begins to smile. Then she realizes that the face above hers isn't the one that she is accustomed to, and the smile becomes a look of abject fear. And then she realizes that, first of all, I am alone – there isn't a whole tribe queuing up to rape and sodomize her – and that, all things considered, I am fucking her gently, with at least some concern for her physical comfort. I am not actually beating her, for example. So the smile that began as she first became aware of me finally returns, and she begins to move her body with mine, thrusting hard upwards as I thrust down. She says something, but it is not in a dialect that I understand. I speak to her and she shakes her head. But she continues to smile and she humps away happily until I begin to spurt my seed into her, at which she moans and closes her eyes, the smile still firmly in place.

I let go of her arms and collapse across her. As my manhood shrinks, I pull it out of her and roll off her. I expect her to make a run for it. But instead she takes my flaccid tool in her hand, and, putting her other hand on my chest and pressing to indicate that I should lie down on my back, she takes me in her mouth and begins to suck at me, suckling my cock as if she were a baby suckling a woman's teat. I have heard from older tribesmen of the secret activities of women who like to be fucked in the mouth, and have always rejected their stories as being boastful male untruths, just as I do those of men who say that there are women who like a man's weapon up their excretory passage.

Her attentions are indeed delightful, and she uses her hand rather as I used to use my own, when my hand was the only thing available to me to fuck. I am quickly stiff again in her mouth, and very quickly after that I again shoot my seed into her, this time between her eager lips. To my surprise, she swallows as I pump away, and when I am finished, she smiles at me and licks her lips lasciviously, indicating that she enjoyed the experience. Her next action has me confused for a while. She puts a forefinger on my mouth, and then she takes it off and, spreading her legs open wide, she puts her finger onto the mouth of her child-hole. As she looks at my puzzled expression, she once more licks her lips, and again puts her finger on my mouth, then down to that other mouth between her legs.

Eventually I realize that, having sucked that which I use to piss through, she now wants me to suck her piss-hole. Can this be so? Can I possibly have misunderstood her? I put my own fingers on my mouth, and then press them against her piss-hole, and I raise my eyebrows quizzically as I then mime a licking motion with my tongue. She smiles broadly, and nods enthusiastically. Since this has been a day of pleasant surprises, I think to myself, perhaps this is but another secret that all men eventually learn about as they are able to practise the humpbacked monster with willing women. Certainly I enjoyed putting my penis in her mouth. Why should I not enjoy trying to take her in mine?

I indicate to her to lie down and she does so, opening her legs for me as she does. I lie down in a position that allows me oral access to her piss-hole and, tentatively, I lick it. It tastes rather pleasant. Rather like those shellfish that are found down at the mouth of the local river. Oysters, they call them. She tastes meaty, but with a slight overtone of fish. I decide that I like it. If it is an acquired taste, then I realize that I have acquired it and I begin to suck at her with enthusiasm. Quite quickly she begins to writhe her hips about beneath my mouth and, as I continue to suck her, she starts again that strange moaning noise which she made when I was first fucking her.

Then, all of a sudden, she is holding my head in her hands and grinding her piss-hole against my mouth as I lick and suck. Then, with a final, high-pitched moan, she lets go of my head, pulls my mouth up to hers, and kisses me. Passionately. What I have been doing to her has aroused me once more, and I thrust my erect cock in between her legs yet again and fuck her, quickly, excitedly, strongly, as we continue to kiss each other. I can taste her piss-hole juice on my lips as I thrust my tongue into her mouth, and the mental image of that first early glimpse of her is enough to take me rapidly beyond the point of ejaculation once more.

And then our sexual introduction was – at least for the moment – over. I walked back to where this woman's man was still tied to the tree. When he saw us, he struggled in his bonds, and shouted at me in their unintelligible language. I expected her to at least comfort him, if not attempt to release him, but no. She first spoke to him, low-voiced and gutturally. Then she spat on the ground in front of him, after which she picked up her small parcel of belongings and, taking me by the arm, she led me off, away into the trees.

I supposed that some member of his tribe would discover him and release him before some wild animal killed him. I didn't feel too strongly about it. He would have done the same with me, given the opportunity. My cock was rising again as the woman led me away. I wondered what else I was soon to discover.

T. L. H. Winchester, Hants.

Probably that it was time to organize lunch! Seriously, maybe there are still a few women out there who are looking for a real caveman. We'll let you know if we hear from any.

COOL AS A CUCUMBER

I met a girl this summer who has made a profound impression upon me, in that she is the finest example I have ever met of whatever the opposite of sexually repressed is. Free, perhaps? Liberal? You tell me. She has no hang-ups whatsoever. She'll take it any time, any place, anywhere. You want it, you can have it. In her mouth. Up her arse. In her hand. You name it, you've got it. She just loves sex. You will remember that this summer just past is on record as the hottest for many years. Would you believe, this girl taught me how to have a cool fuck? No, I'm not kidding. Really. We were lying there in bed one evening, sweating like the proverbial pigs, having enjoyed a serious session of Hide the Sausage, and I said something about wouldn't it be pleasant, in this kind of weather, to have a cool fuck. 'Haven't you ever had one, darling?' she asked. I had to admit that I hadn't. 'No problem,' she said, looking at her watch.

'It's probably too late to arrange it now, but I promise you that tomorrow I'll provide you with the coolest fuck you've ever had.' I fell asleep wondering just exactly what she had in mind. The following day, around mid-morning, after she had been out food shopping, Marie announced that she was ready – and available – for a cool fuck, any time I felt like one. 'How about now, darling?' I asked, never being one to turn down an opportunity. 'I'll see you upstairs in the bedroom in two minutes,' she replied, smiling. Two minutes later, she arrived upstairs, carrying something in an icebox. She stripped off, lay down naked beside me, and opened her legs.

'Can you open that icebox, darling?' she asked. I reached down and picked it up from off the floor where she had left it and opened it up to discover, inside, a large, peeled cucumber. Just shove that slowly and carefully up my cunt,' she instructed. Doing as she asked guaranteed a humdinger of a hard-on. About ten minutes later, she said, 'OK, sweetheart, you can pull it out now, and fuck me.' I did as she told me, and I certainly had the coolest fuck ever. It was a most unusual, and delightful, sensation. I recommend it to anyone who gets bored with lovemaking in the long, hot summertime. And as you can probably guess, after some cool sex, we had some pretty cool cucumber sandwiches for our tea.

S. B. Shoreham-by-Sea, Sussex.

Did you remember to invite the vicar?

BLACK IS BEAUTIFUL

Living as I do in a small town in the sticks, I've grown up – I'm twenty-three – in rather secluded circumstances. We have neither the facilities, nor the anonymity, of big cities, and for this reason, my main fantasy stays as exactly that. I'm happy to say that, yes, we *have* heard of sex down here, and it's in plentiful supply. Country lasses are something else, and they aren't backward in coming forward. But for ages now, I've wanted to indulge in a relationship with a black girl. Of which there are very few around here. Irma, in your last issue, is exactly what I am looking for. She's gorgeous, isn't she? In my fantasy, I can see myself beside her on that lovely big bed, with her wearing just those tiny white knickers – more of a G-string, really – that (I'm sure unnecessary, but very sexy) white brassiere, and those lovely white stockings. She looks fabulous, with that mane of long black hair spread out on the pillow, and with her hand down inside her panties. I can see her thick bush of black pubic hair peeping through the transparency of her knickers, and I can imagine what she is doing to herself. I've always wanted to see a real live girl playing with herself, but that too, sadly, is still a fantasy. Perhaps Irma would like to help me on both counts? I particularly like that large picture where she has her eyes closed, her mouth open, and this time her fingers are outside her panties, but she is still playing with herself. She has also by now taken her bra off, and her other hand is playing with one of her dark – almost black – nipples, pulling and twirling it until it is standing there erectly upon her large, similarly, almost black areola. Her breasts are full and shapely, and I can imagine the feel of them under my fingers. Over the next few pages someone – in my fantasy it is me – is slowly undressing her. First they pull down her virgin white panties. I can imagine easing them over that gorgeous arse, revealing her bushy black pubic hair, out of which are pouting those surprising bright pink inner labia, surrounded by her almost black outer lips. I touch the gusset of her sodden knickers to my nose as I take them off.

Both sets of lips are glistening wetly in the studio lights, and I can see, in one picture, that a thread of mucus is hanging down from her wet pussy, and I imagine myself catching it on my tongue and sucking it into my mouth. I can smell the scent of her cunt, and the taste of it, as I begin to suck her fleshy lips into my mouth. After a while, she sighs and draws her legs up beneath her, raising her arse in the air so that I can see, then touch and feel, then suck, her black anus, peeping at me out of another hairy mound, higher up now than her pussy, in this new position. Her pussy juice is running out of her in a small stream and has run down into her anal crevice and onto her rectum. I put out a finger, and stroke her black, puckered, forbidden entrance. She moans, slightly, and her whole body quivers as she draws in a deep breath. Her full lips are open again, and she is licking them. She is saying something to me. So very quietly. I lean down, my ear to her mouth. 'Your cock,' she is saying. 'Give me your cock. Please. Put your cock in my mouth, so that I can suck you off.' She is lying on her back now, and I kneel over her face, her full breasts beneath my stomach, and she takes my tool in her hand and guides it into her mouth, where she closes her full lips about it and sucks me, as she uses her tongue to tantalize my knob-end. My tool jerks in her mouth at her first oral contact, then it settles down, and I begin to fuck her mouth, very, very slowly.

As I am doing this, I am looking down, immediately below my face and mouth, to her blue-black labia, which are even wetter now, the juices running down her thighs, the pink inner lips open, and silkily wet too. I thrust my middle finger down into her, all the way in to my knuckle. She is delightfully warm, very wet, and unbelievably tight. It is akin to thrusting my finger into a firm, well-made jelly. The aroma of aroused cunt invades my nostrils. She smells like an overripe tropical melon, with an underlying breath of something slightly fetid. It is exciting, tangy, and I reach down and lick her, slowly, running my tongue from just above the wrinkled entrance to her rectal passage, tentatively, enjoyably, lustfully, joyfully, gratifyingly, all the way back to the apex of her wet black outer vaginal lips.

I thrust my tongue down beneath its hood and find her swollen clitoris within reach. I lick and suck at the same time, and she wriggles beneath me and starts to jack me off into her mouth at the same time as she is fellating me. This is oral sex beyond the dreams of ordinary man. This woman is the Sistine Chapel of fellatio. The female God of oral sex. Her mouth should be a national treasure. I pump away at her hand and mouth, and she masturbates and sucks my swollen prick as I thrust away, bringing me quickly to the point of ejaculation. I can hardly tear myself away from my oral devotions at the altar of her increasingly freely moistened cunt. I'd almost rather not come than stop sucking her gorgeously scented, exquisitely tasting, open, wet pussy. But then, there I am, suddenly, exultantly, happily spurting my warm, creamy seed into her all-encompassing mouth. She sucks and swallows me, thirstily, as I spurt my semen into her. I promise to pump my come into her, now and forever more, world without end. Amen.

I wish I had a hundred cocks, so that she could suck all of them. That I could maintain a permanent erection, for her to fellate. Continuously. I wish I could keep my mouth, tongue, lips, nose, forever buried in her hot, black, fleshy cunt. I believe that I am finished. Fucked out. Sucked out. And then she takes my limp cock in her hand, and she masturbates it for me. Exquisitely. So gently. So erotically. It was as if I had never before tossed myself off in my life. Never been given a quick wank by some girl – any girl – anxious to get rid of me but realizing that I needed to ejaculate before she could reasonably expect me to let her go without raping her. At least in my mind.

As if I had never enjoyed a quick one off the wrist from a young lady, one who wanted to say 'Thank you', but who didn't want – for whatever reasons of her own – to drop her knickers for me. Perhaps she had the rags up, as we used to say all those years ago. It was pretty much the only acceptable excuse, in those days. It was many years before *Hustler* magazine in America had turned menstrual copulation into a pastime for the allegedly sexual erudite few. And, I suppose, any girl still a virgin (and wanting to stay that way) but willing to pull a chap's plonker for him, until his semen spurted all over her hand, was generally thought to be pretty good news. At least by the chaps. Better by far than having to go home and do it on one's own. Sniffing the finger that one had reluctantly been allowed to slip up the forbidden vaginal orifice, whilst wanking off madly with the other hand. Oh, the excitement of youth.

So my fantasy continues, despite my sexual excess so far, with this exotic, desirable woman masturbating me back to erection. In my dream, as soon as I am fully erect, she then turns over onto her stomach, draws her knees up underneath her, and pulls herself up into a kneeling position and with her legs apart, offering me both her pussy and her anus. They are both black and beautiful, running with lubrication, and fully available. She turns her head, looks over her shoulder at me lasciviously, and says, 'I love it up my arse. Why don't you fuck me anally?'

As you all know, there's only one answer to that particular invitation. I spat, hugely, onto my fingers, and – despite her own, obviously welcoming lubrication – I rubbed my spittle thoroughly into her anal orifice, making it even wetter. Greasier is probably a better word. She felt gloriously tight. She squirmed, and said, 'Oh, yes. Oh, baby. Oh, God. I'm ready for you. Fuck my arse. Stick your huge cock up my arsehole. Come in my bottom. Fuck me up there. Now. Please, darling. Do it to me. Bugger me. Now. I'm ready.' Her anal hair was wet with her emanations, and I thrust a finger, gently, up her pinkly glistening arsehole. Very tentatively, I have to admit. It slid in, all the way, without the slightest resistance from her. She really *was* ready. And willing. And able. I pulled my finger out, and then I took my cock in my hand and fed it into her anus. She breathed in, strongly, as the tip of my cock entered her. I continued to press, and my knob-end popped into her. She gasped and said, 'Ooooh.' Nothing else. After that, it was roses all the way. I thrust up into her, up to my hilt, my balls slapping against her taut, firm thighs. 'Oh, yes,' she said. 'Don't stop. Fuck me now. Give it to me. Bugger me. Fuck my arsehole. Fuck me now. Oh, Jesus. Do it to me now.'

I began to move my hips, thrusting my already almost bursting penis up into her, then slowly withdrawing it again, revelling in her tightly clenched anal cavity. She became slightly looser – more slippery, perhaps, is a better description – as I continued to fuck her, presumably from the lubricant that her rectal passage was exuding as my cock massaged her internally. Whatever the cause, the effect was absolutely terrific, and I knew that it was only a matter of time – almost certainly a very little time – before I spent myself, spending my jism in the delightful warm, moist constrictions of her bottom-hole.

Why is it that the naughtiest things, the forbidden things, the things that society most disapproves of, are always the nicest things? Why is it that they are that much more enjoyable than the things that nobody cares about? Buggering ladies' bottoms is high on my list of forbidden treats. And, happily, I know a number of ladies who agree with me. But don't tell anyone, please. Sadly, it's still against the law. As I felt my ejaculation building, the girl reached a hand around behind her, took my right hand away from her waist, and put it down between her legs. 'Play with my clitty, darling,' she said. 'Please. Make me come now.' And then she reached behind her again, and took hold of the base of my cock as it thrust in and out of her lovely blue-black tiny little anal flower and, as I masturbated her clit, she wanked the base of my tool. Then we almost immediately came together, laughing at our pleasure.

'Oh, God,' she said, as I started to spurt my come up her arsehole. 'Oh, Jesus. Oh yes. Oh, darling. I'm coming. You're coming in my arsehole, and I'm coming too. I can feel your hot spunk spurting up me. Oh, God. I like it. I love it. Oh, Jesus. Oh, fuck.' I continued to frig her, for as long as she was having what became a long, almost continuous, series of orgasms, and she kept her busy fingers doing the same for my cock, for as long as I kept spurting my semen into her, until finally, we both collapsed, sexually spent, still giggling slightly at our mutual, breathless, completely out-of-condition – but very happy – physically fulfilled state.

After that, we continued to make lazy, self-indulgent love, on and off, for most of the night. We were happy with each other, relaxed with each other. Turned on by each other. Appreciating the feel, the smell, the taste of each other. Loving the sensations that we were able to stimulate in each other's bodies. Liking the excitement produced by each other's hands, mouths, tongues, fingers, sexual organs, orifices, protrusions.

Making a meal of each other's bodies. Until we fell into a deep, satisfied, completely sexually replete slumber. I hope this fantasy explained to you my love of – and lust for – black women. If there are any black female readers out there who want to become an integral part of my single-minded sexual fantasy, please write to me.

P. G. W. Bridgeport, Connecticut.

Sounds like an invitation to become a personal sex slave!

ELIZABETHAN EULOGY

I've always been tremendously excited by what I imagine to be the Elizabethan way of life, particularly with regard to sexual matters. From what I have read about the period, it was one long orgy, provided, of course, that you were rich. It certainly wasn't a great time in which to be poor. I love the thought of myself, with a group of my men friends, sitting down in a private room in an Elizabethan inn and being served a splendid meal by a selection of attractive serving wenches, their ample bosoms barely concealed, as we eat and drink our way through the feast put before us. Naturally enough, when the table is cleared, our thoughts turn to sex with the young women servants, who are not averse to earning a little extra on the side, and the orgy begins. It starts with the girls lining up in front of us and undoing the bodices of their dresses to reveal their naked breasts in all their mammary glory. Nipples are pinched and tweaked into a state of full arousal, and the bulges in our hose indicate that the men are aroused too. There is much jocular banter as we men inspect the objects of our growing desires closely, and we feel and suck the girl's breasts as we inspect, making comparisons, and probably choices, for later, closer attention. We are, of course, quaffing quantities of good French claret as we carry out our inspections, and the ladies join in with us as we drink. The party consequently soon becomes merrier, and it isn't too long before the girls' long Elizabethan skirts are being voluntarily hoisted, and voluminous pairs of drawers opened at the crotch, or dropped, to display an interesting variety of hairy love-mounds sitting between their open thighs. Serving wenches are not renowned for their shyness, and they happily sit on the now cleared long table, spreading their legs, and offering themselves to the highest bidder.

Bidding begins, with the oldest of the wenches acting as auctioneer, and the bids are accompanied – quite properly – by extremely close inspection of the differently hued muffs on offer. Pubic hair is parted, vaginal lips are spread by willing fingers (both male and female) and the girls encourage fingers to be inserted into orifices in order to verify the degree of tightness, the level of elasticity, and the quantity of wetly indicated anticipation and enthusiasm shown by each individual girl. One girl is cheered loudly when she bends down over the table, raises her plump arse in the air and then, putting her hands behind her, pulls her arse cheeks apart, exposing her tightly clenched anus. She is quickly – and expensively – bought.

All of the girls, naturally, pass the tests, and the bidding begins to take on a more urgent tenor. Heavy purses are extracted from hitherto deep pockets, and golden sovereigns are tipped onto the table in seemingly limitless quantities. The next girl to strike a deal gets a cheer, due to the fact that she has been bought entirely due to the quantity of sticky lubrication that is issuing from her cunt, its flow obvious, since she is holding her cunt open widely with her fingers, and asking who wishes to plug it for her. As the bids get higher, the girl masturbates herself frenziedly, to the delight of her cheering audience, and the highest bid is made as she doubles over in the thrill of reaching orgasm as the auction ends. She has attained the astonishingly high price of two guineas. But it is necessary to remember that we are in an age in which a twelve-year-old common prostitute from the streets of London may be used for fourpence.

I have to admit that I am the one who bought the girl who was offering herself anally. The sight of her generous buttocks, their fleshiness plumply surrounding her dark brown, tightly puckered rectal flower, was all too much. It was simply pleading to have me distend its petals. I couldn't look at it without imagining sinking my swollen penis between its tender lips. As I looked, I could practically feel its hermetic rigidity gripping my member as I thrust into it, dilating it, feeling its inner warmth and moistness. I almost came in my hose in frantic, excited anticipation.

The girl was pretty with it too. She had short black hair that shone with health and much brushing, and a black, coarse pubic growth that was repeated all the way up (or down, if you prefer) her anal cleft. She had a small, elfin face, rather heavily made-up, and long, slim legs. When she stripped off, I noticed immediately that her armpits were unshaven, in the Continental manner. When I later took her in my arms, I licked her armpits and they were damp and heavily scented with her bodily secretions. Their odour went straight to my penis, which grew magnificently as a result. Her breasts were heavy, and her nipples and areolae were also surrounded by a sprinkling of long black hairs. I had taken her up to one of the inn's rooms, not wanting to bugger her publicly, and on the way upstairs she had asked me to excuse her and said that she would be but a few moments before she rejoined me. When she arrived and knocked at the door, as I opened it I could see that she came with a dish of mutton grease in her hand. 'All the better to grease your entry,' she said, blushing slightly. A very sensible precaution, I thought. For both of us.

She undressed, as did I, and without further preamble she knelt on the bed, her delightful haunches facing me as I stood there, and suggested that I grease her anus for her. I took the mutton grease from the side table where she had put it and began to anoint her. I slid a finger deep into her and she shuddered and waggled her bottom. 'Mmmm,' she said. Nothing else. Just 'Mmmm.' I took it as a sign that she was enjoying my attention.

She was exquisitely tight, and I felt her rectal muscles grip my finger as I thrust into her, and then withdrew. I took it that she was no anal virgin. I would guess that she made a practice of what she and I were about to do, and probably made an excellent living at it. I greased her thoroughly, and then gave her the dish of fat, with the suggestion that she now perform the same service on my penis. Why keep a dog and bark yourself, as they say? She smiled at me and then, as she greased my cock, she said 'Oh, my. That *is* a big one, isn't it? I hope you're not going to hurt me, sir.' But she smiled as she spoke, and I don't believe that she really thought anything of the kind. She wasn't worried in the least bit about having her fundament uncomfortably stretched. She simply knew that men like to be complimented on the size of their sexual equipment. She finished her job, to her *and* my satisfaction, and wiped her greasy fingers on one of the crisply laundered linen sheets. 'There, sir,' she said, looking at her handiwork. I was fully erect, and extraordinarily well greased. 'I think we're ready now,' she said.

And so saying, she knelt once more on the bed and again put her hands behind her and pulled her buttocks well apart, thus revealing her anus, now partially dilated, extremely well greased, and showing just a smidgen of her own anal lubrication which was beginning to trickle out and run down her anal crevice. For the first time I could now actually see inside her rectal passage. Down through the dark brown, closely puckered surround, held enticingly open by her fingers, she glistened pinkly inside, very like a vagina, apart from the hole itself.

Below her anus, I could see her vaginal lips, hanging down loosely. They were the same dark brown as the flesh of her anus, and they were perhaps the largest outer pussy lips that I had ever seen. They were about four inches long, as far as I could judge, and they were quite fat. 'Fleshy' is perhaps a better word. They reminded me of bats' wings. I could just make out a pink slit at their centre, and unthinkingly I put both hands down to her, and spread her outer pussy lips, and thrust my forefinger up her cunt. It was warm, and very wet, and she shuddered as I fingered her. She looked over her shoulder. 'Have you changed your mind, sir?' she asked. 'I thought that you had got your heart set on a bit of buggery. You won't be dissatisfied, I promise you. If you want a bit of cunt after that, I'm more than happy to throw that in for nothing. But I'd rather have it up my arse first, if it don't make no difference to you, sir.' 'And so you shall, my darling,' I told her. I took my finger out of her cunt and, taking hold of my rampant erection, I began to feed it up into her anus. She pulled her cheeks apart again with her agile fingers, and at the same time she pushed back against me, enabling my cock to slide all the way into her. As I slid in, she let off a small, squeaky fart. 'Oops,' she said. 'Pardon me, sir.' I found it rather endearing.

As I started to bugger her, she clasped hold of my cock with her anal muscles, as tightly as it had ever been grasped by any woman before, and as I thrust deeply in and out of her greasy back entrance she thrust back towards me, as hard as she knew how, and squeezed me hard with her powerful rectal muscles. I wondered how many of the local gentry, with whom I foregathered at this very public house of a Saturday evening, had been up her delightful tight young arse before me. Quite a few, I would imagine. She was no stranger to what I was doing to her, that was for sure, and it must have taken a great deal of very regular practice for her to get her rectal muscles into the highly developed condition that they were presently in.

So joyful was our congress that in no time at all I was shooting my hot spunk up her back passage, to cries, from her, of 'Oooh', and 'Ohhh', and, finally, 'Ohhhh, Jesuuuusssss, yeessss'. She squeezed and sucked my jism up into her arsehole, with seeming pleasure, until I was completely spent. As my penis shrivelled back to its more normal state, it plopped out of her, and she got up off her knees, turned around, and sat down beside me. She stroked my hair, as I lay there. I was sexually more than replete, at least for the moment.

'I enjoyed that, sir,' she said. 'I think you've probably buggered a few of us young girls, before me.' 'I have that,' I told her. 'But never one that I have enjoyed as much as you. You've got a regular customer, if you are looking for one.' 'That's very kind of you to say that, sir,' she said. 'There's a good few young women in this part of the world would give a lot to hear a gentleman like yourself say that to them. I appreciate it. Thank you.' 'My pleasure, darling,' I told her. She lay down beside me, and we lay together in silence until we were both rested. After a while, she reached out a hand and took hold of my flaccid penis. It began to swell under her touch. She sat up and said, 'I'll just get a flannel, and wash this little man here, before he becomes a big man again. And then we'll find a different place to put him. Is that all right with you, sir?'

'That's very all right with me, darling,' I said. 'Feel free.' She went over to a corner of the room, where there was a washbasin and a jug of water. It must have been hot when we first came upstairs, for it was still warm now. She came back with the basin half full of water, and a flannel, and began to wash my cock, carefully and gently. By the time that she had finished, it was beautifully clean, and wonderfully erect. She put the basin and the flannel down on the floor beside the bed and, leaning down, she took my now fully erect penis in her soft, warm mouth. She held it delicately in her right hand, slowly masturbating it into her mouth, whilst she kissed it, and tongued it, and sucked it. She ran her tongue the full length of it, from its swollen purple tip to its base, down by her fingers, wetting it all over with her saliva. She then held it steady in front of her mouth, and gently blew on it, making it cold, and all the more sensitive to the attentions that she was giving it.

She saw me watching her, and she took me out of her mouth and smiled at me. 'It's all right, sir,' she said. 'You can fuck me with this any time you like. I just thought that I'd give it a little treat before you started. I don't know if you're married or not – and I don't want to know—' she said, hurriedly. 'But a lot of the married gentlemen I service tell me that their wives won't take their cocks in their mouths. They say they don't like the taste of them. Me,' she said, positively grinning at me now, 'I *love* the taste of them. And the feel of them in my mouth. And the taste of come. If you want to spunk in my mouth, then that's fine with me, sir,' she said. 'I'll swallow every drop. You just try me.'

'I'm not actually married, darling,' I told her. 'But I'd love to come in your mouth. It's the final pleasure.' Then I thought for a moment of the gorgeous sensations that I had enjoyed recently, shooting my semen up this young girl's anus, and so I slightly changed my statement. 'Well,' I said, '*One* of the final pleasures. And I still haven't fucked you . . .' She grinned at me again. 'Don't worry, sir,' she said. 'I don't know about you, but I've got all the time in the world. For what you're paying me, you can fuck me, suck me, bugger me, frig me, and then play noughts and crosses with me, all day and all night, for a week.' And so, in my fantasy, I do all the things that she suggested. Well, except the noughts and crosses. And in slightly less than a week. My own, private, Elizabethan orgy.

P. C. Newton Abbot, Devon.

Cakes and ale and *crumpet. What fun!*

MALE MENAGERIE

My boyfriend and I love to read your excellent magazine together. We delight in the girl sets. They turn us *both* on (no, I'm not a lesbian). And the features and stories give us lots of lovely ideas for ways to bring both fun and variety into our sex lives, for which I, for one, thank you. But may I make one small complaint, please? We enjoy your letters columns too, and my own favourite topic is that of reading about other people's fantasies. But you seem to concentrate on publishing letters from men. Reader's letters from women, describing *their* fantasies, are few and far between. So how about publishing mine?

My fantasy is like a favourite film. I can run it any time I like. At home. In the office. In a restaurant. I like it best when I'm in a situation where I can slip my fingers down between my legs, and masturbate while I run it through. Without anyone seeing me, of course. Sometimes – particularly in the office, – that means that I have to go and lock myself in a cubicle in the ladies' loo, drop my panties, and finger myself off in there, which means I often go back to my desk looking rather flushed. In my fantasy, I am rich. Very rich. I live in an enormous penthouse apartment, on the top floor of a very high building. I have an enormous bedroom with – what else? – an enormous bed. I have my own private, fully equipped gymnasium, and a terrace which runs all the way around the apartment. I have a retinue of servants. All men. All handsome, physically fit, attractive men. All men who like to fuck. Me.

Some of them do other things, like cook and look after the apartment, take care of my clothes, and so on. But they are *all* capable of taking care of me. Fantasies being what they are, there are no jealousies, no squabbles, no problems. Life is tranquil. There is, essentially, much variety. I have in my collection black men, white men, brown men. Some are employed full-time, some have fixed-term contracts, some are rented by the day or week. If I get bored with any one of them, they are immediately discharged. Paid off. All are totally obedient.

If one of them passes through a room when I am in it, and I snap my fingers, he comes and stands in front of me. If I want to unzip his trousers, put my hand inside, and play with his cock until he has a raging erection, then that is what I do. If I say to one of them, 'Get your cock out and toss yourself off', then that is exactly what he will do. If I am watching television and I feel like having someone suck my pussy as I watch (and that's whenever Richard Burton is on, for a start) then I simply summon whichever one sucks pussy best at that particular time and tell him to get on with it. All I have to do is spread my legs. I let *them* pull my panties down. If I want to get fucked all night, I have them stand in line outside my bedroom door and as one ejaculates and pulls out of me I press a bell to summon the next one in. In order not to waste time, I have a pretty girl standing inside the bedroom door to jack them off, or suck them off, until they are fully erect, and then I just plug them in and let them fuck me until they come. I never, ever, *ever*, suck their cocks myself. As a matter of principle (sorry, chaps). But I have girlfriends who love to come and suck cock at my place (amongst other things!) and it amuses me to watch my fellas ejaculating down their throats, if that is what one or other of the girls happens to feel like on a particular day. Some of us girls obviously *do* enjoy it. I have done it – and will do it – for men I love. But not for my fantasy team. With just one exception (tell you later).

The nicest thing about my fantasy is that it is almost infinitely variable. It allows for endless new recruits, or the permanent retention of an old favourite. I can be fucked endlessly, even mindlessly, if that seems appropriate. I can enjoy continuous orgasms. I can choose quality or quantity, or both. I never, *ever*, have to say to myself (or to anyone else) gosh, I really feel like a fuck (or having someone masturbate me, being sucked off, fucked up the arse, *anything*). I just snap my fingers. Literally.

I only take it up my arse in my fantasies. In real life, I'm too nervous. Originally, I intentionally hired a man with rather a small cock (most unusual in most of my fantasies!) to initiate me. Now I can take anyone up there. I love it. In my daydreams. But don't ever believe those stories, girls, about 'It's not how big it is, it's what you do with it.' They're put about by men with small cocks. Big cocks are the greatest. Take it from me. And of course I've tried out all kinds of sexual acts that I don't do in real life. Being fucked, for example, up my arse, up my pussy, and sucking a man off (well, that was the exception I mentioned earlier: just that once!) all at the same time. Just for the novelty of it. It wasn't any great experience, really. In point of fact, I discovered that I didn't know whether I was coming or going. I simply didn't know which one to concentrate on. Each one seemed to detract from the other. It's more fun in succession. One after the other. Of course, it isn't all serious sex. Not really. We have fun too! Particularly when two or three of my girlfriends are with me.

What I like to do is to have dinner in the apartment. You know, lashings of good food, and delicious wine, and plenty of liqueurs with the coffee. That sort of thing. And sometimes I tell the chaps to serve it with them all completely naked. So that, if any of the girls sees something that she particularly fancies, then she asks his name, and he is hers afterwards. Well, usually she's first. It's not an exclusive arrangement. And one evening, one of the girls suggested a competition. She suggested that we have a contest where we would compete to see which one of us could make the most men ejaculate in the shortest possible time. We all thought that was a terrific idea. Well, we were all well pissed at the time! And so we worked out a set of rules.

First of all, it had to be public. In other words, the competition had to take place with us all in the same room. There was no question of going off into a spare bedroom and coming back and saying, ten minutes later, that you'd made ten men ejaculate. Then, we decided, we would have to have an official, a judge, to keep the scores. Scoring would be simple. One man, one ejaculation, one point. Next, we decided that it would be both more practical, and more fun, if each girl entered individually. Meaning that we each made our attempt on our own, with the others watching. (If they wanted to. And, of course, they did!) Which would make it a long night, but most of the evenings thus spent with the girls *were* long nights! We decided that we would draw lots to decide the order of entry. And, naturally, the judge's decision was final. There were no objections to these rules.

I won't bore you by describing every act that every girl performed that evening, but I'll relate, if I may, a couple of the more amusing incidents. First of all one girl – Amanda – was disqualified, after the judge had decided that she wasn't entering into the true spirit of the game. In other words, instead of seeing how many man she could bring to ejaculation in the shortest possible time, she was simply seeing how many times she could get laid. Full stop. Speed wasn't a part of her game at all. She had achieved getting fucked by seven different men by the time the judge stepped in and disqualified her. She then carried on in one of the upstairs bedrooms. 'Whatever turns you on' is the rule of the evenings at my fantasies!

And the winner was the first amongst us (a sexy redhead called Jennifer) to realize that we had omitted to make a rule, which, had we thought about it, would have made it a much more even contest. But Jenny realized right from the start that we hadn't specified how many men an entrant could attempt to bring to orgasm at any one time. Consequently, when her turn came, she had a line of men queuing up to take the places of earlier men as each one with her was brought to orgasm. And she started off with five men. *Five!* One in each hand, being tossed off. One being sucked off in her mouth. One fucking her normally. And finally, one fucking her anally. It was the equivalent of one of those one-man-band buskers that you used to see outside cinema queues in Leicester Square.

As each man with Jenny came to orgasm, and was checked off by the judge, he was immediately replaced by another. After she had wanked off three pairs of men, Jenny stopped using her left hand, and concentrated on her right hand, while she gave up being buggered after the second man had spurted his come up her backside. It was too distracting, she said, in a quick moment of respite between gobbling two men off. Nevertheless, she had brought twenty-three men to orgasm when the rest of us threw our hands in and gave her best, to a rousing cheer from the men she had worked with to achieve this figure. It ought to be in the *Guinness Book of Records*, but we didn't approach them, on the basis that we didn't think that they accepted sexual contests. Maybe they should?

H. K. V. Abingdon, Berks.

I bet you girls would make a sharks' feeding frenzy look like a vicarage tea party. Seriously though, your fantasy sounds like a lot of fun. It's certainly in our *record book.*

ICE MAIDENS

May a mere male confess to a full, red-blooded appreciation of the wonderfully sexy costumes worn by (maybe that should be *almost* worn by) those amazingly attractive young girls entering the international ice-dancing championships so beloved by television companies these days. And for the best possible reasons. All those gals are so eminently fuckable, aren't they? I don't know anything of the technicalities – or the buzzwords – used in ice dancing, but I just adore the way that the girls skate about on one foot, with the other foot raised up behind them, parallel to the ground, exposing their pretty little crotches to all and sundry, glimpsed from underneath their tiny thigh-length skirts. I can watch for hours, fantasizing about what lies beneath those narrow strips of gauzy material, and imagining, as the girls get worked up and excited during their performances, just how wet and sticky the inside of those panties must be. I'd love to be a dresser in the girls' dressing rooms.

P. B. Hastings, Sussex.

We're with you. It's a really heart-warming experience. Would an ice-pack help?

WILD VIBRATIONS

As a single woman presently without a regular male partner, and not being much of a girl for one-night stands, I recently made use of one of the mail-order advertisements in your splendid magazine and ordered myself my first vibrator. This may not sound greatly exciting to those of your female readers accustomed to these delightful additions to every woman's list of essential items to carry around in her handbag. But it was something completely new in my life, and I had a lot of fun that first evening (and most evenings since!) trying out the various heads with which the vibrator came equipped. As a variation on the old UYOF (use-your-own-fingers) technique, learned at boarding school, the vibrator is a distinct improvement. The only disadvantage that I can see (feel?) so far, is the fact that I may never need a man in my life again! Positive advantages noticed so far are (i) the variety of heads, and the variable speeds, giving me what is tantamount to a whole wardrobe of men. I can choose one to suit any mood. (I love the anal probe. It has brought a new kind of love to me.) (ii) The vibrator's erection never fails. It can fuck me all day, and all night, and then some. (iii) It never wants to fuck me when I've got my period.

Disadvantages noticed so far: (i) It *is* a bit noisy. But who cares? (ii) I love to suck cock, but, much as I like the flavour of my own pussy juice, it's not much fun to suck. (iii) It doesn't ejaculate. (My girlfriends tell me that I should buy one of those dildos that *does* ejaculate, and which takes a vibrator as an insert. I'm looking for one.) (iv) I haven't succeeded in wanking it yet. (Although I did tell it one evening that I had a headache). On second thoughts, is there a woman out there who would like to swop her man for one fairly new vibrator? Five heads. Well run in. Still in its original packaging. Low mileage. Four spare batteries.

J. M. C. Glasgow, Scotland.

It does make sex sound somewhat mechanical. Why not use it as an adjunct to, rather than as a substitute for, the real thing?

BATH TIME

I think I'm a fairly normal man as far as most sexual matters are concerned, but with one exception: I love the combination of sex and water. Water as in a bath, or a jacuzzi, a swimming pool, or even the ocean. Bath water is my favourite fantasy. Add together *two* naked girls, one giant size bath-tub, lots of hot, soapy water, and me, and you have the basis of my sexual dreams. I will always remember once, on a business trip to New York, going to a so-called 'leisure spa', in Manhattan, and bringing all my water fantasies to life. It was fantastic! The spa was on Third Avenue, between 50th and 51st Streets. I was taken there by a man from the company that I was doing business with.

We went into what appeared to be a normal bar, with the exception that there were a number of girls there – all very pretty – dressed in a sort of Hawaiian costume. Basically minuscule bras, and very brief hula-hula skirts. We drank exotic, allegedly Hawaiian cocktails, and the girls were all over us. The guy who I was with said, 'Choose any two you like, Mac. It's on the house.' By which I took it that he meant that he would be picking up the tab. I chose a couple of attractive girls and they took me down along a corridor, then down a small staircase, and opened the door into what I can only describe as a sort of fucking parlour.

The floor was upholstered as if it was an enormous mattress, the whole thing covered with silken sheets. The curved walls and the ceiling were entirely of mirror glass, while over in one corner was a huge jacuzzi. The whole place was full of exotic tropical flowers, and it smelt of incense and scented water. The girls turned on the jacuzzi, and poured me yet another rum cocktail from a cabinet at one end of the room. They next undressed themselves, and then me. One of them grabbed my cock and quickly masturbated me to a splendidly huge erection. They then brought out a bottle of sun oil, and suggested that I oil their bodies for them. This I spent a long time doing. Oiling their bodies included oiling anything that I wanted to oil, and I oiled all four breasts, and both their pussies, bringing them both to orgasm as I attended to their quims. They were both doing the same to me, and I came a number of times during this delightful experience. I found the girls gorgeously attractive, and they were really friendly. There was none of the 'Let's get this over as quickly as possible, and get our money and get out' approach that one might have expected. I sucked their lovely breasts, and then their lovely pussies, and then they took it in turns to suck my dick. We were in the bath, out of the bath, and back in the bath again. We were fucking, sucking, and playing with each other, taking everything in turns. I fucked both girls. Both girls sucked me off. I sucked both girls off. They sucked each other off, whilst I tossed myself off. There was nothing that we didn't do, a number of times over, until I was completely sexually replete. Not to put too fine a point on it, I was fucked. So were the girls. I'm pleased to be able to tell you that finally, when I came out of the room relaxed, refreshed, and feeling on top of the world, my business friend had gone. But he had settled my bill. To this day, I have no idea how much that tremendous service cost.

D. H. Montreal, Canada.

An arm and a leg, we would guess. Sometimes it's better not to know these things.

SMALL IS BEAUTIFUL

Why the obsession in your letters columns with the sheer size of everything? Huge boobs. Giant buttocks. Colossal pussy lips. Enormous nipples. If I were a woman, I could understand a preoccupation with mammoth cocks, but that's about as far as I can go. As a man, I just love everything about my women to be small *but perfect*. Small, but elegantly shaped buttocks. Small, but firm, exquisitely shaped breasts. Tiny, fully erect, hard little nipples. Not forgetting small but elastically tight cunts. Doesn't anyone out there realize that small is beautiful?

H. Y. Bridport, Dorset.

Beauty, my friend, is in the eye of the beholder. We don't disagree with you. Nor with anyone to whom big is beautiful.

THROUGH THE LOOKING GLASS

As a woman, I am full of admiration for the lovely girls who pose for the pictures in your excellent magazine. I'm fascinated, too, by their ability to look both beautiful *and* sexy at the same time. That combination, I find, is not the easiest to assume. It's something I've been practising in front of my bedroom mirror for a while now, and I think that at last I'm beginning to get the hang of it. This is how one of my sessions goes.

First of all I have a long, languorous bath. I soak out the day's hassles with hot water, and lots of bath essence. I put silk scarves over all three of my bedroom lamps – to give a soft, sexy light – and I dress myself in some of my sexiest underwear. Tiny, flimsy nothings that reveal everything that they pretend to cover. Then I lie across my bed, beside which I have placed one of those old-fashioned pier mirrors. You know the kind? They are long and narrow, and you can tilt them to any angle that you wish. Then I pour myself a glass of champagne, and I lie there for a while, looking at myself, and thinking sexy thoughts. I think about my fantasy man, sitting beside me on the bed, fully dressed. I see the bulge in his trousers as he looks at me, and I reach out and undo his zip, and then I reach inside his fly and pull out his swollen cock. I examine it closely, pulling down his foreskin and exposing his purple cock-head, with its skin stretched so tightly. I see the blue veins standing out down his rigid length, and the coarse pubic hair below, in which nestle his balls. There is a drop of colourless liquid exuding from the tip of his cock. I make a few masturbatory movements with my hand, pulling his skin up and down his shaft, until he is completely erect, and then I lean forward and take him into my mouth. I suck him off as slowly as I know how, tantalizing him with my tongue, licking him, sliding him between my wet lips, sucking him until my cheeks are hollow with my efforts. Reasonably enough, it is not too long before he spurts his jism down my throat.

I keep sucking, and I swallow his salty, creamy, warm come. Every drop. By the time I have sucked him dry, he is fully erect again. He pulls down my panties and rams himself up into my welcoming wetness. I masturbate him with my vaginal muscles. He feels stiff and hard – like a thick steel rod – and, to my noisy delight, he fucks me practically senseless, until I am lying there, having huge orgasm after huge orgasm. I have to plead with him to stop. He knows me too well, of course, to take any notice of my entreaties, and he goes on fucking me until he explodes into me once more. He jets his spunk into my pussy. I can feel it erupting into my womb. The spasms of my orgasms make my whole body shudder: I climax endlessly.

The reality of course, is somewhat different. Back at the beginning, as I look at myself in the mirror, and think about my fantasy man, my hand slips – inevitably – inside my panties, and I spread my dry, tight, pussy lips. I slide two fingers inside myself. Soon I'm really wet, and I begin to masturbate as I think of that lovely, engorged cock in my mouth, extending my lips to their fullest with its circumference, stretching my mouth almost to its limit. My fingers move faster, and I feel my first orgasm beginning to build. This is when I next look at my face in the mirror and try and look sexy. At first glance, I just look like me masturbating. Slightly frenetic. But then I rearrange my face.

I open my mouth a little, wet my lips, and realign them

into a sexy pout. I pull my fingers out of my pussy long enough to use both hands to slip my knickers down my thighs, until they are stretched tautly between my open legs, a moist, grey spot showing on their – up until then – virginal white gusset. I slip my fingers back inside myself, and start frigging again. Harder this time. I come. I lie back and enjoy it until it is over and that first – essential – orgasm has been and gone. I then look at myself in the mirror again, and – thinking of the pages of photographs of your models in the magazine – I realize that I have forgotten a number of essential positions.

So I start again. I've done the hands-inside-my-knickers-playing-with-myself shot, so I don't need to do that again. But I haven't done the no-knickers-on, is-my-middle-finger-really-*just*-inside-my-slit? picture. I get a comb, and comb my long, curly pubes, until they are in a more suitable state to be photographed. Then I try a number of I've-got-my-finger-in-my-pussy poses, until I find the one that pleases me. I hear the click of an imaginary camera. Next I do the one where my black, silk-stockinged thighs are spread widely, with my knees drawn up – no knickers, of course – for the would-you-like-a-really-close-look-at-my-wet-pussy? pose.

I'm just admiring myself in this position, when I realize, God damn it, that my nipples aren't erect. I spend pleasurable minutes pulling and twirling at them, until they stand up proudly, like a pair of baby cocks. A men's magazine's model's job ain't *all* bad! I decide against the would-you-like-a-close-up-of-my-anus? shot, simply because I'm much too shy. I'm not against anal sex. Absolutely not at all. Given the opportunity, I quite enjoy it. It's just that I have a very hairy anal cleft, and what seems to me to be a rather large arsehole, not to put too fine a point on it. But there is another problem . . .

By this time, I realize that I need to come again. As soon as possible. The hell with being a model. I revert back to being just me, and go and get my vibrator out of the drawer where I keep it. I'm nice and wet, so I don't need any kind of lubricant. (I always think that should be lubri*cunt*!) I lie back down on the bed, on my back, and slide the vibrator up my waiting pussy. I switch it on, turn the handle to the fastest speed, and produce a series of seriously fast orgasms. I enjoy those, and then I turn the speed down and enjoy a lovely, long session of increasingly slow, but also increasingly intense, orgasms. After about half an hour, I'm fully relaxed, sexually replete, and happy. I guess it's time now to go and wash my vibrator. I hope you print my letter. Who needs men?

J. K. Twickenham, Middlesex.

Some do. Some don't. Whatever turns you on. Your letter certainly turned us on.

HAIR OF THE BITCH . . .

What is it about a great mass of female pubic hair that I find so attractive? I don't really understand it myself, but it is a fact that I find girls with big bushes the most sexy. You can keep your pictures of glistening open cunts, and gaping, fleshy labia, so long as you keep on printing the occasional shots of girls with thick growths of pubic hair. Linda, in your January issue, is just too much. Thanks for that tremendous picture of her, side view, squatting down, where you can see her long, thick mane of pubic hair hanging down between her legs. It's gorgeous. It completely hides any sign of her cunt or her arsehole. How I would love to nestle and snuggle my nose and mouth down there. And then there's that fabulous picture of her bending down, with her arse towards the camera, and her huge bush sprouting out of her anal cleavage. It's magic. I fantasize myself lying there and licking those beautiful cuntal tresses all day long. Your Linda is almost as beautifully endowed with her pubes as is my live-in girlfriend Diana. She is the most pubically hirsute woman I have ever come across (and I mean that literally). She loves me to lick and stroke and suck her locks before we fuck. Those of your readers who constantly extol the virtues of shaven pudenda are simply missing out.

F. A. Z. Oldham, Lancs.

We won't split hairs with you about your preference, but for our money, it's shaven lasses, by a hair's breadth.

NOT SO SOLITARY SEX

Many of your letter writers seem to manage eventually to achieve their fantasy ambitions. If one can believe them, of course. My own major fantasy is something that I have – so far – been totally unable to bring to fruition. It's quite a simple one, really: that of watching a woman masturbate, without her knowing that I am watching her. I've watched girlfriends masturbating, but always with their knowledge and agreement. Most of them seem happy to perform this erotic task on request, and for my pleasure. And highly erotic it is, too. But I have never managed to catch a girl wanking herself off, unaware of my presence as an observer. I would love to be able to look in on any girl's bedroom as she lies on her bed, playing with herself. I would like to see her slip her fingers inside her knickers, and begin by stroking herself slowly to wetness, at first just rubbing her outer labia, and then progressing to inserting one or two fingers up into herself. I'd love to see her fingers disappearing up in between her vaginal lips, and then delving deeper and deeper inside her pink cunt, nestling there in amongst her soft brown curly pubic hair.

I'd love to see the sticky, liquid wetness on her fingers as she withdrew them from her moist pussy and then sucked them clean, tasting herself, licking her own pussy juice off her fingers. And then I'd continue watching as she delved deeply inside herself once more and found her clitoris. Then, as she began to manipulate herself to orgasm, she would use her other hand to pull and tease at her nipples, tugging and twisting at them until they stood up erectly, tiny, stiff sentinels, standing guard on the peaks of her firm, pointed breasts.

She would start off wearing transparent pale pink nylon knickers and, at the beginning of her masturbatory session, she would start to rub herself through the thin material. As her wanking became more urgent, she would raise her pretty young bottom up off the bed and hurriedly pull her knickers down. Down around her buttocks, down past her shapely thighs – pulling in her spread knees as her knicks travelled down past them – and finally pulling her feet out of them and discarding the panties upon the floor. She wouldn't bother to take her matching bra off. She would simply pull it up, off her lovely breasts, to allow her fingers free access to her nipples. In my fantasy Peeping Tom capacity, I would be able to stretch out from my hiding place and pick her knickers up off the floor beside the bed. I would press the damp moistness of their sodden gusset against my nostrils and sniff the odour of her wet pussy. The inhalation of the scent of her vulva would instantly produce an excruciatingly stiff erection. And dreams being what they are, as soon as I had watched my lovely lady wanking herself to an all-embracing, highly vocal, shuddering climax, she would look up and – for the first time – see me. She would immediately catch sight of my hard-on, and she would get up and (not questioning my presence there) smiling at me the while, she would slowly and gently – but expertly – masturbate me to *my* climax, finally allowing my sperm to jet in warm, globular spurts onto her soft, quivering breasts as I came.

P. S. K. Blackpool, Lancs.

Wanks for the memory, as the old joke goes . . .

RAKES AND LADDERS

It is only recently that I have realized that I am a stocking fetishist. For a long time, looking at the many magnificent girls in your mag, I believed that I was looking at their crotches. Their tits. Their cunts. Their sexual paraphernalia. You know what I mean. But with your current issue, with those wonderful pictures of Madelene, I realize that what is *really* turning me on is that amazing pair of self-supporting black nylon hose that frames her pussy so elegantly. With her legs drawn up somewhere around her ears, I can see the seams of her stockings running all the way down the back of her beautiful long legs. And those exquisitely decorated lacy stocking tops – it all joins together to make the perfect frame for her pretty little snatch. Tell me, do your photographers sell off the used stockings after they have finished shooting a girl set? I can just imagine myself as the proud owner of numerous pairs of stockings, perhaps still warm from the gorgeous open thighs of the models themselves. Sheer black silk stockings. Pale brown, almost flesh-coloured stockings. White stockings, with extravagantly patterned stocking tops. Black mesh stockings. Soft blue nylon stockings, with slightly darker blue stocking tops. Black stockings with the tops rolled down tightly, looking like the rolled base of a condom. All of the above with, preferably, matching or contrasting suspender belts, and with long thin black elastic suspenders with silver attachments.

A. T. Newark, New Jersey.

David Jones

I'm told that the stockings and the lingerie we use in our photographic sets are normally a perk of the models themselves. What they do with them, I don't know. But we all know what you want in your stocking next Yuletide.

CHINESE CRACKERS

I've just come back from my first trip to the Far East. I've been to Hong Kong. I realize, naturally, that one can go a lot farther East then there, but by God! What a revelation, those Hong Kong Chinese girls. I could hardly tear myself away. Living in the country, as I do, I've never been to the Chinese areas of big cities such as Liverpool or London. But I shall certainly make sure that I do now. My life has been completely taken over by daydreams of those small, petite little bodies with their tiny, perfectly-shaped breasts and their slim waists and slender, taut little bottoms. I shacked up for four weeks (I was there on business) with a Chinese girl student, from Hong Kong University. I'd heard, of course, all those schoolboy jokes about Oriental girls' vaginas being horizontal, rather than vertical. But no one told me of their exquisitely soft, long, wispy black pubic hair! Having just spent four weeks running my fingers, my tongue, and my lips over – and down through – this delight, I can't wait to spend the rest of my life doing just that. My girl – Tsai – had beautiful long black tresses to match, and a flat, smooth stomach beneath those charmingly girlish breasts, and she had the longest, softest pubes I've ever seen! She wore black stockings, kept up by garters. (Something else I've never seen before. Not in everyday use, anyway!)

Her always instantly available snatch, nestling permanently wetly amidst that lovely mane of pubic hair, was long – about three inches, I would guess – which *is* long for a small girl – fleshily plump, and with outer labia that were almost black in colour (as were her tiny nipples). She was the deepest shade of pink inside. The lips of her mouth were full, and looked absolutely charming as they surrounded my engorged cock, something of which Tsai seemingly couldn't get enough. Whilst young, Tsai was also obviously sexually experienced. Far more than I, in fact. To my intense, enthusiastic, daily – and nightly – pleasure.

Tsai seemed completely relaxed about sex in a way that I have never come across in English girls, and obviously found sex as normal – and as necessary – as eating and drinking. Her skin was perfect. Her whole body was completely without blemish. Something which was pleasantly demonstrated when she introduced me to anal sex. The sight of her gorgeous, pale, creamy, perfect buttocks surrounding that tiny, almost black, fully dilated, puckered little rectum, was something that I shall always remember with consummate pleasure. All that, and I did some excellent business out there too.

P. S. Y. Llanarmon Dyffryn Ceiriog, Clywd.

Patently your Far Eastern trip was Far Out . . .

HAND TO MOUTH

May I take up a little of your space to disagree with most of the men who write to you about watching girls or women masturbate? I too find watching women jack off extremely stimulating, but I'm of quite the opposing opinion to those readers who say that their fantasies are all about watching women masturbate without the women knowing that they are being observed. My greatest pleasure is to have a woman masturbate in front of me, specifically for the mutual pleasure of watching and being watched. You may be surprised to know that there are many women who get enormous sexual pleasure from masturbating in front of a man.

I love it when a woman will agree to sit or lie down, pull up her skirt, pull down her panties, spread her legs, and finger herself to orgasm while I watch. I particularly enjoy it when the woman frigs busily away at her cunt whilst keeping full eye contact with me as she is doing it. Best of all is when the woman has a big, fleshy wet cunt that has produced enough liquid to make squishy noises as she wanks herself off. It is important to me, too, that the woman has a hairy cunt. There's something so much raunchier to watching a woman with a hairy great cunt tossing herself off than there is looking at someone playing with one of those prissy, tidy, shaven little holes that seem to me to be completely devoid of all sexual character. And the ultimate pleasure, of course, is to pull out my cock and masturbate in front of the woman who is masturbating in front of me. Having both got our rocks off in this delightful way, we can then get

David Jones

down to first some oral sex, and then to some serious fucking!

W. G. Portsmouth, Hants.

I think it's called keeping your hand in.

WHITER THAN WHITE

May I thank you for recently proving something to my friends? I have always known, ever since I've been old enough to get laid, that the most erotic lingerie is not the overly popular black of so many readers' fantasies, but is sheer, unadulterated white. Deanna, the girl on page 23 of your September issue is the ultimate proof of my theory. First of all, of course, Deanna is herself a very pretty girl. She would look good in anything, let's face it. She has a lovely face, an eminently kissable mouth, gorgeous blue eyes, and great tits with delicate areolae and perfect nipples. Add to all that a wonderful body with a fantastic arse, a lovely, blonde, hairy little pussy with neat pink lips, and what have you got? Perfection. I agree. But the white lingerie that she is almost wearing adds about another one hundred per cent plain, straightforward, sexual attraction.

That tiny white completely transparent brassiere, with one side just falling off a perfect breast, is so much more enticing than simple nudity. Isn't it? That minuscule white suspender belt, with its long, narrow, elastic suspenders running down Deanna's thighs, are enough to give the Pope a hard-on. Just look at them! And then those fabulous plain white tiny knickers, with their lace edging, showing everything that Deanna has got down there. I'm lost for words. They just make you want to tear them off and fuck her. Or suck her. Or both! Her pale pink pussy lips are exquisitely accented by the whiteness of her stocking tops framing her spread thighs, while her transparent white knickers, now pulled aside to allow her busy fingers access to her wet pussy, are an immaculate snowy hymn to sexual titillation. You can have my share of girls in sexy black lingerie any day. Give me the lovely Deanna, in her anything-but-virginal, pure white get-up. Now! Please!

P. R. Hounslow, Middlesex.

You're obviously pale with excitement. But we hear what you say. We must admit, as far as coloured lingerie is concerned, to being fans of the Henry Ford persuasion.

PUSSIES GALORE

As I'm only eighteen, you'll appreciate that I am not as sexually experienced as all that, although I'm not in any way complaining. I've got most of my sexual experience ahead of me! But I'm writing to tell you that I'm already fascinated by the different kinds of pussy that there are out there, even within my limited experience. There seems to be an infinite variety. It would be intriguing if you were to get a row of girls, all chosen for their original pussy shapes, and photographed them in a row, with their legs apart, so that we readers could see some of the many variations. There are girls with every shape of labia, from tight, neat, almost non-existent lips, through small, tidy lips, to larger lips, fleshier lips, fatter lips. There are longer thin lips, and shorter fat lips, and medium long/medium size lips. Pubic hair comes not only in colours ranging from pale dyed blonde through darker natural blonde to light brown, medium brown, and dark brown, to black, to blue-black, but there is also a tremendous range of auburn pubic hair, from carroty ginger to dark, almost claret-coloured red hair. The hair itself comes straight, curled, wispy, thick, grossly thick – and shaved. It's heavy, it's sparse. I haven't really got any special preferences as to pussy size or shape as yet. I love them all. Not to mention that smaller hole, situated lower down, but only a few inches away. But that's another story. One thing at a time!

S. K. R. Croydon, Surrey.

We wish you well with your first hole in one.

SMACK ON TARGET

I've fantasized for years about being caned, but I've never dared to tell any man in my life about this fantasy, in case he might insist that I try to turn my fantasy into reality. May I confess all in your pages? I'm twenty-four and 32-22-34, which will tell you that I have a nicely rounded arse. I love to flaunt it at men, in tight, short skirts, hot pants, swimsuits – anything that will let them see the shape of my buttocks against my deliberately, provocatively tight clothes. I love men feeling me up back there. Squeezing my buttocks, and fingering my anal cleavage. And my anus. And, yes, I *do* take it up my arse. That's a reality. And the final reward. But first – strictly in my fantasies – I like to be caned, or spanked. I like to be roughly handled.

I imagine being tricked into visiting an ex-boyfriend's house where I am overpowered by mystery masked assailants. I am tied, roughly – my legs spread-eagled – to some kind of frame. My back is to my audience. I am in a large room. I can see a neglected garden through a window at the far end of the room. There is virtually no furniture, and I am bound tightly with cord to a timbered cross-frame, set against the wall. I can hear three men behind me, talking in low voices, but I can't see them.

The next thing that I know, rough hands are stripping off my clothes. My jacket is torn off my back, followed by my skirt. Then my knickers are torn off. Fingers feel between my legs. They are calloused, hard working fingers. They feel me, intimately but surprisingly gently. And then I hear a sudden *swish*, the noise of someone trying out a cane for size, through the air. The fingers are still between my legs. 'Yer wet, yer dirty cow,' says a flat East London accent. 'Yer cunt's all wet. Ready for a fuck, ar' yer?' He takes his hand away. I don't reply, and then I hear the *swish* again, but this time a stinging pain cracks across my buttocks as the cane lands upon me. I wince at the agony of it, and draw in a deep breath, quite involuntarily. 'Jesus,' I say, through teeth clenched with pain. Whoever is caning me takes no notice, and the thin switch stings my flesh, again and again. Soon, I can feel a harsh glow as my bum skin reddens. To my surprise, I can also feel a copious lubrication erupting from my pussy. The caning is non-stop. Relentless.

I begin to sob, and I hear someone step nearer to me. Then, a moment later, something is thrust into my mouth from behind, effectively putting an end to my making a sound of any kind, unless I want to risk choking. I realise, after a moment, that it is my bunched-up knickers that have been pushed brutally into my mouth. I can taste myself – my intimate juices – upon them. I suffer the continuing thrashing with nothing more than the occasional groan, and I wonder about the damage that is being done to the skin of my behind. I am still exuding pussy juice. Suddenly the caning stops. I hear the cane being dropped on the floor, and then I hear the small – but quite unmistakable – sounds of a belt buckle being undone and a zip pulled down. I brace myself for what I know is coming.

I am right about that which I am anticipating, for seconds later hands grip my shoulders and a huge rock-hard tool is thrust up my cunt from behind. The rapist fucks me, without thought for me. But what rapist cares about his victim? I smell his bad breath, and feel it upon my neck. He grunts as he thrusts, and in no time he is spurting into me. I come with him. Violently. But I try not to let him know that. On reflection,

I doubt that he ever *would* know. He pulls out of me seconds later, says, sarcastically, 'Thank you, darlin'' and another man takes his place. This one is altogether gentler. His breath doesn't smell. His tool is huge, but he slips it up me as would a lover rather than a rapist, and he fucks me gently, almost lovingly. The contrast with the previous lout is so great that, after a while, I begin to respond to his thrusts, clenching my cunt muscles, pushing back against him as far as I can which, because of my bonds, isn't very far. When he comes, I come with him too, and I wriggle my sore arse as he squirts his load up me. His come feels hot as it hits the neck of my womb. I wonder why this man, who has at least some of the attributes of a man who knows what love is, needs to rape. Perhaps it's as simple as just liking the excitement. Perhaps the brutality of it turns him on. Suddenly he's finished ejaculating up me, and he pulls out.

His place is taken by what I hope is the last of the three men who have tethered me. He puts one hand on my shoulder and starts rubbing something greasy up my bottom with the other. *Oh, Christ*, I think. Rape is bad enough. Now it's going to be anal rape. I can smell alcohol on this man's breath. He's breathing hard, and his finger is invading my most private of places. Very few men have done what this stranger is doing to me forcibly. The others have been there by invitation only. 'Do you like it up your arse?' a voice says, thick with lust. It's not the flat accent of earlier in the day. It's difficult to place. More South than East London, I would guess.

I don't reply. I can't. 'Well, like it or not, up your arse is where you're going to get it, darling,' he says. ''Ere it is, then,' he says next, and I feel a sharp stab of acute, horrendous pain as he thrusts an enormous, ramrod-stiff dick deep into my anus. Thank God for the grease that he's rubbed into me, but the pain is still awful. 'Oh, she's lovely and tight. Really tight, Harry,' he says to one of this companions. *Terrific*, I think. He's fucking me like a rutting animal, thrusting savagely up me. I can feel my rectum dilating, stretching to accommodate this abhorrent, agonizing invasion.

I try to relax my rectal passage, attempting to accommodate him, as if he were a lover I was welcoming up my bottom. This is simply to try to lessen the pain, but it doesn't work. I can't relax while I'm being anally raped. He's breathing hard now, in my right ear. 'I'd rather have it in your mouth, you dirty cunt,' he says. 'But seeing as this is the way you're tied, and you're offering me your arsehole, that's what I'm taking. I love it. There's nothing like a bit of enforced buggery, is there? I bet you're loving every moment of it, you dirty whore.'

He reaches around me with both hands, takes hold of my breasts and squeezes them, brutally hard. If I had any way of being able to do it, right now I would kill him. I'm seeing red. Literally. Blood red. I try to calm myself. All I'm going to do, getting angry like this, is choke myself to death with my knickers. I can feel that my tormentor is approaching ejaculation. His cock is throbbing as he thrusts it up me. I tense myself, anticipating the final act of this, the most insulting of all sexual assaults. He comes with a rush, his filthy semen jetting into me. The final bloody insult, I think. He groans as he pumps into me, and then it's over. He pulls out. 'Very nice, darling,' he says. 'Very nice indeed. Thank you. We must do it again some time.' He laughs to himself. He reaches around me, puts a stinking finger and thumb between my lips, and pulls my knickers out of my mouth. 'I may as well use these to wipe my cock clean with,' he says. I don't reply to that either. Although I am now physically able so to do, I'm in too much pain. All I want is to be untied and set free. I'm terrified that they might start on me all over again.

Well, there you go. I can end my caning and bottom-fixation

sexual fantasies in a variety of different ways. All of which make me as horny as hell. And all of them accompanied by, at worst, my fingers. At best, my vibrator. Do you think I'm wise to keep these fantasies as fantasies? Or should I try to act them out, turn them into realities, with a sympathetic boyfriend?

K.O'D. Kilburn, London.

You seem to have got pretty much to the bottom of the problem. But the fact of the matter is, you're *the only person who can answer those two questions satisfactorily. Sorry.*

VALUE FOR MONEY

Do you remember the old song which starts, 'She was poor, but she was honest...' and which includes the chorus, 'It's the rich wot gets the pleasure, and the poor wot gets the blame. It's the same the whole world over. Ain't it all a bleedin' shame?' It has always seemed to me that the rich don't get half as much pleasure as they could do, if they really tried. But maybe I do them an injustice. Because I know exactly what I would do if I were seriously rich. And I have never – ever – come across a reference anywhere, in books, magazines, on television, or even in a movie, where there is any kind of mention of them doing what I would do. Which is simply fill the place with women. Every imaginable kind of woman. Blondes. Redheads. Black-haired women. Women with brown hair. Long hair. Short hair. Bald women. Fat women. Thin women. In-between women.

Tall ones. Short ones. Women with huge breasts. Women with tiny breasts. The same with bottoms. Huge, fat bottoms. Lovely slim, tight bottoms. Hairy bottoms. Shaven bottoms. Shaven quims. Hairy quims. Legs. Long legs. Short legs. But always open legs, when wanted. And I'd fuck myself silly. Morning, noon, and night. Some would be elegantly, fully dressed. Others would be completely naked. Some wearing the most expensive, sexy underwear that money can buy. They would all be there voluntarily, and they would all be well paid. No one would need to stay, if they didn't like it. They would all be ready to do anything that I wanted. At any time. If I pointed at one, and said, 'Come over here, darling, and suck my cock', that is exactly what darling would do. If I fancied sticking my hand up the skirt of a beautiful girl who was passing, and having a good feel, that's what I would do. And she would smile at me, and wait for me to finish what I was doing. If I then said, 'Get your knickers off', she would get her knickers off. What fun!

If I called over three of them at a time and said, 'Take it in turns to toss me off', then they would take it in turns to toss me off. All it would cost would be money. But I've never heard of anyone doing it. Can any of your male readers think of a better fantasy? Or, assuming winning the National Lottery, a better reality? But there must be dozens of men out there rich enough to afford to put my fantasy into practice right now. Why aren't they doing it? They must be out of their tiny minds.

P. H. T. Dungarvan, Waterford, Republic of Ireland.

It's almost impossible to disagree with anything that you say. We wish you good luck with the Lottery.

THE PLAIN TRUTH

I have always been fascinated by the letters in your correspondence columns. Particularly those concerned with what I would call fetishes. Men who infer that they can't get it up unless their beloved (or the immediate object of their desires) is wearing (a) black silk knickers, (b) rubber knickers or (c) crotchless knickers. This because I have always found the completely naked female body far more attractive, far more sexually tantalizing, than when adorned with whatever item of lingerie it is that turns others on. If I have a fetish at all – and I would be unusual if I did not, would I not? – it is that I am enormously aroused by a sweating naked woman's body. For this reason (and this reason only) I have had a sauna built into my flat here in Rotherhithe. Thus, under the pretence of enjoying the health-giving properties of saunas, I am able to indulge my own particular fetish. I have yet to meet a woman who can be persuaded into bed who would not, first, be persuaded into a sauna. There I lie back sweatily myself as I watch my loved one's body becoming hot and wet. Her nipples will become erect as the sweat breaks out upon her full bosom. Her pubic hair will become full of drops of her bodily secretions, like moss after a spring shower of rain. The petals of her vaginal flower will slowly open as her cunt begins to sweat, along with the rest of her, and I will inevitably get an erection – albeit entirely involuntarily – as I feast my eyes upon these delightful happenings. Seeing my erection will usually bring my fetish to a happy conclusion, for the woman will normally reach out and take it in her hand, leading to a sexual act which is often of my choosing. Perhaps oral. Maybe vaginal. Even, on occasions, anal. But whatever the sexual act, the major enjoyment for me, at this stage, is to conjoin in whatever way with a body that is wet all over with perspiration. And then, after the sauna and the sex, we will have a shower and depart off to bed, to further consummate our sexual relationship in rather more usual ways.

H. D. O. Rotherhithe, Kent.

That got us all quite hot under the collar.

LESBIAN CURIOSITY

As a 'normal' heterosexual woman, may I be allowed to tell you of my wildest, deepest fantasies? Are you sitting comfortably? Then I'll begin. I love to fuck. I enjoy it, and I enjoy giving and receiving sexual pleasure in any way that my man of the moment likes it. I have no hang-ups (that I'm aware of) and there is nothing that I won't do for you, if I love you. Or even if I only think that I love you. I'll happily suck your cock all day and all night, if that's what you want. And you can come in my mouth. Or I'll deep-throat you properly, if you feel like that. Not too many girls can, you know? I'll wank you like you've never been wanked before, if that's really what you fancy. I'll wank myself off in front of you too, very slowly, while you watch me, if that turns you on. You can fuck me in any position that you can think of, and when you've run out of ideas, I'll show you one or two positions that you probably haven't come across before. And yes, of course you can bugger me, if you're into anal sex. I love it up my arse. All of which *should* tell you that there isn't too much about male/female sex that I'm not rather more than familiar with. So what, then, do you think my biggest fantasy is? Shall I tell you? I spend many a night playing with myself until I fall asleep, just thinking about it.

I want to be made love to by a woman. Women. Girls. Lots of them. I want slim, feminine fingers playing with my pussy. I want a head with long, blonde tresses sunk between my open thighs, with a female tongue and lips playing beautiful music upon my wet cunt. I want to be frigged by a young girl. Sucked off by a mature woman. I want to *soixante-neuf* with another female sex, instead of with a cock. I want to slip my hand up beneath skirts, pull down pretty panties, slip my fingers into eager, waiting, wet little pussies. I want to be kissed by soft feminine lips, to taste tongues that are as agile and as gentle as mine is. I want a really pretty girl to use her vibrator on me, until I'm screaming for her to finish me off with her mouth.

It doesn't seem a lot to ask. I've been to any number of lesbian clubs, to suss out the situation, and I've had them queuing up to get my knickers down. But somehow, so far, I've always resisted. And then, when I get home, I cry myself to sleep again from sheer frustration at not having had the nerve to ask any of them back with me, and let them do their worst (best?). It's not that it's just a one-way thing, either. I want to do all those lovely, dirty things to them too. I don't just want to lean back and enjoy it. I want to give as good as I get. But when the opportunity presents itself, or whenever I've engineered myself into a situation where my fantasy is about to be turned into reality, I back off. Can anyone explain to me why I do that?

B. S. Bristol, Avon.

Beats us. But if you'd rather keep it all as a fantasy, there's nothing wrong with that either.

GOOD VIBRATIONS

Let me ask your readers a question. How would they feel if they had been pursuing a new girlfriend for three weeks, had finally got her into bed, and then, the second time that she lay back with her legs spread, and they were just about to gain entry for their once more rigid penis, the girl said, 'Hang on a moment, darling. If you feel under the mattress at the side of the bed, just about here' (pointing) 'you'll find a vibrator.' Taken more by surprise than by anything else, you feel down there, underneath the mattress, exactly where she had indicated, and you find the said vibrator. When you pull it out, it's off-white, slightly sticky, and *very* BIG. 'That's the one, darling,' she says. 'Now, how would you like to vibrate me, before you fuck me?' What exactly are you supposed to think? Is she telling you that you're a lousy fuck? First indications are that yes, she is. You look at the vibrator again. It's about twice the size of any cock you ever saw in the changing room at the rugger club. You're no expert on cock size (unlike most girls) but you've never had any complaints before. Quite the reverse, in fact. You've been told, on occasions, that your cock is 'a lovely big one, darling.' But it pales into insignificance, in terms of size, beside this intimidating plastic sexual weapon. Or do you simply take the view that this is a lady who likes to get her rocks off, and prefers a vibrator to plain fingers when she's on her own? If that's so, then why does she need it now, when the real thing is ready, willing, and totally available? On the occasion to which I refer, I simply took the course of least resistance and did as I was asked.

I must admit that I found it sexually extremely stimulating. The actuality of leaning over this woman's – up until this moment – largely unexplored vagina, prying it open with my fingers, finding the lady's clitoris, and then finally switching on the dreaded machine and stroking her to almost instant orgasm, got me harder than I ever remember being. Her vocal, highly sexual accompaniment to my shagging her with the vibrator was also highly enjoyable (I love women who talk dirty) whilst the physical result of my efforts was to produce a soaking wet cunt that fucked like a dream when I finally got around to it. Maybe I've answered my own question by relating this experience to you?

Since the first occasion, I have become accustomed to using the vibrator on my new girlfriend in this manner, before fucking her myself. It certainly gets her in the mood, and I have recently added a variation of my own which, whilst she was initially slightly resistant to my innovation, she now tells me that she thoroughly enjoys. It is simply that, having first 'vibrated' her to orgasm in the normal way, I then turn her over onto her stomach, and pull her up into a kneeling position. This is so that I can fuck her doggy fashion. Whilst I am fucking away, I slowly insert the vibrator up into her bottom (which, naturally enough, I have greased well beforehand). I love to watch the diameter of the vibrator dilating her secret entrance, and then disappearing up into her anus. When the plastic cock has all but disappeared, I switch it on, having previously set it at the right speed. The right speed, for this girl, is as fast as it will go. The vibrations quickly bring the two of us to the finest mutual climax that you can possibly imagine. Maybe these vibrators aren't quite so intimidating as I originally thought!

J. F., Wellingborough, Northants.

She sounds as if she likes it shaken, not stirred!

MOUTHWATERING

All my sexual fantasies are about oral sex. I dream that I have been commissioned by your magazine to investigate the world's best brothels, and I am currently in the Far East – Bangkok, in fact – looking for the finest blow-job that money can buy. I am sitting in a comfortably furnished room. I have a long, cool, iced drink in my hand. A fan is turning slowly in the ceiling. Through the open window, the usually strident noises of the street seem pleasantly far away. I look down at the long, soft, shining black hair on the head of the girl that is bobbing up and down between my knees. She looks fifteen, but the madame swears that she is eighteen. She is very beautiful. Who am I to argue? 'Does she suck cock?' I asked, as I ordered my drink. 'Like angel,' says the madame. 'Best blow-job in all Thailand.' 'How much?' I ask. 'You fuck her after?' she asks. 'She almost virgin. Maybe anal sex? She like it up small arsehole. Very tight.' 'We'll see,' I say, putting my hand in my pocket, and trying to hold my rampantly erect prick down. We haggle for a while, and finally the woman agrees an amount of *bhats*, the local currency, which totals approximately fifty pence in English money. As a *farang* – a foreigner – I am probably getting ripped off. Who cares? It's all legitimately on my expenses. And it's tax deductible, too.

I don't know whether anyone else would call what I am getting the best blow-job in all Thailand, but it is most certainly extremely expert. The girl is really working hard at it. She began by taking my cock in her small, long-fingered, shapely little hand, and pulling down my foreskin. After a couple of semi-wanking style movements – ensuring, I think, my full erection – she examined my swollen prepuce expertly, and then she slowly licked it, all over. She next looked up at me and, maintaining her eye contact, she took it slowly, deeply, into her mouth. Her mouth feels warm, and her tongue is soft. She uses it to stroke and lick my length, lovingly, carefully. And then she starts to suck me. The trouble with my fantasies about oral sex is that I am never given a bad blow-job. All these little Thai girls are experts. They suck cock like Scots girls used to bone herrings. Cleanly, quickly, and expertly. Although I must admit that this girl is in no hurry. I wonder idly what percentage of the fifty pence is hers, and whether it is more, or less, than half.

She is producing exquisite sensations in my prick, and I can feel my ejaculation gathering. I consider marrying her, and taking her back to Maida Vale, which is where I live. She could suck my cock all day, every day. With time off, of course, to explore her pretty little cunt, covered as it is with long, soft pubic hair. And not forgetting her nether entrance, enthusiastically described by the brothel keeper as 'very tight'. Right then my orgasm peaks, and I begin to ejaculate into the girl's mouth. I reach down and hold her head in my hands, as I pump my spunk between her full, sexy lips. I fuck her mouth for the time it takes me to ejaculate. She looks up at me as she swallows and sucks, in a long, sensual, continuous motion until, finally, my spasms fade slowly away, and I pull out of her wet mouth. She smiles at me, and some of my come dribbles out of the corner of her mouth. She puts up a finger, pushes it back between her lips and then swallows again. She grins at me. 'You like?' she asks. 'Feel good? Tina suck well?' I didn't know her name was Tina. 'Yes, darling,' I say. 'I like. Tina suck very well. Very well indeed. Thank you.'

She gets up off her knees and stands in front of me. She is completely naked. I love her on her knees. I like the natural subservience of Oriental girls. They are bred to perform sexual acts. They are born to it. And they love doing it. She will probably suck off her boyfriend at lunch time. My cock is getting erect again as I look at her. She can't be more than five foot tall, at the very most. Her small breasts are exquisitely shaped, with almost black nipples and areolae. She reaches out and takes hold of my cock.

'What you like now?' she asks. 'I do anything you like. You fuck me. Bugger me. You spank me. I spank you. Toss you off. I get other girl, we suck each other, then you fuck both of us. What you like? You tell me? You like something very special? All you need do is tell me?' I was literally speechless at the list of acts offered. What on earth could be 'special' after that menu? Tina looked downcast. Patently she felt that somehow she was failing in her duties.

She let go of my now rigid cock and, putting both her hands down between her legs, she took her minuscule outer labia in her fingers and pulled them apart, revealing for me a shiny, wet, bright pink, tiny little cunt beneath those almost black lips. 'Nice cunt,' she said. 'Look. Very tight. Feel with finger.' I put out a hand and she took it, guiding my extended forefinger deeply into her pussy. It really was tight, and very wet, and she began to fuck my finger as it slid into her, right up to the knuckle. Her vaginal muscles were doing things to my finger that I wouldn't have believed that a woman could do with her cunt. I almost came as I sat there, my finger up this delightful girl's vagina. She smiled at me. 'Feel good?' she asked. 'Feel much better on cock.' She suddenly looked at me, and pulled my finger out of her pussy. Then she put my finger in her mouth, and sucked it clean. She smiled at me. 'Don't want finger to smell of pussy,' she said. *You speak for yourself*, I thought. Frankly, I would rather have sucked it myself.

As I was contemplating the varied sexual delights on offer, Tina turned around and, with her back to me, she spread her legs, bent down and putting her hands behind her onto the cheeks of her buttocks, she pulled them apart, revealing the 'very tight' arsehole discussed earlier. I could see her peering up at me between her legs. 'Very tight,' she said. 'Feel with finger. Tight. Like Tina's cunt.' I reached out a tentative finger, and thrust into her tightly closed anal sphincter with it. 'Push in,' she commanded. 'You not feel properly unless you push right in.' I did as I was told, and then, wonder of wonders, she started to massage my finger with her rectal muscles. In exactly the same way as her vaginal muscles had done only a few minutes earlier. That decided me. 'How much for up your arse?' I asked. 'Nothing extra,' said Tina. 'All paid for up front. Tina yours all day. All night. No extras. Just tip at end, if you happy.'

She was telling me that the approximately fifty pence that I had handed her mistress earlier had bought her for twenty-four hours. To do anything I wanted. 'Arsehole it is, then, darling,' I told her. Tina went over to the bed that was up against the far wall and turned it down. She then went to a cupboard and brought back a small round wooden box, of the kind old-fashioned apothecaries used to use in Britain before World War II. 'You like to grease Tina's arsehole?' she asked. 'Most men like.' She took the lid off the box and held it out to me. I looked at it. It contained some pale, yellow-coloured kind of unguent. It looked a bit like axle grease. I sniffed it. It smelt faintly herbal. Quite pleasant, in fact. Tina got up onto the bed and, kneeling, looked over her shoulder at me.

I looked at her perfectly formed plump little buttocks, now some six or eight inches away from my face, and at the long black hair covering her anal cleft and surrounding her puckered little anal rosebud. I leant forward and kissed it. Dead centre. It tasted of slightly over-ripe mango, and smelt quite strongly of rotting, exotic fruit. I felt it dilate beneath my lips, and I stuck my tongue down deeply into its centre. This time, it tasted like some unfamiliar, slightly alien truffle. Earthy almost. My cock almost exploded. It was so stiff that it hurt. 'Hmmmm,' said Tina. 'I think you bugger many girls. You like to fuck arseholes. Yes?' 'Yes, sweetheart,' I said. 'Emphatically, yes. I adore them. Especially tiny ones, like yours.' 'What you mean, em . . . emfat . . . what you said?' she asked. 'You like little boys too?' I sighed.

'No, darling,' I said. 'Girls yes. All orifices. Anywhere. All the time. Boys, no. At any time.' She looked at me again, over her shoulder. 'Englishmen strange,' she said. 'Don't worry about it,' I told her. 'It's just the habit of a lifetime. I'm too old to change now.'

I began to anoint her anus with the grease that she had supplied, and I enjoyed the sexually exciting sensations of pushing my finger in and out of her bottom, knowing that almost any minute now I would be doing exactly that with my cock. She gripped my finger as it entered her, and as I drew it out, she held it so tightly with her rectal muscles that it made a long, slow sucking noise. Tina laughed. 'Rude,' she said. 'Very rude noise.' I had to laugh, too. Here I was, greasing her arsehole, immediately prior to buggering her, and she was seemingly embarrassed by a slow fart. Oh, well. It takes all sorts. After I had rubbed as much of the lubricant in and around her anus as possible, I carefully rubbed my John Thomas all over with it, after which I wiped my greasy hands on my handkerchief, climbed up onto the bed immediately behind Tina, grabbed her by her waist, and thrust myself into her. I watched as my cock distended her sphincter as it entered her, and as soon as she felt it inside her, she began working her rectal muscles energetically. It was sensational. I considered marrying her. Well, think about it.

I'd not fucked that many girls up the arse, despite my boastful conversation with Tina. English girls (other, I'm told, than those from aristocratic families, whose male line go to Eton, Harrow, Winchester, Belmont, and the like) tend not to be greatly enthusiastic about anal sex. I've never fucked a woman with a title, so I can't tell you if the rumour that they are expected to submit, once married, to what their husbands get a taste for whilst at boarding school is true or not. It's a lovely thought. A topic for dinner conversation. 'Do you take it up the arse, ma'am?' Much better than 'Did you see so and so on the box last night?' I'm having the best anal fuck that I've ever had in my life. It is thrilling. Truly, voluptuously, breathtakingly sensational. But I'm not going to last more than a few seconds.

Never mind. We can do it again. And then again. I look closely at my swollen cock as it travels lustfully in and out of that dear hole. The unguent is creating a small, glutinous ridge around her anus, as its tightness strips it off my cock. I can smell the sharp scent of her rectal odour acridly upon my nostrils as I lean over her buttocks, the better to bury my prick as deeply as possible into her. I treasure the sight of her dark brown buttocks, her blue-black rectal flesh, her black anal hair, and I pull her towards me, trying to get even further up her, as I suddenly explode into her, spurting my semen like a demented rapist up her rectal passage. I shout out, 'I'm coming. I'm coming. I'm coming up your arsehole. I'm coming as I bugger you.' She manages a moan, reaches around behind her, and energetically wanks my tool into her, as I spend my jism in hot, spasmodic jets. And then, suddenly, it is all over. I decide that I'm going to stop trying to find the East's finest blow-job for you, and start looking for the best anal sex available. You don't want to commission me to undertake that particular search? Then the hell with you. I'll do it for myself. Freelance.

A. H. Maida Vale, London.

Do you have to be such a pain in the backside?

TONGUE-TIED

I love my new boyfriend, and we have terrific sex, but recently he has started to insist on tying me up during our sexual encounters. He doesn't want to beat, or cane, or whip me, thank goodness. He says that he just loves to fuck me while I'm tied up. Or down, as the case may be. He's obviously into submissive sex. He strips me down to my knickers, and then he spreadeagles me on the bed and ties my wrists and ankles to the four corners of it. He'll suck my breasts for what seems like hours, until my nipples are sore. And then he loves to suck my pussy through my knickers, before he finally tears them off. (If you think about it, that's the only way that they can come off, with my legs tied to the bed.) Then he'll suck me some more, before he finally fucks me. I don't mind all that pussy-lapping. I get lots of lovely orgasms, and my previous boyfriend wouldn't suck me down there. He said he didn't like the taste of cunt. So it's still something of a treat. But after a while, not being able to touch him, or stroke him, or play with his cock – masturbate him, even – while he is sucking me is extremely frustrating. It's not that I want to control him. I just want to be able to react with him, sexually. Do you think I'm being silly? Should I just let him get on with it?

P. T. Ipswich, Norfolk.

Tell him what you're telling us. Sex is for both parties to agree about. If you're not entirely happy, tell him why not.

RUBBER SOUL

I've recently been experimenting with rubberwear, which I find sexually very stimulating. So far, I've acquired rubber stockings, which are black and which come halfway up my thighs, and long red elbow-length rubber gloves. I've tried rubber knickers, but they don't affect me in the same way as the gloves and stockings do, so now, when I've got the stockings on, held up by a sexy black satin suspender belt, and I'm wearing tiny black satin knickers, I'm ready for anything. The problem is that I don't dare tell my husband about this obsession with rubberwear. He's pretty straight as far as sex is concerned, and I think he would find my growing fetish bizarre, if not just plain perverted. This leaves me with my old and trusted friend, my vibrator, which services me whilst my husband is out at work. How can I get to meet like-minded people, or meet men who find women wearing rubber sexy? I'd love to wear it for someone who got as much of a kick out of it as I do, and who would enjoy fucking me while I have it on. Do any of your readers live in Norwich? If so, and they are into rubber, perhaps they would like to write to me? I'm thirty, blonde, blue-eyed, and I'm told I'm pretty.

S. K. Norwich, Norfolk.

You could look for discreetly-worded advertisements in the personal columns of your local newspaper, or check the personal ads in some of the more downmarket men's magazines.

David Jones

But why don't you start off by finding out if your husband gets turned on by rubber? All you have to do is ask him. You don't have to let him see you wearing it until you know it's the right answer. He might find it the most sexually exciting thing that's ever happened to him. We'll happily forward any mail.

SHARE AND SHARE ALIKE

My wife is bisexual, and always has been. It is something that I knew before we got married, and it has never been a problem since she shares her lesbian sex with me, in that I have always been welcome to watch her at play with her friends, provided that I don't interfere in any way. Up until now, I have always believed that our own sex has been stimulated, even improved, by this situation. It certainly adds spice to my life to watch another woman sucking my wife's cunt, and to watch my wife sucking another girl's cunt. I enjoy seeing them fuck each other with strap-on dildoes, and wank each other with vibrators or their fingers. I love it when they suck each other's nipples, and play with each other's pussies, and I have had many a happy wank watching my wife at sex-play with other women. Now, for the first time ever, we have a disagreement over one of these women. Put at its simplest, I want to fuck my wife's latest girlfriend. My wife says that she doesn't object in principle, but she refuses either to suggest it, or to let me suggest it, to this adorable girl. I think she is being unfair. What do you think?

A. B. Gosport, Hants.

I think you're moving the goalposts. If your original – and seemingly long-lasting – arrangement was that you didn't interfere in any way, I believe that you should stick with that. If you don't like the heat, stay out of the kitchen.

KEEPING ABREAST OF IT ALL

Fantasies are made of what the lovely Bernadette reveals in your December issue. Or they are for me! She's everything I have ever fantasized about since I was old enough to get a hard-on. She's got a mouth that was made for sucking cock. Just *look* at those lips . . . All I've got to do is shut my eyes, and I can feel those luscious, full, wet lips softly sucking around my throbbing cock. She must have been invented to illustrate the word 'cocksucker'. Her face is that of an angel's. A sexy, gorgeous, dirty-minded angel. It is surrounded, halo-like, by her beautiful, auburn hair. Then her breasts. Her perfect breasts, surmounted by those long, erect nipples, sitting there like tiny sentries, guarding her areolae, waiting for me to suck them. I can feel them hardening in my mouth, whilst I fuck my erect dick in between Bernadette's lovely cunt lips. Following the natural line of her body, downwards, we come to her exquisite thighs, spread wide just for me. Her white panties are pulled tightly over her hairy cunt. Happily, her panties are transparent enough for me to be able to see the lovely lips of her cunt, peeping wetly at me through the translucent material. It's translucent because it's wet. Wet with her cunt-juice, trickling, exuding freely from between her dark pink, fleshy cunt lips and staining the cotton crotch of her silky panties, shading the white a slightly darker, rather greyish off-white. Stray hairs from her thick pubic bush peep out at me from the sides of her lacy-edged silken gusset. I can smell the heady, matchless aroma of wet pussy, as I peer closely at her crotch. This girl is made to fuck. I fantasize about pulling those lovely white knickers down, revealing her plump pudenda, thatched thickly with her dark brown, three-inch-long pubic hair. I want to pull it, tease it, play with it, part it to show her outer labia. I want to pull her moist lips apart and lick her inner, secret places. I want to taste her, smell her. Sniff her.

In her next picture she has turned over and taken her knickers off. I leer at the plump cheeks of her ass. They expose a completely white-skinned bikini shape, apart from which her buttocks are deeply tanned, a dark, mahogany brown. I want to run my hand over those firm ass-cheeks, squeezing, feeling, playing. I want to run my tongue deeply down and into her anal crevice, tonguing her long anal hair, sucking her cleavage, smelling her intimate smells, licking her forbidden entrance, watching closely as it clenches against my would-be forced lingual entrance. My cock stirs and raises its head as I tongue her backside. I think about greasing her rectum with oil. Pungently scented, syrupy, viscous, glutinous, cock-sliding oil. My erection thrusts itself fully upwards. I want to fuck this delightful girl's pretty bottom. Dilate her arsehole with my huge, throbbing cock. Bugger her. Down, boy. There's no hurry.

I can't believe it. On the next page she's playing with herself. Oh, Bernadette, darling. Why wank, when I can fuck you? Why play with your pussy when I can ravish you, forever and a day? Why waste all that finger energy, when I can fuck you stupid, morning, noon and night, with my massive, eager cock? When I can make you cry, make you plead with me to stop? Make you beg for mercy? To think that you are actually *real*. That, whilst you're a fantasy to me, you're a reality to someone, somewhere. That someone actually fucks you. That you really do take someone's cock between your luscious lips. That you suck him off. Swallow his semen. Wank him, slowly, whilst he sucks your cunt. Jesus.

F. L. Harrisburg, Pennsylvania.

Are you practising your breast-stroke, F. L., along with all those other manual strokes?

WANKS FOR THE MEMORY

I was lucky enough, the other evening, to pick up a new girlfriend in a local pub. Well, actually, to be honest, she picked *me* up. Quite unwittingly, later on that evening, she fulfilled one of my earliest teenage fantasies. I'm only twenty now, and I don't mind admitting that my sexual experience is not all that amazing. But I keep trying. Like everyone says, my life is all before me. It can only get better. But I was going to tell you about Susie. I was sitting there up at the bar in my local, minding my own business, daydreaming about spare cunt, when this gorgeous blonde comes up to the bar, and orders herself a glass of cider. She looks at me and smiles. 'Do you live around here?' she asks me. It's not the most subtle of lines, but why should I give a shit? The lady wants to talk to me. Who am I to complain? Moments later, we're sitting at a table, well away from the bar (and the competition) and we're getting on like a house on fire. Later that evening, after a few more drinks, a lot more conversation, and a curry at the local Indian, we're back at my place, and she's stripping off before I've even said, 'Would you like a glass of red?' I can't believe my luck. She's really gorgeous. I keep humming 'If you knew Susie' to myself.

She's tall, (I'm six foot, and she's well over my shoulder), blonde, with what look like terrific tits beneath the tight sweater that I've been lusting over all evening. I live in a bedsitter, so there's not a lot of privacy. She's stripping off while I'm looking for a bottle of plonk that I know I've got stashed away somewhere, and then I'm trying to find the corkscrew. She drops her skirt, and pulls the sweater up over her shoulders, showing me that they really *are* fantastic tits, and that she neither needs, nor wears, a bra. Which leaves her in baby-pink panties (the kind with just a thin ribbon around her waist and a tiny triangle of transparent material over her pudenda), pale-beige self-supporting stockings, and a pair of beige, high-heeled patent leather shoes. Fuck-me shoes, I think they're called. I'm having trouble finding the corkscrew.

Frankly, I've got such a hard-on, I'm having trouble doing anything. And then she starts doing it. My teenage fantasy. She's lying on my bed, with just her knicks on. Like I said. And she's looking at me, and whilst she's looking at me, she slips a hand down inside her knickers, and she starts playing with herself. Or whatever girls call it. Frigging? 'Just keeping it warm for you, darling,' she says. 'And wet, of course.' I nearly come in my trousers. I mean, there's a beautiful girl – what would she be? – Nineteen? Twenty? At the most. She's lying, almost naked, on my bed, tossing herself off, and looking at me while she does it. I mean, you know. Christ. Her hand, down inside her knickers, is just a blur of movement. Right now, she isn't looking at me any more. She's let her head drop back upon the pillows and she's wanking herself silly. She's making little moaning noises, and she's obviously – even to my inexperienced eyes – about to come. Her legs are spread wide, and her arse is moving up and down on the bed, in what I can only describe as fucking movements. Like a fiddler's elbow, as they used to say. Suddenly she starts shouting. I pray that my fellow bedsitter neighbours have all got their televisions well turned up. 'Oh, Jesus,' she shouts. 'I'm coming. Oh, fuck. Oh, God. Oh yes. Ohhhhh.' She would have collapsed, all of a heap, were she not already collapsed all of a heap, as it were.

I don't say anything. Eventually, she opens her eyes. She

looks up at me and grins. 'There's nothing like a quick wank, if that's what you feel like, is there?' she asks me. I'm speechless. My hard-on is so hard on, it hurts. 'Don't just stand there,' she says. 'Why don't you come and fuck me? Don't you like girls?' I look down at her. Her legs are still wide apart and I reach down and pull her knickers slowly down her legs. She has to squeeze them together so that I can get them off. Once they're off, she opens them wide again.

'Do you like what you see?' she asks, seeing me looking at her wet cunt. It's a beautiful cunt. All open and pink and wet and hairy. I can smell it from where I'm standing. 'You seem to have a problem, darling,' she says. 'Sort of a stiff prick. I think I can help you make it feel better. Much better. Come over here.' I do as I'm told, and she takes hold of my rampant cock and pulls me towards her. She's lying on the bed, and I'm standing beside her, and she takes my cock deeply into her mouth. 'Mmmmm,' she says, not greatly intelligibly, bearing in mind that she's got her mouth full. Of my dick. I'm practically coming already, and it's only been a matter of seconds.

I look down at her splendidly, moistly open pussy. It's surrounded by lovely long blonde pubic hair, and her brownish pink outer lips are pouting loosely up at me, after her manual attentions to them of a few moments back. I can see the ribbed walls of her inner, paler pink, fleshy cunt. I can see it shining wetly up at me, and I want to touch it. So I do. I reach out and push one of my fingers into it. It closes around my finger like those pictures you see on telly of insect-eating plants. Her pussy goes *splat*, around my fingers, and begins to throb and pulsate around my enthralled digit. *Jesus*, I think. *The sooner I get my dick in there, the better.* Meanwhile she's doing unspeakable things to my cock, with her lips and tongue, and all I want to do is keep it there forever, and fuck her mouth, and come down her throat.

What a delightful sexual dilemma! To fuck, or not to fuck? To come in her mouth, or not? After seconds of indecision, she makes up my mind for me, because she puts her hand around my swollen shaft and starts to wank me into her mouth. At the same time I begin to frig her cunt with my finger, and mere seconds later, I'm spurting millions of frantic sperm into her mouth. She slurps, and swallows, and grins up at me around my swollen member. At one stage I've pumped so much of my involuntary stockpile of semen into her that it's dribbling out of the corner of her mouth and down her chin. 'Thank you for coming,' she says. It's an old joke, but, in the circumstances, a pleasant one. I remember my line. 'My pleasure, my darling,' I tell her. 'Thank you for having me.' She laughs, and pats the bed beside her.

I lie down with her, my arm about her shoulders, and she takes hold of my cock again, working it competently, and fairly rapidly, back to full erection. At which point she says, 'I think you're ready again, sweetheart. If you fancy a quick fuck – or even a slow fuck – I know someone not a million miles away from here who'd be happy to entertain you.' She lets go of my stiff tool and I climb on top of her. She spreads her legs wide, and uses her fingers to part her outer vaginal lips. I can see the pinky-brown of her puckered anus an inch or so below her now open pussy. I take my dick in my right hand, and, with the other, I feel how wet she is inside. There's no need for foreplay, or lubrication, or anything, other than a rampant prick. This I have to hand, so I insert it into her and thrust. It slips in like a well-oiled piston into a cylinder. 'Ooooh,' she says. 'That's nice. That feels really good. Now fuck me senseless. Please.' I look down at her again. The lips of her cunt have closed around my cock, and I can feel her muscles working at me.

I begin to move my hips, and I slip my hand underneath her buttocks and pull her up towards me. Her buttocks are firm and sexily plump and I squeeze them as I fuck her. 'Touch me,' she says, and for a moment I'm not sure what she means. 'Touch me,' she says again. 'You know. Down there.' And then I realize that, in holding her buttocks, the fingers of my right hand are only centimetres away from her tightly clenched anus. I move my fingers just the tiniest bit, and they are in her anal cleavage. I move my forefinger around, feeling her anal hair carefully until, quite quickly, I find that forbidden entrance. 'Yes,' she breathes, as I slide my finger into it. 'Oh, yes. Nice. Yes.' I finger-fuck her anally as I continue to fuck her normally, and then suddenly I'm shooting my load into her in the most exciting way. She comes with me. I can feel her orgasming as I shoot my sperm into her, and finally we both relax, our breathing heavy, our efforts leaving us both breathless. 'Wow,' she says. 'That was terrific. Nice. Really good. Thank you.' I say pretty things back to her. But at the back of my mind remains that magic, delightful picture of her with her fingers down inside her sexy pink panties, masturbating herself whilst I watched. It was a one-off for me. I shall always remember it, and I hope it's something that I shall see many times again. But often, the first time stays forever as the best.

P. F. Stoke-on-Trent, Staffs.

Well, you'll never be able to say that you don't give a toss any more, now will you?

LINGERIE TO LINGER OVER

I've always been into two things, from way back. Farther back than I care to remember. One, girls. Two, naughty knickers. The combination of the two together has kept me self-indulgently happy ever since. Add to that the fact that a woman only has to wear three things, actually, to get into my record book. Naughty knicks, as already mentioned. Almost any kind of stockings. And high-heeled patent leather 'fuck-me' shoes. My favourite fantasy begins with my selecting a woman from a long line of women. They are all naked, and they all want me to fuck them.

As I walk along the line, they do and say things which each one believes individually will cause me to choose them over and above any of the others. This may be anything from a shy, reserved smile – presumably indicating unknown pleasures in store – to vulgarly (and delightfully) obvious things like pulling their vulvas open, or bending down, their slim fingers opening up their plump buttocks to my eager sight. Some of them masturbate themselves, their fingers playing with their pussies frenetically, showing – I assume – their enthusiasm for fucking. Some of them talk dirty. This has always been a big turn-on for me. You've only got to get a woman to whisper in my ear, 'How would you like to play with my wet cunt?' or, 'Would you like me to toss you off while you suck my pussy?' and I'm theirs. Instantly.

So, walking along this line of immediately debauchable women, all of them, of course, with perfect bodies, I select a chosen few. I take some with shaven pussies, because I love the sight (and taste, and feel) of baldly available cunt lips. I take some with over-sized nipples, for I adore to suck big teats. I take some with hairy pussies, for the opposite of shaven turns me on just as much. The hairier the better. I take some with big, fat, fleshy, cunt lips, for I love to suck them, and then watch my cock disappear between them. I take some with tiny, prettily puckered anuses, for I love to watch my cock dilate them. I choose some Japanese girls for they are, to me, the most beautiful women in the whole wide world. And I take some simply because I like the idea of fucking them. And then the fun begins.

I let them loose in the world's most expensive lingerie shops, having given each one of them a blank cheque. Then they come home and change into their choice of sexy underwear, and when they're ready, I take them, one by one, and play with them. They are all wearing stockings of some kind. The stockings may be self-supporting, as with modern stockings, or they may be hooked to suspenders, or they might even be held up with garters. Tights are out. It's that magic expanse of thigh, that few inches of naked flesh between stocking-top and knicker-bottom, that is one of the sexiest sights in the world. The girls' feet will be shod in high-heeled, strappy sandals or court shoes, and all of the girls will wear knickers of some sort. Bikini knickers, camiknickers, teddys, G-strings. French knickers, navy blue schoolgirls' knickers, crotchless knickers, suspender knickers. You name it, they'll be wearing it! And in every imaginable colour and kind of material. Plain white cotton. Black satin. Silk in every shade of the rainbow. Rubber knickers. Nylon. Wool. Lace. Striped knickers. Patterned knickers. Flowered knickers. Totally transparent knickers.

Sometimes I'll peel them off myself. At other times, I get the girls to do a slow striptease for me. I love getting them to pose as if for your magazine, pulling the crotch of their knickers aside to expose their vulvas to me. I adore sucking pussy through silky knickers. It's all spelt F.E.T.I.S.H., with a capital F!

P. G. Basingstoke, Hants.

We're with you, P. G. Enjoy.

SPELLBOUND

I often have this terrific fantasy where I'm able to hypnotize women. Think about it! It means that I can fuck any woman that I want to. Let's say I'm in a restaurant, and I fancy the pretty young waitress who is serving me. I simply look her straight in the eyes and hypnotize her. Then I say to her, quietly, 'Go out the back to the men's room and go into the first cubicle on the left. Pull your knickers down, and wait for me.' Off she goes, in a trance. Two minutes later I follow her out, and there she is, her knickers down around her ankles. I have a quick feel, and she's a bit dry, so I say to her, 'Play with your pussy until it's nice and wet.' She reaches down an obedient hand and frigs herself until I can see the juices running out of her pussy, at which point I say, 'OK. You can stop that now, and I'll shag you.' So she opens her legs, and I stuff her silly, until I've spurted all my come into her. I get myself together and then I say to her, 'Pull your knickers back up, go into the ladies and tidy yourself up, and then come back to me at my table in the restaurant.' I leave her there, go back to my table, and a few minutes later, she follows me. I snap my fingers, she comes out of her trance, and I say, 'Just the bill, thank you.' And that's it. Great, isn't it? I do similar things with girls in big stores, and in supermarkets. I have even stopped girls in the street, hypnotized them, and taken them home for the night. They tend to look a little puzzled the following morning, when I take them back out onto the street where I picked them up, and unhypnotize them, but that's not my problem. I don't always fuck them, either. Sometimes, depending upon there being a suitable place to do it, I'll have them give me a blow job, or maybe just a quick wank, if I'm in a hurry and I simply feel like getting my rocks off. I don't even have to pretend that I love them.

Sometimes, of course, it's much more subtle than that. For example, I might meet a girl at a party and fancy her. Well, I can always try my luck, of course, like anyone else. But why should I risk a failure, when all I've got to do is look the girl straight in the eyes, put her into a trance, and say to her, 'When you come out of this trance, you'll want to fuck me more than you have ever wanted to fuck any man in your life before. You'll ask me to take you home, and you'll get me to fuck you all night long, for as long as I can and as often as I can. You'll perform every possible sexual act upon me. You'll suck my cock, masturbate me, have me fuck you up the arse. You'll do anything that I want you to, and you'll love every moment of it.'

Then I just snap my fingers, and she's all over me. She can't get me out of there and back to her place quickly enough. She practically rapes me in the taxi. So much so that the cab driver says, 'You've got a right little goer there, mate', when I pay him off. By the following morning, I can hardly walk, I'm so well fucked. She's done all the naughty, lovely things to me that I've told her to do, and she's pleaded with me to do the naughty things to her that I asked her to. And she's asked me back again for another session this evening. I'm not sure if I'm up to it. But I'll try!

E. H. L. Maidenhead, Berks.

It sounds entrancing.

BOTTOM LINE

I just adore the female ass on display in your magazine. It's seriously high quality. But where I guess a lot of your readers get off on thoughts of fucking those lovely ladies, I get my sexual highs imagining *spanking* them. If you've never tried it, you should. That moment when a girl first exposes her naked ass to you, by dropping her panties. Or maybe you're in luck, and she's let you peel her panties down her thighs yourself. Those wonderful, white, plump buttocks, with her anal hair curling away out of sight, down her anal cleft. The magic of her ass, framed by her skirt – pulled up, of course – her black stocking tops, and her panties, pulled saucily half way down her legs. You reach out and touch that smooth white flesh. It's cool and firm. You squeeze it, and pinch it. Maybe hurt her a little. Run a finger up her cunt, if that's what you want to do. Or up her ass, if – like me – you're into anal sex. But first the spanking. It's better if you can tie her down. That means she can't get up and run away in the middle of the proceedings. It also tells her who's boss. So, tie her down. Strap her wrists and ankles to something solid. I've got a whipping block in my basement. If you haven't got a block, use a broom handle to stretch her legs apart, with an ankle tied to each end, so that when you've spanked her enough to make her cry, you can fuck her whilst she's still tied down. In her mouth. Up her ass. Wherever you want. But the sound of the smack on her naked flesh as your bare hand comes down is the ultimate cock-hardener. You increase the frequency of strokes. And the momentum. I love it!

B. D. Denver, Colorado.

I hope your ladies like it too.

KEEPING YOUR HAND IN

May I suggest that those of your readers who so vociferously extol the virtues of traditional heterosexual sex – i.e. plain, old-fashioned fucking – are possibly ignoring what is for me one of the most exciting and stimulating of sexual activities possible between man and woman? I refer to mutual masturbation. If they have never experienced the joy of watching a woman slowly undress, knowing that she is going to sit or stand immediately in front of them, only inches away, and masturbate herself to orgasm, then they have truly missed out. First the blouse is slowly unbuttoned and allowed to hang half open, revealing firm, braless, naked breasts for just a moment. They are then allowed to disappear again. As the woman bends down and lifts her skirt, she exposes to your lascivious gaze the stocking tops that are covering her plump white thighs, themselves a darker brown than the nylon gauze of the stocking itself, attached to suspenders. She hoists her skirt even higher, and reaches to unclip the suspenders, and then lets her skirt fall back into place, as she rolls down first one, then the other stocking. The almost obscenely rolled nylon reminds you of an unfurled French letter, and your cock starts to harden. You wriggle on your seat, finding a more comfortable position. One that will allow you to adjust yourself, when necessary. It won't be long now. As she bends down to pull the stockings off her feet, her blouse gapes open wide, and you get your first real glimpse of her erect, dark brown nipples. Now she stands up, and discards the blouse altogether. Her areolae are large, and her erectile nipples are swollen with passion. You need your hand, this time, to adjust your own erection. Your lady unzips her skirt now, and bends down to step out of it, exposing her completely see-through white nylon knickers for the first time. You can see the dark brown of her pubic hair through the transparent material, and is that a . . . ? Yes. It is. You lean forward, and you can see a tear-drop of moisture that has just oozed from her aroused vulva, staining the crotch of her knickers, and as you lean forward, you inhale the aroma of her freshly awakened sex. She looks down at you, and smiles as she begins to peel off the knickers. You can feel your heartbeat increase as you watch her. Soon you will need to let your cock free of its restraint.

She rolls down the waistband of her knickers, knowing how this excites you, and you watch as the top of her pubic hair is exposed. It is dark brown, long, soft and straight. Wispy. As she pulls her knickers slowly down her thighs, you can see that the cotton lining of the crotch is adhering to her moist inner lips, and as she continues slowly to pull them further down, the crotch is pulled out of her quim, and she reveals the inner pinkness of her vagina, shining wetly at you. The scent of aroused woman is much stronger now. You run your tongue over your dry lips and watch intently as your woman pulls the white nylon knickers all the way down her long legs, and off, over her shapely ankles, and finally her feet. She doesn't drop them on the floor, as you anticipate, but she reaches out with them in her hand and presses them to your nostrils. You breathe in, and as you once more inhale that divine scent, and feel the dampness of the material against your nose, you hastily unzip your fly and pull your now fully erect cock out of its prison. She laughs with you as you stand up and struggle out of your clothes, and then you sit down again, now as naked as she is, your erection proudly at attention. She spreads her legs, the better to offer you the full, erotic intimacy of her actions, and thrusts two fingers slowly, and deeply, up herself. She draws them out, carefully, and holds them out to you. Her fingers glisten with the wetness of her sexuality. You reach out a hand, and pull her fingers up to your mouth and suck them, savouring the taste of her wetness. Her tangy, strong, female flavour and odour does things to your taste-buds and nose, and via those, to the rigidity of your cock.

Having sucked her fingers thoroughly, you release them. Next she teases you, first using the febrile fingers of both hands to pull her labia wide apart, showing you the depth of her pale-pink love slot, and then she begins, oh so slowly, to massage her outer lips. As her fingers move over her labia, now fat with desire, so do her hips begin to move, keeping erotic time with her sensual fingers, a masturbatory hymn to her femininity. Your hand picks up her rhythm, and you start to masturbate in time with her, sharing the sexual intimacy, the voluptuous carnality, of that which lesser beings only indulge in isolation.

Her expression is dreamy now. Her body language speaks of languorous sensuality, of lazy, pleasurable, sexual warmth. As you watch, her forefinger strays, almost as if by accident, into her vulva, until her expression tells you that she has found her clitoris. Her sexual parts are so wet now, with her lubricious emanations, that her fingers are making tiny squelching noises as she massages her swollen cunt-flesh. Her movements increase just slightly, and she is beginning to make small noises somewhere deep in her throat. Almost a purr. Her knees are now slightly bent, and she is patently nearing her first orgasm.

You are sufficiently familiar with her masturbatory habits to know that when it arrives, this first orgasm will be but the harbinger of further, numerous, and increasingly intense successors, until she builds up to a final, earth-shattering, body-racking crescendo, accompanied by heavy breathing, then screams, and then shouts, a mixture of expressions of love, oaths, dirty language and the strident taking of God's name in vain. There is no need to try and keep up with this progression, nor is there any urgency on your part, since your lady will continue to masturbate indefinitely, should that be your wish. She will also, once she has reached her first serious orgasm, masturbate you if you so wish, something that experience tells you is infinitely more pleasurable than continuing to do it for yourself. She is beginning to sweat a little now. You can see a trickle or two of perspiration running down from her hair line, and her fingers – the two now firmly inside her cunt – are stiffer than they were initially, and her rhythm is faster. Her sexual lubrication is running freely down her thighs. You reduce your own rhythm, now simply pleasuring yourself with the occasional idle pull of your foreskin. Just enough to keep you erect and send small, erotically pleasant messages to your brain, whilst awaiting the culmination of your lady's first real orgasm, and her subsequent manual devotion to your sexual interests. Her mouth is open now, and there is a tiny dribble of saliva in both corners. Her fingers are moving faster now, and her hips are bucking wildly. She's fucking her fingers. There's no other way to describe what she's doing. 'Oh, yes,' she says, suddenly. Loudly. 'Oh, Jesus. Yes.' *This is it*, you say to yourself. Here we go for the jackpot. It won't be too long now, and those lovely long slim fingers, with their immaculately painted finger-nails, will be wrapped lovingly around your cock. You hope she won't be long.

'Oh, yes,' she says again. 'Oh, fuck. Oh, God.' Her fingers are a blur now. 'I'm coming,' she shouts. Bored with her announcements, in that they're not doing a lot for you sexually, you pick her knickers up off the floor and press them up to your nose again. And there it is. The unmistakable scent of cunt. Wet cunt. If only you could bottle it, you'd make a fortune. 'I'm coming,' she shouts. You wonder if the neighbours are listening. 'I'm coming. Oh, Jesus. Yes. Yes. Now. Now. Oh, dear God.' Suddenly she drops down onto her knees, her fingers working overtime, as she wanks herself silly. She's obviously coming in large, regular, enjoyable instalments. *This is it, baby*, you think to yourself. *Enjoy. And hurry.*

And then she's finished. She's exhausted. She's half crying, half laughing. 'Christ,' she says. 'That was a good one. Terrific. Now let me finish you off.' *Please God*, you say to yourself. She takes your cock in her hand and begins to do wonderful things to it. She squeezes, pulls, wanks, rubs, caresses it. She's making love to you with her fingers. You reach out and begin to finger her cunt. It's soaking wet. She wriggles. 'Hmmmm,' she says. 'That's nice. I love it when I'm tossing you off, and you play with my pussy.' You can feel your ultimate ejaculation building, somewhere way down in your prostate. She's kneeling on the floor between your knees now, masturbating you with malice aforethought. She leans forward, and says – quietly, in your ear – 'Do you like it when I jack you off? Do you like me giving you one off the wrist? Are you going to fuck me, after I've made you come all over my fingers?' 'Yes, darling,' you say. You're breathing hard now. You can feel your ejaculation coming up out of your boots.

'Oh, yes,' you say, panting. 'Now. Please. Make me come now. Right now.' She moves her supple fingers just that little bit faster, and then yes, Jesus, you're spurting your come like a hot little geyser. She takes your cock and aims it towards her lovely breasts, so that your ejaculate is spurting all over them. She uses her other hand to rub your sticky come into them. Her nipples stand up again beneath this close attention. 'Oooh, nice,' she says. 'I love your come on my tits.' She keeps up her expert manipulation of your dick, until every last drop of jism has been extracted. 'I think that's it for now, darling,' she says. 'But we'll start up again in a little while.

Would you like me to toss you off again? Or would you rather fuck me? Or shall I suck you off, this time? I quite fancy you sucking me off, so we could start with a little *soixante-neuf*, and see how we go on from there. What do you think?'

My cock is half way hard again already. I'm too far gone to make any kind of a decision. 'You tell me, sweetheart,' I say. 'Whatever you fancy.' She smiles at me, and leans up and gives me a sexy wet kiss. 'I think I'll suck you off for a little while,' she says. 'And then I'll ask you again. OK?' 'OK,' I agree. That's the lovely thing about mutual masturbation. It leaves you absolutely relaxed, and ready for anything.

R. P. Lee-on-Solent, Hampshire.

We like a woman who will enter into the spirit of things and give us a helping hand.

BEST FOOT FORWARD

I think I must have a foot fetish. Or a shoe fetish, thinking about it. Yes. That's more like it. A shoe fetish. I'm fixated on girls who are naked, apart from their shoes. They have to be high heels. That's absolutely vital. I love it when they're naked, and they're sitting down, and lying back, with their legs crossed in front of them, showing their shoes, just in front of their beautiful love-holes. The strappier the shoes, the happier I am. Lydia, in your November issue, had me jacking off for days. I've got her picture beside my bed, and I jack off to it every night, before I go to sleep. She's perfect. Her lovely blonde hair, framing her innocent-looking little face. (I'm sure she's not innocent at all. That's half the attraction.) Her fabulous breasts. They're not too big, but they're nicely plump and in wonderful shape. I can imagine sucking those teats between my hot lips. And that lovely, hairy cunt, with its gorgeous, fleshy cunt lips. They're wide open in your photographs, and that's the way I'd like to see them. I'd like to thrust my tongue up between them first of all, and suck Lydia to a wild orgasm, before I rammed her with my massively erect tool and fucked her brains out. But it would be an essential part of the deal that she kept those fantastic red sandals on while I do all those things to her. As to that tiny little peep-hole, an inch or two below her cunt, well, what can I tell you? Not a lot.

    S. L. K. Hull, Humberside.

It's largely a question of keeping body and sole together.

KISS OF LIFE

My fantasies all revolve around girls' lips. Ever since I was sucked off by my secretary at my firm's annual Christmas party last year, I haven't wanted to know about fucking as such. Why waste time pushing your dick up something a woman pisses through when you can have her put it between her elegant lips and mouth you off? I read, all the time, of women whose cunts 'caress like fingers', 'suck like mouths', 'massage like experts', but I've never met one. The only girls who suck *me* off, suck me in their mouths. And that's where I like to be. Now, at parties, or when I meet new women, I don't look at their tits, or at their legs, or up their skirts, or wonder about their cunts. I look at their luscious lips, and imagine thrusting my cock into their hungry mouths and spurting my come down their welcoming throats.

Angela (my secretary) says she loves me to come in her mouth. She also lets me come on her tits, in her hand, over her stomach, and anywhere else I want, after she has sucked me to the point of ejaculation. She doesn't particularly want to be fucked afterwards either. She's happy for me to wank her off, or watch her while she wanks herself. Sometimes she sits beside me in my office, apparently taking dictation (just in case anyone else should come into my office) but in fact she's tossing me off, her hand down my flies. Then she'll toss herself off, and I'll lick her fingers clean for her afterwards. Oh, happy days.

W. T. New York, N. Y.

She's obviously taking you for a sucker.

BLACK LOOKS

As an admirer of the female form, may I relate my favourite fantasy for the benefit of your other readers, who may share my tastes? I'm the only man on board a sailing clipper, sailing the Caribbean. The rest of the crew are all women. They're professional sailors, and completely capable of handling the ship in any kind of weather, but they're also chosen for their looks and their enjoyment of things sexual. They come in all shapes and sizes. There are American girls, European girls, Asian girls, African girls, Chinese and Japanese girls and, naturally enough, girls from the various Caribbean islands. There are very few rules, but there are two upon which I insist before the girls sign on. One, all girls are totally naked, at all times. Two, all girls are available for any sexual act, at all times. The girls are, of course, well paid, and the crew lives in considerable luxury. Domestic requirements, like cooking and cleaning ship, are shared equally amongst all the crew. There are no ranks. I am nominally the captain, but, like the crew, I don't wear a uniform. Certain members of the crew have certain responsibilities, in line with their nautical training, otherwise everyone is equal. When we go ashore, to collect provisions or for medical needs, for example, or simply to enjoy a meal in a restaurant, we all dress, (for want of a better word) in civilian clothes, so as not to embarrass anyone. In my fantasy, the weather is always perfect, and the long, Caribbean days are full of beautiful bodies on deck, some managing the ship, others simply improving their tans. I have my eye on a lithe, long-limbed Caribbean lady called

Joan. She is black, with long black hair in corn rows, which are then tied back. Her breasts are full, and crowned by dark-skinned, almost black, silver dollar-sized areolae, mounted by hugely erect nipples, the size of my thumbs. I can see her generous growth of black, tightly curled pubic hair, and I can also see, down the centre of her pubis, a dark pink, almost black gash, shining wetly in the sunshine.

As I watch, Joan is aware of my interest. It is that, I believe, which is causing her nipples to become so stiffly erect, and it is also the reason for the moistness at her crotch. She is standing facing me, about four foot away from me, leaning against the rigging. As I watch, she turns and leans against the ship's rail, her legs almost up to her waist, her perfectly shaped taut buttocks facing me roundly and revealing the growth of anal hair that is presently hiding her anus. Joan and I haven't fucked yet. She looks over her shoulder at me and smiles. 'Pussy all wet, man,' she says, in that lovely, husky voice that the girls from the Islands all seem to have. 'Pity to waste it,' she continues. 'What you say?' She turns back to face me and spreads her legs wide apart. I can see the glistening, clear liquid which is now trickling down her pubic hair and making its slow journey down towards her strong thighs. She puts a finger between her legs and strokes her pussy lips.

'You like to fuck Caribbean girls?' she asks. 'This girl ready to fuck.' What can I tell you? I stand up, my rampant erection an answer in itself. I grin at Joan. 'Just follow me, darling,' I say. 'Today's your lucky day.' Well, I *am* the captain, when all's said and done. As I stand up and my erection makes my objective obvious to the entire crew, Joan and I get a round of applause from the others. That's nice, isn't it? The stuff of dreams. I lead the way down to my master cabin and through my lounge to the bedroom. It is air conditioned and pleasantly cool. My king-sized bed has been made up with fresh linen and is turned back, ready for the day's activities. Joan looks around her. She obviously likes what she sees.

'Hmmm,' she says. 'Nice.' 'Thank you,' I say. There is a light sheen of sweat all over her perfect body, but it is quickly disappearing in the coolness of the cabin. 'How do you want me?' asks Joan. 'Do you want me to suck your cock a little first? Do you want to suck my pussy? Do you just want to lie there and let me fuck you?' She smiles at me and she's fingering her pussy again. 'I think that, maybe to start off with, I'll just watch you playing with your pussy, darling,' I tell her. 'Then we'll think again.' 'Sure, baby,' she says. She goes over to the bed and sits on the edge, and then she spreads her thighs and begins to masturbate herself. I go and kneel down in front of her, so that I can fully appreciate the sight, sounds, and scents of what she is doing. My cock is standing fully to attention. I take hold of it and begin to stroke it, gently.

Joan's cunt is a deep purple colour, down inside her pinky black labia, and I can see how wet it is. She is fingering herself deeply, but I don't think she has started manipulating her clitoris. She is simply thrusting her fingers in and out of herself. She looks at me, lazily. 'You like what you see?' she asks. She licks her full lips and I wonder, for a moment, what it is going to feel like when she sucks my cock. 'Yes,' I tell her. 'I like. I think I'll suck you now.' So saying, I pull her hand away from between her legs, press her thighs farther apart, and lean forward to take her swollen labia between my lips. She tastes strongly of her feminine juices, mixed with tropical fruits, and with an unusual, overriding sweetness that I don't recognize. It's probably called Jamaican cunt.

Whatever it is, I like it. I find her clitoris and concentrate on it, and she begins to wriggle. I stop what I'm doing for a moment, just long enough to push her flat down upon the bed on her back, straddle her face, and bury my mouth between her legs again. She obediently takes my cock in her mouth (in that position, she can hardly avoid it) and I start to feel what it's like to be sucked by those delightful lips, aided by that busy, experienced tongue. It feels good. So good, in fact, that I quickly shoot my load down her throat. She doesn't show any signs of being irritated by this event and sucks and swallows until all my ejaculate has disappeared.

I continue sucking her pussy, and soon she too achieves a series of orgasms so I feel that I've at least given as good as I've received. I get up off her and go through to the lounge cabin where I open my concealed fridge and extract a bottle of champagne. It's the real stuff. Vintage Mumm. As I open it, I call through to Joan and ask her if she wants to join me. She does, she says. I pour two glasses, and carry them through to the other cabin. 'Cheers, darling,' I say. 'Cheers,' she says. She puts her glass down and takes hold of my cock, which she begins to play with. She rapidly teases it back into a full erection as I watch. I enjoy the sensations which she is so expertly producing. 'You've done that before,' I say. She grins at me. 'If a girl wants to get well fucked, that's something she has to learn how to do,' she tells me. I grin back at her. 'Since you're so expert,' I said, 'keep on doing it. Jerk me off. I'd like that. Then you can make me hard again, and then we'll fuck. OK?' She began jerking me off, energetically. 'You're the boss,' she said. 'Whatever turns you on, baby.'

I began playing with her pussy while she masturbated me. It was very wet, and accommodated my fingers easily. 'You're not doing too badly yourself,' she said. 'Have you frigged a lot of girls?' 'That's almost a "When did you stop beating your wife?" question,' I said. 'But yes. I've frigged a few girls in my time. But I'd far rather watch them doing it themselves, as you already know. This is just so's not as to completely waste the time, since you're so busy jerking me off. I just love the feel of wet pussy.' I dipped my forefinger farther in and began to frig her clitoris. She came very quickly, gasping and muttering under her breath and jerking her hips about on the bed, but she didn't falter in her five-finger exercise with my cock.

'I'm going to make you come now, honey,' she said. And she did. She pressed a knowing finger deeply into me, somewhere just at the base of my cock, underneath it, where my scrotum joins it. The result was instant. It was as if she had massaged my prostate. I shot my ejaculate all over her busy fingers. 'Hmmm,' she said, not for the first time that day. 'That's nice. Was it nice for you, baby?' She wiped her hand clean on the immaculate sheet beneath her and then she leaned forward and, taking my cock in her mouth, she sucked and licked it scrupulously clean. 'Now we can start afresh,' she said. 'Pussy wants you now. Joan wants to be fucked. But tell me,' she said, 'which of the other girls are you going to fuck next?'

'Why do you ask?' I said. 'Because that's how I'm going to get you going again,' she said. 'Tell me.' 'Well, I don't really know,' I told her. 'I hadn't given it a lot of thought. The nice thing about this boat of mine is that all the lovely girls are fuckable. Anythingable. I don't have to work at getting my rocks off. But since you ask, I've been looking at that little Chinese girl. You know the one. Five foot nothing, tiny tits, slim little legs, and great big thick bushy pubes. I'll stake my reputation that she's got a lovely, tiny, tight little cunt hidden away in that bird's nest between her legs.' 'That's Tsai,' said Joan, laughing gently. 'She's lovely. Shall I tell you what she really likes? We girls talk about these things, you know.' 'I guess you do,' I said. 'Yeah, go on, then. Tell me.' Joan took hold of my semi-erect cock once more. Thinking about the Chinese girl had already got me going in the right direction.

'She likes to dress up in sexy lingerie,' Joan told me.

'Black silk or satin. Lots of lace. Black silk stockings. Suspender belts. That sort of thing. And then she likes someone to rip it all off her. Spank her a little. Nothing too serious, mind. Rape-fantasy stuff. You must have come across it?' She looked at me, expectantly, as if she expected me at least to nod my head. 'No, honey,' I told her. 'I've never come across a girl who liked to be roughed up.' All the time we were talking, Joan was slowly kneading my dick. Pulling on it. Peeling back the foreskin. It jumped to almost fully erect, listening to what little Chinese Tsai liked to have done to her. 'But the best is yet to come,' said Joan. 'She likes it up her ass. Do you like to fuck girls in the ass?' 'Some,' I said, lying in my teeth. A lot of girls don't like you even to suggest anal sex, never mind actually doing it. 'Yes,' Joan went on. 'She likes to have someone pretend to rape her anally. Apparently she likes to scream, and shout, "No. Please, God, no. Not up there. Not in my asshole. Please. Please." '

Joan's imitation of Tsai pleading for the virginity of her asshole was almost too much for me. I quickly pulled my cock away from her naughty fingers. 'If you seriously want to get fucked, darling,' I said to her, 'now's the time.' 'OK, baby,' she said. 'No problem. You just lie back there and relax, and I'll fuck you like you've never been fucked before.' I lay back as directed. She stood up over me, on the bed, and put one foot each side of me. I looked up into her hairy snatch. It was literally dripping with her mucus-like lubrication. She put her fingers down and pulled her pussy-lips wide open. 'Here it comes, baby,' she said. 'Genuine one hundred per cent, dyed-in-the-wool real Jamaican nooky. You'll never have better.' She grinned, bent her legs, and ended up kneeling over my thighs, a long leg each side of me, impaling my cock with what felt like her almost liquified cunt as she so did.

She was tight, and she was hot. Literally. Really hot. It was like sticking my dick into a private, miniature, cock-encompassing, slippery steam bath. 'How does that feel, honey?' she asked me. Her cunt-muscles gripped me as she spoke and she began to ride me, working away at me as she rose up and down, gleefully, vociferously, on my joystick. 'Oh, yes, baby,' she intoned. 'This's what Joan's been waiting for. Lovely, big, stiff cock. Every girl's best friend. Oh, yes. I love it.' She threw her head back, and laughed out loud as she rode me.

I soon took hold of her gorgeous buttocks, and gripped them as she rode me. Tempted by her earlier conversation about Tsai, I slowly moved my hands down and then, when they were in the right position, I slipped a finger into her anal cleavage, and felt around for her anus. She was as hirsute there as was her snatch, and I couldn't feel her actual asshole for the quantity of her thick anal tresses. As soon as she felt me fingering her ass, she sat up straight, took hold of my searching finger, and moved it onto her dimpled little anal rosebud. 'If that's what you're looking for,' she said, 'there it is. Don't fuck about. You want to finger-fuck my asshole while I fuck you? I'd like that.'

I slipped my finger into her and felt her tight little hole dilate as my finger entered into it. I had to time the insertion and withdrawal of my finger from up her asshole quite carefully, to coincide with her movements as she rose and fell the length of my cock. If it hadn't been for the number of times that she had already brought me to ejaculation, I would have already come by now, so erotic were the things that she was doing to me as she fucked me. She brought the expression 'I'm going to fuck your brains out' to reality for me. Looking back, I think she probably knew that right from the beginning, and had almost certainly engineered my earlier ejaculations, in order to ensure that she eventually got herself well fucked, once she finally got me around to it. Either way, I was very happy. I was overjoyed.

D. O'M. St Petersburg, Florida.

Some trip. It seems you were fucking up a storm. We'll keep our fingers crossed that you didn't have a mutiny on your hands!

APHRODITE DIET

My girlfriend and I were discussing the theory of aphrodisiacs the other day, and we went through all the old theories that we had read about, from Spanish Fly (which I'm told is the ground-up powder from a dried insect) through oysters – and yes, I've heard the joke about the guy who ate a dozen oysters and his wife complained that one of them didn't work – to raw meat. I've eaten oysters, of course, but never with the intention (or hope!) of improving my sexual performance, and I have to say that there was no noticeable difference, either way. Nor with Steak Tartare – probably not a very popular dish in these days of BSE. But I have always maintained that there is no aphrodisiac in the world that works as efficiently as a new woman. Discovering all her secret places for the first time. Touching them, feeling them. Sucking them, licking them. Inhaling her intimate scents, tasting her forbidden fruit. The first time you insert your penis into her wet vagina. Finding out what turns her on, what makes her scream with pleasure. Learning how best to bring her to orgasm. My girlfriend agrees, and says that the same applies for her with a new man! Thus, whilst I stay faithful to my girlfriend, my fantasies encompass an endless supply of beautiful women, kept in a large house, to which I am the only male who is permitted access. The house is in the country and includes stables, with horses, indoor and outdoor pools, professional cooks (female!) and servants for cleaning, looking after laundry, and the rest. In my fantasy, when I visit the house the girls are instructed to assemble in the main sitting-room (where there is a bar) and I mingle with them, going from group to group, chatting, enjoying a glass or two of champagne, until I see one who appeals to me.

I will then take her up to her room, and the detailed introduction takes place. I undress her, or watch her undress, depending upon my mood. When she has taken off her outer clothes and is standing there in her undies, I will probably tell her to hold everything for a moment, and I'll go over to her and caress her breasts (preferably, at this stage, through a sexy brassiere). I'm not a stockings and suspenders man, so I don't mind whether the woman is wearing those or tights. Whichever she has on, I'll feel between her legs while she is still wearing them and, of course, her panties. This feeling and stroking of flesh and private parts through layers of material is an essential (and exciting) part of my fantasy ritual. The girl responds to my touching her up, pressing herself and her thighs and everything that they conceal up against me.

Next I take off her brassiere, and suck and squeeze the newly revealed breasts. If I'm lucky, the girl will have quite small breasts. From choice, I am not overly attracted to large breasts, but to small, firm, well-shaped ones. I like pretty nipples, which swell beneath my ministrations. After some time playing with the girl's breasts, I will move down and, depending upon whether she is wearing stockings or tights will remove her knickers and then her leg apparel, or vice versa, exposing her pubic bush, and her pudenda, to my delighted eye. You may be wondering about girls who shave between their legs. I find the sight of labia pouting baldly at me most unattractive, and any girls thus shaven are either eliminated (by a written examination) early on, or they are instructed to grow their pubic hair back. All the women are asked to let their pubic hair grow as thickly as it will. Trimming is absolutely not permitted. Once the girls are naked, I take them over to the bed for the next part of my 'getting-to-know-you' introduction. What happens then depends entirely upon mood. I may play with their pussies for a while. I may suck them. I may have them suck me. We may do both those things together. I will, of course, eventually fuck them, but it is this discovering their sexual secrets, slowly, over a period of time, as I said at the beginning of my letter, which gives me so much intense erotic enjoyment.

R. C. Y. Harrogte, Yorkshire.

We certainly agree with the main point of your philosophy, as far as a woman being the only real aphrodisiac is concerned. But aren't you making rather a meal of it?

HOT LIPS

As a woman who is seriously into sex, I love looking at the photographs of the sexy ladies that you publish. But I am embarrassed to see – over a period of time – that the lips of my sex can (by comparison with those of the pretty girls in your pages) only be described as gross. I enclose a photograph taken recently by my boyfriend. You see, I never went to boarding school or played team sports, served in the armed forces, or did any of those things where a woman lives with other women and has an opportunity to compare her body with other women's bodies. Your magazine has given me that opportunity, and, frankly, I'm horrified. My current boyfriend is my first really sexual relationship, and because he says he loves my fleshy labia, I have always assumed that they look like any other girl's vulval appendages. Wrong! Since looking at some recent issues of your magazine, I see that my outer labia look more like swollen bats' wings than the attributes displayed by your models. Can anything be done to make them more normal? Plastic surgery, for example?

K. R. Cardiff, Glamorgan.

To take your last question first, yes, specialist plastic surgeons can reduce the size, and alter the shape, of women's labia, should that be necessary. But before you rush off to make an appointment, think on this. One: pussy lips come in all shapes and sizes. Every variety has its enthusiasts. Two: we all love yours. Three: a quick straw poll of our male editorial and design staff produced over fifty per cent who prefer larger, rather than smaller, labia on their ladies. And research through our files reveals that of all the models photographed over the past ten years (well over 700 girls) 460 of them have large labial lips. Now read on:-

LUSCIOUS LIPS

Diana, on page 72 of your last issue, has my blood racing. Into my cock. It's swollen with desire. She fulfills my ultimate fantasy. I have *never*, EVER seen such gorgeously shaped, full, elongated, tumescent, wonderful cunt lips. Please, PLEASE pass my name and telephone number to Diana. *Please*. I have to have those rare, enormous, immense, suckable labia in between my own lips. I have to suck them. I have to lick their length and breadth, and thrust my tongue (and, later, my cock) between them. They look like pinkish segments of ripe orange, peeping wetly from within Diana's glorious thatch of pubic hair. Diana is a cunt-lapper's delight. Imagine easing down a girl's knickers, the first time that you took her to bed, and exposing fabulous lips like those beneath them! Imagine running your tongue down their centre, and parting them, to delve between them! I'm in love. I can't eat or sleep, for thinking about how they would feel in my mouth. Imagine *fucking* them, watching them open to absorb your swollen cock, dilating as you entered them, closing tightly around your tool as it sank deeply in! Imagine watching Diana's fingers idly playing with those lips, as she waited for you to tear off your trousers! In anticipation.

H. A. Highgate, London.

We passed H. A's letter on to Diana, who sent him an autographed colour photograph of herself, emphasizing her special attributes.

WHITER THAN WHITE

I've always had a thing about white panties, and I see from your current issue that at least one of your team of photographers and/or your picture editor are white-pantie freaks too. Those fabulous photographs of Prudence, the tiny Oriental girl, with her legs spread and the crotch of her white knickers stretched tightly over her plump little pudenda, are too much. They tell me precisely the size and shape of her glorious sex mound, and clearly show the outline of her labia through the thin material. What a pity the photographer didn't talk about sex to Prudence, in order to induce her to wet her knickers, as it were, whilst he was taking his photographs. You know what I mean. Get her juices running, so that they stained the perfect white of her knicker crotch and turned the material from transparent to translucent. I love the shot of Prudence with her hand down inside her white panties. We all know what she's doing. In fact, we can more or less *see* what she's doing, and the expression on her face says she's enjoying herself. Later on in the set, she turns around for us and shows us her arse through those skimpy white knickers. I get real horny seeing her plump arse cheeks and the dark shadow of her anal hair, of which wisps peep out from beneath her knicker-leg. Fantasies are fantasies, of course, and fucking is fucking, and for me the first is but the prelude to the second. I love the final picture, where Prudence has taken those lovely knickers off and is holding her pussy open with her delicate fingers, showing us the deep pink hole down which, no doubt, some lucky guy regularly thrusts his prong.

David Jones

I'd love to eat it out and then fuck it, very, very slowly. I'd make a real Chinese meal of it.
  G. E. D. Salisbury, Wilts.

One large helping of number sixty-nine, please, waiter!

DIGGING THE DIRT

I had a new experience recently, which I would like to share with your readers. I'm nineteen and am still learning (albeit enthusiastically and energetically) about sex. I picked up a girl in my local pub the other day, who seemed to take an immediate shine to me. So far, this is a pretty rare occurrence in my life and one not to be taken lightly. Usually, I have to work very much harder to get anywhere near getting a girl to drop her knickers for me. So when she said, 'Why don't we go back to my place and get to know each other better?' I didn't waste any time, other than to stop off at an off-licence on the way to get a bottle of wine. Mary, her name was. She only lived around the corner from the pub, and when we got there I learned that she lived in a well-furnished one-bedroom flat that she was buying on a mortgage. She worked as a legal secretary, and made quite good money. Once inside, she grabbed hold of me and kissed me, at the same time unzipping my trousers and reaching inside to play with my dick. I won't bore you with a blow by blow account, but I will simply tell you about the bit that I found so exciting. Well, I found it *all* exciting, really, but the difference was that, as she got close to her first orgasm, she started talking dirty to me. Very dirty. I'd always been under the impression that girls thought sex and love were interchangeable, and that love-making went on in a gentle atmosphere of sweetness and light. Not with this girl. No way.

She had her clothes off quick as blinking and was lying on her bed naked, her legs apart, playing with her pussy while she waited for me to undress and join her. My hard-on slowed me down a bit, but I didn't waste *too* much time. We were, I guess, about halfway along the road to mutual orgasm when she started talking dirty to me. 'Oh fuck,' she said, breathing hard in my ear. 'Oh, Jesus. I love your cock. Your cock is fucking my cunt. You're going to make me come. Oh, God. Fuck me harder. Fuck me with your great big cock. Fuck me like there's no tomorrow. Oh, yes. You're fucking me. I'm coming now. *Now*. NOW. I'm coming.' I can't tell you how exciting I found it, listening to this delightful young girl using words I'd never heard any woman use, ever before. She was *saying* what I was *thinking*. I'd never heard a girl say 'fuck' before. I nearly came, instantly. I loved it. And this wasn't some downmarket, uneducated little tramp. She'd been to Cheltenham Ladies' College, she'd told me earlier in the pub, and then on to Cambridge, where she'd studied English Literature. To cut a long story short, I *did* come, very quickly. But it was only the first of many times, that memorable night. If you haven't tried it, I recommend it. Get a pretty girl to talk dirty to you while you fuck her. You'll love it.

E. Z. Edgeware, London.

Sounds like you cleaned up, sexually. Congratulations.

LOOK OUT FOR *THE WORLD'S BEST SEXUAL FANTASY LETTERS VOLUME 2*, EDITED BY DAVID JONES, TO BE PUBLISHED BY NEW ENGLISH LIBRARY IN JULY 1997.